Mark

THE CROSSWAY CLASSIC COMMENTARIES

Mark

EXPOSITORY THOUGHTS ON THE GOSPELS

by

J. C. Ryle

Series Editors

Alister McGrath and J. I. Packer

CROSSWAY BOOKS • WHEATON, ILLINOIS
A DIVISION OF GOOD NEWS PUBLISHERS

Mark.

Copyright © 1993 by Watermark.

Published by Crossway Books
    A division of Good News Publishers
    1300 Crescent Street
    Wheaton, Illinois 60187.

Art Direction: Mark Schramm

First printing, 1993

Printed in the United States of America

Library of Congress Cataloging-in-Publication Data
Ryle, J. C. (John Charles), 1816-1900
    Mark / J. C. Ryle.
        p.   cm. — (Expository thoughts on the Gospels)   (Crossway
classic commentaries : v. 2)
        1. Bible. N.T. Mark—Commentaries.   I. Bible. N.T. Mark.
English. Authorized. 1993.   II. Title.   III. Series.   IV. Series: Ryle,
J. C. (John Charles), 1816-1900. Expository thoughts on the Gospels.
BS2585.3.R955 1993   226.3'07—dc20   92-45785
ISBN 0-89107-727-8

01		00		99		98		97		96		95		94		93
15	14	13	12	11	10	9	8	7	6	5	4	3	2	1

Contents

Series Preface

The purpose of the Crossway Classic Commentaries is to make some of the most valuable commentaries on the books of the Bible, by some of the greatest Bible teachers and theologians in the last five hundred years, available to a new generation. These books will help today's readers learn truth, wisdom, and devotion from such authors as J. C. Ryle, Martin Luther, John Calvin, J. B. Lightfoot, John Owen, Charles Spurgeon, Charles Hodge, and Matthew Henry.

We do not apologize for the age of some of the items chosen. In the realm of practical exposition promoting godliness, the old is often better than the new. Spiritual vision and authority, based on an accurate handling of the biblical text, are the qualities that have been primarily sought in deciding what to include.

So far as is possible, everything is tailored to the needs and enrichment of thoughtful readers — lay Christians, students, and those in the ministry. The originals, some of which were written at a high technical level, have been abridged as needed, simplified stylistically, and unburdened of foreign words. However, the intention of this series is never to change any thoughts of the original authors, but to faithfully convey them in an understandable fashion.

The publishers are grateful to Dr. Alister A. McGrath of Wycliffe Hall, Oxford, Dr. J. I. Packer of Regent College, Vancouver, and Watermark of Norfolk, England, for the work of selecting and editing that now brings this project to fruition.

Introduction

Crossway Classic Commentaries are selected with the purpose of making available some of the best quality help ever produced for the understanding of the Bible's practical message. All the books of Scripture were written to nurture faith and promote godly living, and expositions in this series are explicitly attuned to this aim, which on the whole was better understood by the church's older teachers than by its more recent ones. The first Crossway Commentary was J. C. Ryle's layman's exploration of Matthew's Gospel, and no apology is needed for the choice of his exposition of Mark as the second.

Ryle was a remarkable man. A banker's son, plunged into poverty by the failure of the family firm, he served for most of his life as a country clergyman who by his ability as preacher, writer, and statesman, and by the spiritual force of his ministry at all levels, became the leader of the evangelical wing of the Church of England in the second half of the nineteenth century and finally served for twenty years as first bishop and ministerial architect of the diocese of Liverpool, to which he was appointed in 1880, at the age of sixty-four. His roots were firmly fixed in the heritage of the Reformers, the Puritans, and the eighteenth-century evangelicals, from which he drew the vision and resources that shaped his own rugged, down-to-earth, no-nonsense ministry. The aim of his writings, as of his life, was the Apostle Paul's aim — to present everyone before God's throne perfect and mature in Christ (Colossians 1:28) — and his expositions are very obviously honed to this end.

If growth in faith and holiness is what you are after, therefore, Ryle is the man for you! The wisdom, clarity, force, and piercing quality of his commentaries are classic in every sense.

Pairing Ryle's expositions of Matthew (1856) and Mark (1857) is truly appropriate, for the two Gospels are noticeably parallel in their narrative — either because Matthew wrote with the Gospel of Mark in front of him, or because Mark wrote with the Gospel of Matthew in front of him, or because both drew on the same stock of organized material. (Scholars have been debating the pros and cons of these three possibilities for more than a century, and are still at it, without any certainty forthcoming.) But Bible students do not need to know why the narrative framework of the two books is so similar; what is important is to grasp the distinct design of each, and to appreciate the portrait of Jesus and the presentation of his grace that each presents. So Ryle thought, and surely he was right.

To dismiss Mark as "a mere abridgment of St. Matthew," says Ryle, is "an entire mistake." Matthew highlights Jesus as King and teacher, "great David's greater son," and the new Moses, fulfilling and transcending the Old Testament order of things. Mark's focus is on activity — the historical journey of Jesus, the God-appointed Savior of Isaiah 53, from his baptism through growing hostility to his cross and empty tomb, and the personal journey of disciples out of spiritual blindness and incomprehension into faith, repentance, self-denial, and cross-bearing, whereby they follow their Master. Ryle notes the difference, and his comments faithfully pursue it, so his two expositions, the one centering on Jesus' words and the other on Jesus' works, are quite different.

In both, however, Ryle's exegesis is accurate within its limits, his applications are consistently searching, and the truths explored are permanently valid. I confidently predict that any who have appreciated either will then want the other, and I am delighted that this series should make both available.

J. I. PACKER

Preface

by

J. C. Ryle

The volume now in the reader's hands is a continuation of a work already commenced by *Expository Thoughts on St. Matthew.*

The nature of the work has been so fully explained in the preface to the volume on St. Matthew that it seems unnecessary to say anything on the subject. It may be sufficient to repeat that the reader must not expect to find in these *Expository Thoughts* a learned, critical commentary on the Gospels. If any expect this they will be disappointed. The work makes no pretense at being anything more than a continuous series of short practical expositions.

The main difference between this volume and the one which has preceded it will be found to consist in the occasional explanatory footnotes. [These have been printed in the main text of the present edition, in square brackets. – *Ed.*] The subjects of these notes will generally prove to be difficult passages or expressions in the inspired text. I cannot pretend that I have thrown any new light on the difficulties in St. Mark. But I can honestly say that I have endeavored to put the reader in possession of all that can be said on each difficulty.

In composing these expositions on St. Mark, I have tried to keep continually before me the threefold object which I had in view when I first commenced writing on the Gospels. I have endeavored to produce something which may be useful to heads of families in the conduct of family prayers – something which may assist those who visit the poor and desire to read to them – and something which may aid all readers of the Bible in the private study of God's Word. In pursuance of this threefold object, I have adhered steadily to the leading principles with which I began. I have dwelt principally on the things necessary to salvation. I have purposely avoided all topics of minor importance. I have spoken plainly on all subjects, and have tried to say nothing which all may not understand.

I cannot expect that the work will satisfy all who want some book to read at family prayers. In fact I know, from communications which I have received, that some think the expositions too long. The views of the heads of families as to the length of their family prayers are so exceedingly various that it would be impossible to please one group without displeasing others. In some households the family prayers are so short and hurried that I should despair of writing anything suitable to the master's needs. In such households a few verses of Scripture, read slowly and reverently, would probably be more useful than any commentary at all. As for those who find four pages too much to read at one time, and yet desire to read my *Expository Thoughts*, I can only suggest that they have an easy remedy in their own hands. They have only to leave out one or two divisions in each exposition, and they will find it as short as they please.

In preparing for publication this volume on St. Mark, I have looked through Chrysostom, Augustine, Theophylact, Euthymius, Calvin, Brentius, Bucer, Musculus, Gualter, Beza, Bullinger, Pellican, Ferus, Calovius, Cocceius, Baxter, Poole, Hammond, Lightfoot, Hall, Du Veil, Piscator, Paraeus, Jansenius, Leigh, Ness, Mayer, Trapp, Henry, Whitby, Gill, Doddridge, Burkitt, Quesnel, Bengel, Scott, A. Clark, Pearce, Adams, Watson, Olshausen, Alford, Barnes, Stier. After careful examination, I feel obliged to say that, in my humble judgment, very few commentators, whether ancient or modern, seem to give this Gospel the attention it deserves. It has been too often treated as a mere abridgment of St. Matthew. This view of it I believe to be an entire mistake.

The only large separate commentary on St. Mark that I have been able to meet with is a remarkable work consisting of 1666 folio pages, by George Petter, Vicar of Brede, in the county of Sussex, published in the year 1661. It is a work which from its scarcity, price and size is much less known than it deserves. The greater part of the impression is said to have perished in the great fire of London. Some account of this book may not be uninteresting to some readers.

Petter's commentary was originally preached by him in the form of expository lectures to his own congregation. He began to preach on it on June 7th, 1618, and continued preaching on it most Sundays with very little intermission till May 28th, 1643. The dates of each sermon are given in the margin.

The doctrine of this remarkable book is excellent – Protestant, evangelical and spiritual. The learning of the author must also have been not inconsiderable, if we may judge by the number and variety of his quotations. His faults of style and composition are the faults of the day in which he lived, and must therefore be charitably judged. But for laborious investigation of the meaning of every word, for patient discussion of every question bearing on the text, for fullness of matter, for real thoughtfulness and for continual practical application, there is no work on St. Mark which, in my opinion, bears comparison with Petter's. Like Goliath's sword, "there is none like it."

I now send off these *Expository Thoughts on St. Mark* with an earnest prayer that it may please God to use the volume for his glory. It has been written under the pressure of many public duties, and amidst many interruptions. No one is more conscious of its defects than myself. But I can honestly say that my chief desire, if I know anything of my heart, in this and all my writings is to lead my readers to Christ and faith in him, to repentance and holiness, to the Bible and to prayer.

If these are the results of this volume in any one case, the labor I have bestowed on it will be more than repaid.

J.C. RYLE
Helmingham Rectory
September 1857

Mark
Chapter 1

The Gospel begun: John the Baptist's ministry *(1:1–8)*

The Gospel of St. Mark, which we now begin, is in some respects unlike the other three Gospels. It tells us nothing about the birth and early life of our Lord Jesus Christ. It contains comparatively few of his sayings and sermons. Of all the four inspired histories of our Lord's earthly ministry, this is by far the shortest.

But we must not allow these peculiarities to make us undervalue St. Mark's Gospel. It is a Gospel singularly full of precious facts about the Lord Jesus, narrated in a simple, terse, pithy and condensed style. If it tells us few of our Lord's sayings, it is eminently rich in its catalogue of his doings. It often contains minute historical details of deep interest, which are wholly omitted in Matthew, Luke and John. In short, it is no mere abridged copy of St. Matthew, as some have rashly asserted, but the independent narrative of an independent witness, who was inspired to write a history of our Lord's *works*, rather than of his *words*. Let us read it with holy reverence. Like all the rest of Scripture, every word of St. Mark is "God-breathed," and every word is "useful for teaching" (2 Timothy 3:16).

[As Stier says in his *Words of the Lord Jesus*:

St. Mark has the special gift of terse brevity and of graphic painting in wonderful combination. While on every occasion he compresses the discourses, works and history into the simplest possible kernel, he on the other hand unfolds the scenes more clearly than St. Matthew does, who excels in the discourses. Not only do single incidents become in his hands

1

complete pictures, but even when he is very brief, he often gives, with one pencil stroke, something new and peculiarly his own.]

1. The dignity of Christ's person

First, let us observe in these verses what a full declaration we have of the dignity of our Lord Jesus Christ's person. The very first sentence speaks of him as "the Son of God."

These words, "the Son of God," conveyed far more to Jewish minds than they do to us. They were nothing less than an assertion of our Lord's divinity. They were a declaration that Jesus was himself true God and "equal with God" (John 5:18).

There is a beautiful fitness in placing this truth at the very beginning of a Gospel. The divinity of Christ is the citadel and keep of Christianity. Here lies the infinite value of the satisfaction he made upon the cross. Here lies the particular merit of his atoning death for sinners. That death was not the death of a mere man like ourselves, but of one who is "God over all, forever praised!" (Romans 9:5). We need not wonder that the sufferings of one person were a sufficient propitiation for the sin of a world, when we remember that he who suffered was "the Son of God."

Let believers cling to this doctrine with jealous watchfulness. With it, they stand on a rock. Without it, they have nothing solid beneath their feet. Our hearts are weak. Our sins are many. We need a Redeemer who is able to save completely, and set us free from the wrath to come. We have such a Redeemer in Jesus Christ. He is "Mighty God" (Isaiah 9:6).

2. The beginning of the Gospel fulfilled Scripture

Second, let us observe how the beginning of the Gospel was a fulfillment of Scripture. John the Baptist began his ministry as "it is written in Isaiah the prophet" (verse 2).

There was nothing unforeseen and suddenly contrived in the coming of Jesus Christ into the world. In the very beginning of Genesis we find it predicted that the woman's offspring would crush the serpent's head (Genesis 3:15). All through the Old Testament we find the same event foretold with constantly increasing clearness. It was a promise often renewed to patriarchs, and repeated by prophets, that a deliverer and redeeemer would one day come. His birth, his character, his life, his death, his resurrection, his forerunner were all prophesied long before he came. Redemption was worked out and accomplished in every step, just as it was written.

We should always read the Old Testament with a desire to find something in it about Jesus Christ. We study this part of the Bible with little profit if we can see in it nothing but Moses, David, Samuel and the prophets. Let us search the books of the Old Testament more carefully. It was said by Jesus, whose words can never pass away, "these are the Scriptures that testify about me" (John 5:39).

3. The effects of John the Baptist's ministry on the Jews

Third, let us observe how great were the effects which the ministry of John the Baptist produced for a time on the Jewish nation. We are told that "the whole Judean countryside and all the people of Jerusalem went out to him. Confessing their sins, they were baptized by him in the Jordan River" (verse 5).

The fact here recorded is one that is much overlooked. We are apt to lose sight of the person who went before our Lord, and to see nothing but our Lord himself. We forget the morning star in the full blaze of the Sun. And yet it is clear that John's preaching arrested the attention of the whole Jewish people, and created an excitement all over Palestine. It roused the nation from its slumbers, and prepared it for the ministry of our Lord when he appeared. Jesus himself says, "John was a lamp that burned and gave light, and you chose for a time to enjoy his light" (John 5:35).

We ought to remark here how little dependence is to be placed on what is called "popularity." If ever there was one who was a popular minister for a little while, John the Baptist was that man. Yet of all the crowds who came to his baptism and heard his preaching, how few, it may be feared, were converted! Some, we may hope, like Andrew, were guided by John to Christ. But the vast majority, in all probability, died in their sins. Let us remember this whenever we see a crowded church. A great congregation no doubt is a pleasing sight. But the thought should often cross our minds, "How many of these people will reach heaven at last?" It is not enough to hear and admire popular preachers. It is no proof of our conversion that we always worship in a place where there is a crowd. Let us take care that we hear the voice of Christ himself, and follow him.

4. John the Baptist's clear teaching

Fourth, let us observe what clear doctrine characterized John the Baptist's preaching. He exalted Christ: "After me will come one more powerful than I" (verse 7). He spoke plainly about the Holy Spirit: "He will baptize you with the Holy Spirit" (verse 8).

These truths had never been so plainly proclaimed before by mortal man. More important truths than these are not to be found in the whole system of Christianity today. The principal work of every faithful minister of the Gospel is to set the Lord Jesus fully before his people, and to show them his fullness and his power to save. The next great work he has to do is to set before them the work of the Holy Spirit, and the need of being born again and inwardly baptized by his grace. These two mighty truths appear to have been frequently on the lips of John the Baptist. It would be good for the church and the world if there were more ministers like him.

Let us ask ourselves, as we leave the passage, how much we know in our own experience of the truths which John preached. What do we think of Christ? Have we felt our need of him, and fled to him for peace? Is he King over our hearts, and all things to our souls? What do we think of the Holy Spirit? Has he done any work in our hearts? Has he renewed and changed them? Has he made us participate in the divine nature? Life or death depends on our answer to these questions. "If anyone does not have the Spirit of Christ, he does not belong to Christ" (Romans 8:9).

Christ's baptism, temptation, and the calling of his first disciples (1:9–20)

This passage is unusually full of matter. It is a striking instance of that brevity of style which is characteristic of St. Mark's Gospel. The baptism of our Lord, his temptation in the wilderness, the commencement of his preaching and the calling of his first disciples are all related here in eleven verses.

1. The voice from heaven

First, let us notice the voice from heaven which was heard at our Lord's baptism. We read: "a voice came from heaven: 'You are my Son, whom I love; with you I am well pleased'" (verse 11).

That voice was the voice of God the Father. It declared the wondrous and ineffable love which has existed between the Father and the Son from all eternity. "The Father loves the Son and has placed everything in his hands" (John 3:35). It proclaimed the Father's full and complete approval of Christ's mission to seek and save the lost. It announced the Father's acceptance of the Son as the mediator, substitute and surety of the new covenant.

There is a rich mine of comfort in these words for all Christ's believing members. In themselves, and in their own doings, they see nothing to please God. They are daily aware of weakness, shortcomings and imperfection in all their ways. But let them recollect that the Father regards them as members of his beloved Son Jesus Christ. He sees no flaw in them (Song of Songs 4:7). He sees them as "in Christ," clothed in his righteousness and invested with his merit. They are "accepted in the beloved" (Ephesians 1:6, KJV), and when the holy eye of God looks at them, he is "well pleased."

2. The nature of Christ's preaching

Second, let us notice the nature of Christ's preaching. We read that he came saying, "Repent and believe the good news!" (verse 15).

This is that old sermon which all the faithful witnesses of God have continually preached, from the very beginning of the world. From Noah down to the present day the burden of their sermon has always been the same: "Repent and believe."

The apostle Paul told the Ephesian elders, when he left them for the last time, that the substance of his teaching among them had been: "turn to God in repentance and have faith in our Lord Jesus" (Acts 20:21). He had the best of precedents for such teaching. The great head of the church had given him a pattern. Repentance and faith were the foundation-stones of Christ's ministry. Repentance and faith must always be the main subjects of every faithful minister's instruction.

We need not wonder at this, if we consider the necessities of human nature. All of us are by nature born in sin and are children of wrath, and all need to repent, turn to God and be born again if we want to see the kingdom of God. All of us are by nature guilty and condemned before God, and all must flee to the hope set before us in the Gospel, and believe in it, if we want to be saved. All of us, once penitent, need daily stirring up to deeper repentance. All of us, though believing, need constant exhortation to increased faith.

Let us ask ourselves what we know of this repentance and faith. Have we felt our sins, and forsaken them? Have we taken hold of Christ, and believed? We may reach heaven without learning or riches or health or worldly greatness. But we shall never reach heaven if we die unrepentant and unbelieving. A new heart and a living faith in a Redeemer are absolutely necessary to salvation. May we never rest till we know them by experience, and can call them our own! With them all true Christianity begins in the soul. Religious life consists in the exercise of them. It is only through the possession of them that people have peace in the end. Church membership and priestly absolution alone save no one. The only people who die in the Lord are those who "repent and believe."

3. The occupation of Christ's first disciples

Third, let us notice the occupation of those who were first called to be Christ's disciples. We read that our Lord called Simon and Andrew, when they were "casting a net into the lake" (verse 16), and James and John while they were "preparing their nets" (verse 19).

It is clear from these words that the first followers of our Lord were not the great of this world. They were men who had neither riches, nor rank, nor power. But the kingdom of Christ is not dependent on such things as these. His cause advances in the world " 'not by might nor by power, but by my Spirit,' says the LORD Almighty" (Zechariah 4:6). The words of St. Paul will always be found true: "Not many of you were wise by human standards; not many were influential; not many were of noble birth. But God chose the foolish things of the world to shame the wise; God chose the weak things of the world to shame the strong" (1 Corinthians 1:26–27). The church which began with a few fishermen, and yet spread over half the world, must have been founded by God.

We must beware of giving way to the common notion that there is anything disgraceful in being poor, and in working with our own hands. The Bible contains many instances of special privileges conferred on working men. Moses was keeping sheep when God appeared to him in the burning bush (Exodus 3:1–3). Gideon was threshing wheat when the angel brought him a message from heaven (Judges 6:11). Elisha was plowing when Elijah called him to be prophet in his place (1 Kings 19:19). The apostles were fishing when Jesus called them to follow him. It is disgraceful to be covetous, proud, a cheat, a gambler, a drunkard, a glutton or unclean. But it is no disgrace to be poor. The laborer who serves Christ faithfully is far more honorable in God's eyes than the nobleman who serves sin.

4. The task to which the disciples were called

Fourth, let us notice the task to which our Lord called his first disciples. We read that he said, "Come, follow me, and I will make you fishers of men" (verse 17).

The meaning of this expression is clear and unmistakable. The disciples were to become fishers for souls. They were to labor to draw people out of darkness into light, and from the power of Satan to God. They were to strive to bring people into the net of Christ's church, so that they might be saved and not perish everlastingly.

We ought to note this expression well. It is full of instruction. It is the oldest name by which the ministerial function is described in the New Testament. It lies deeper down than the name of bishop, elder or deacon. It is the first idea which should be before a minister's mind. He is not to be a mere reader of services, or administrator of sacraments. He is to be a "fisher" of souls. The minister who does not try to live up to this name has mistaken his calling.

Does the fisherman try to catch fish? Does he use every means, and grieve if he is unsuccessful? The minister ought to do the same. Does the fisherman have patience? Does he toil on day after day, and wait, and work on in hope? Let the minister do the same. Happy is the person in whom the fisherman's skill, diligence and patience are all combined!

Let us resolve to pray much for ministers. Their function is no light one, if they do their duty. They need the help of many prayers from all praying people. They have not only their own souls to care for, but the souls of others. No wonder St. Paul cries, "Who is equal to such a task?" (2 Corinthians 2:16). If we never prayed for ministers before, let us begin to do it today.

An evil spirit cast out; Peter's mother-in-law healed *(1:21–34)*

These verses begin the long list of miracles which St. Mark's Gospel contains. They tell us how our Lord cast out demons in Capernaum, and healed Peter's wife's mother of a fever.

1. Uselessness of mere intellectual knowledge

First, we learn from these verses the uselessness of a mere intellectual knowledge of religion. Twice we are specifically told that the evil spirits knew our Lord. In one place it says, "they knew who he was" (verse 34). In another, the demon cries out, "I know who you are – the Holy One of God!" (verse 24). They knew Christ, when teachers of the law were ignorant of him and Pharisees would not acknowledge him. And yet their knowledge did not save!

The mere belief of the facts and doctrines of Christianity will never save our souls. Such belief is no better than the belief of demons. They all believe and know that Jesus is the Christ. They believe that he will one day judge the world, and throw them down to endless torment in hell. It is a solemn and sorrowful thought that on these points some professing Christians have even less faith than the devil. There are some who doubt the reality of hell and the eternity of punishment. Such doubts as these find no place except in the hearts of self-willed men and women. There is no unbelief among demons. "The demons believe . . . and shudder" (James 2:19).

Let us take care that our faith is a faith of the heart as well as of the head. Let us see that our knowledge has a sanctifying influence on our affections and our lives. Let us not only know Christ but love him, from a sense of actual benefit received from him. Let us not only believe that he is the Son of God and the Saviour of the world, but rejoice in him, and cling to him with heartfelt determination. Let us not only know him by hearing with our ears, but by coming to him every day for mercy and grace. "The life of Christianity," says Luther, "consists in possessive pronouns." It is one thing to say "Christ is a Saviour." It is quite another to say "He is my Saviour and my Lord." The devil can say the first. The true Christian alone can say the second.

[As Petter says in his 1661 commentary on Mark:

> Rest not in an historical knowledge or faith. If thou do, it will not save thee; for if it would it would save the devils: for they have their literal knowledge and general belief of the word. Dost thou think it enough to know and believe that Christ lived and died for sinners? The devil and his angels know and believe as much. Labor then to outstrip them, and to get a better faith than is in them.

2. The Christian's first remedy in trouble

Second, we learn what remedy a Christian ought to turn to first, in time of trouble. He ought to follow the example of the friends of Simon's mother-in-law. We read that when she "was in bed with a fever," they "told Jesus about her" (verse 30).

There is no remedy like this. We must use whatever means are available in time of need, without question. In cases of sickness, we should send for doctors. When property or character needs defense, we should consult lawyers. We should seek the help of friends. But still after all, the first thing to be done is to cry to the Lord Jesus Christ for help. No one can relieve us so effectively as he can. No one is so compassionate, and so willing to relieve. When Jacob was in trouble he turned to his God first – "Save me, I pray, from the hand of my brother Esau" (Genesis 32:11). When Hezekiah was in trouble, he first spread Sennacherib's letter before the Lord – "deliver us from his hand" (2 Kings 19:19). When Lazarus fell sick, his sisters immediately sent to Jesus – "Lord," they said, "the one you love is sick" (John 11:3). Now let us do the same. "Cast your cares on the LORD and he will sustain you" (Psalm 55:22). "Cast all your anxiety on him" (1 Peter 5:7). "In everything, by prayer and petition, with thanksgiving, present your requests to God" (Philippians 4:6).

Let us not only remember this rule, but practice it too. We live in a world of sin and sorrow. The days of darkness in people's lives are many. It needs no prophet's eye to see that we will all shed many a tear, and feel many a heart-wrench, before we die. Let us be armed with a recipe against despair, before our troubles come. Let us know what to do when sickness, bereavement, cross, loss or disappointment breaks in upon us like an armed man. Let us do what they did in Simon's house at Capernaum. Let us at once "tell Jesus."

3. Jesus' perfect cure

Third, we learn from these verses what a complete and perfect cure the Lord Jesus makes when he heals. He takes the sick woman by the hand, and helps her up, and "the fever left her" (verse 31). But this was not all. A greater miracle remained. At once we are told "she began to wait on them" (verse 30). That weakness and enervated state which, as a general rule, a fever leaves behind it was in her case entirely removed. The fevered woman was not only made well in a moment, but in the same moment made strong and able to work.

[Let us not fail to observe here that Peter, one of our Lord's principal apostles, had a wife. Yet he was called to be a disciple, and afterwards chosen to be an apostle. More than this, we find St. Paul speaking of him as a married man, in his letter to the Corinthians, many years after this (1 Corinthians 9:5). How this fact can be reconciled with the compulsory celibacy of the clergy, which the Church of Rome enforces and requires, it is for the friends and advocates of the Roman Catholic Church to explain. To a plain reader, it seems a plain proof that it is not wrong for ministers to be married men. And when we add to this striking fact that St. Paul, when writing to Timothy, says that "the overseer must be . . . the husband of but one wife" (1 Timothy 3:2), it is clear that the whole Roman doctrine of clerical celibacy is utterly opposed to holy Scripture.]

We may see in this case a living picture of Christ's dealing with sin-sick souls. That blessed Saviour not only gives mercy and forgiveness, he gives renewing grace as well. To all who receive him as their physician, he gives power to become the children of God. He cleanses them by his Spirit when he washes them in his precious blood. Those he justifies, he also sanctifies. When he gives an absolution, he also gives a new heart. When he grants free forgiveness for the past, he also grants strength to "wait on" him for the future. The sin-sick soul is not merely cured and then left to itself. It is also supplied with a new heart and a right spirit, and enabled so to live as to please God.

There is comfort in this thought for all who feel a desire to serve Christ but at present are afraid to begin. There are many in this state of mind. They fear that if they come forward boldly and take up the cross they will shortly fall away. They fear that they will not be able to persevere, and will bring discredit on their statement of belief. Let them fear no longer. Let them know that Jesus is an Almighty Saviour who never deserts those who once commit themselves to him. Once rescued by his powerful hand from the death of sin, and washed in his precious blood, they will go on "waiting on him" to their life's end. They will have power to overcome the world, and crucify the body, and resist the devil. Just let them begin, and they will go on. Jesus knows nothing of half-cured cases and half-finished work. Let them trust in Jesus and go forward. The pardoned soul will always be enabled to serve Christ.

There is comfort here for all who are really serving Christ, and are still cast down by a sense of their own weakness. There are many in such a state. They are oppressed by doubts and anxieties. They sometimes think they will never reach heaven at all, but will be cast away in the wilderness. Let them fear no longer. Their strength will be sufficient for each day. The difficulties they now fear will vanish out of their path. The lion in the way which they now dread will prove to be chained. The same gracious hand which first touched and healed will uphold, strengthen and lead them to the end. The Lord Jesus will never lose one of his sheep. Those whom he loves and pardons he loves to the end. Though sometimes cast down, they will never be cast away. The healed soul will always go on waiting on the Lord. Grace will always lead to glory.

Christ's private prayers; the purpose of Christ's coming (1:35–39)

Every fact in our Lord's life on earth, and every word which fell from his lips, ought to be deeply interesting to a true Christian. We see a fact and a saying in the passage we have just read, which deserve close attention.

1. An example of Jesus' prayer habits

First, we see an example of Jesus' habits in private prayer. We are told that "very early in the morning, while it was still dark, Jesus got up, left the house and went off to a solitary place, where he prayed" (verse 35).

We will find the same thing often recorded of our Lord in the Gospel story. When he was baptized, we are told that he was "praying" (Luke 3:21). When he was transfigured, we are told that "as he was praying, the appearance of his face changed" (Luke 9:29). Before he chose the twelve apostles, we are told that he "spent the night praying to God" (Luke 6:12). When everyone was speaking well of him, and wanted to make him a king, we are told that "he went up on a mountainside by himself to pray" (Matthew 14:23). When tempted in the garden of Gethsemane, he said, "Sit here while I pray" (Mark 14:32). In short, our Lord always prayed, and did not give up. Sinless as he was, he set us an example of diligent communion with his Father. His divine nature did not make him independent of the use of all human methods. His very perfection was a perfection kept up through the exercise of prayer.

We ought to see in all this the immense importance of private devotion. If he who was "holy, blameless, pure, set apart from sinners" prayed continually like this, how much more ought we who are subject to weakness? If he found it necessary to offer up prayers and petitions with loud cries and tears (Hebrews 5:7), how much more necessary is it for us, who offend daily in many ways?

What shall we say to those who never pray at all, in the face of such a passage as this? There are many such people, it may be feared, in the list of baptized people – many who get up in the morning without prayer, and without prayer go to bed at night – many who never speak one word to God. Are they Christians? It is impossible to say so. A praying master, like Jesus, can have no prayerless servants. The Spirit of adoption will always make people call on God. To be prayerless is to be Christless, godless, and on the high road to destruction.

What shall we say to those who pray, yet give only a little time to their prayers? We are obliged to say that they show at present very little of the mind of Christ. Asking little, they must expect to have little. Seeking little, they cannot be surprised if they possess little. It will always be found that when prayers are few, grace, strength, peace and hope are small.

[As Traill wrote in 1696:

Ministers must pray much, if they would be successful. The apostles spent their time this way (Acts 6:4). Yea, our Lord Jesus preached all day, and continued all night alone in prayer to God. Ministers should be much in prayer. They used to reckon how many hours they spend in reading and study. It were far better both for ourselves and the Church of God, if more time was spent in prayer. Luther's spending three hours daily in secret prayer, and Bradford's studying on his knees, and other instances of men in our time, are talked of rather than imitated.]

We would do well to watch our habits of prayer with a holy watch-fulness. Here is the pulse of our Christianity. Here is the true test of our state before God. Here true religion begins in the soul, when it does begin. Here it decays and goes backward, when a man backslides from God. Let us walk in the steps of our blessed Master in this respect as well as in every other. Like him, let us be diligent in our private devotion. Let us know what it is to "go off to a solitary place and pray."

2. Christ's purpose in coming into the world

Second, we see in this passage a remarkable saying of our Lord as to the purpose for which he came into the world. We find him saying, "Let us go . . . to the nearby villages – so that I can preach there also. That is why I have come" (verse 38).

The meaning of these words is plain and unmistakable. Our Lord declares that he came on earth to be a preacher and a teacher. He came to fulfill the prophetic role, to be the "prophet greater than Moses" who had been long foretold (see Deuteronomy 18:15). He left the glory which he had shared with the Father from all eternity, to do the work of an evangelist. He came down to earth to show people the way of peace, to proclaim freedom for the prisoners and recovery of sight for the blind (Luke 4:18). One principal part of his work on earth was to go about telling good news, to offer healing to the broken-hearted, light to those living in darkness, and pardon to the chief of sinners. "That is why I have come."

13

We ought to observe here what infinite honor the Lord Jesus puts on the job of the preacher. It is a job which the eternal Son of God himself undertook. He might have spent his earthly ministry instituting and keeping up ceremonies, like Aaron. He might have ruled and reigned as a king, like David. But he chose a different calling. Until the time when he died as a sacrifice for our sins, his daily, and almost hourly, work was to preach. "That is why I have come," he says.

Let us never be moved by those who cry down the preacher's job, and tell us that sacraments and other ordinances are of more importance than sermons. Let us give to every part of God's public worship its proper place and honor, but let us beware of placing any part of it above preaching.

By preaching, the church of Christ was first gathered together and founded, and by preaching it has always been maintained in health and prosperity. By preaching, sinners are awakened. By preaching, inquirers are led on. By preaching, saints are built up. By preaching, Christianity is being carried to the heathen world. There are many now who sneer at missionaries, and mock those who go out into the highways of our own land to preach to crowds in the open air. But such people would do well to pause and consider calmly what they are doing. The very work which they ridicule is the work which turned the world upside-down, and cast paganism to the ground. Above all, it is the very work which Christ himself undertook. The King of kings and Lord of lords himself was once a preacher. For three long years he went about proclaiming the Gospel. Sometimes we see him in a house, sometimes on the mountainside, sometimes in a Jewish synagogue, sometimes in a boat on the sea. But the great work he took up was always one and the same. He came always preaching and teaching. "That," he says, "is why I have come."

Let us leave the passage with a solemn resolution never to "treat prophecies with contempt" (1 Thessalonians 5:20). The minister we hear may not be highly gifted. The sermons that we listen to may be weak and poor. But after all, preaching is God's grand ordinance for converting and saving souls. The faithful preacher of the Gospel is handling the very weapon which the Son of God was not ashamed to employ. This is the work of which Christ has said, "That is why I have come."

A man with leprosy cleansed *(1:40–45)*

We read in these verses how our Lord Jesus Christ healed a man with leprosy. Of all our Lord's miracles of healing none were probably more marvelous than those performed on people with leprosy. Only two cases have been fully described in the Gospel story. Of these two, the case before us is one.

1. The nature of the disease
First, let us try to realize the dreadful nature of the disease which Jesus cured.

Leprosy is a complaint of which we know little or nothing in our northern climate. In Bible lands it is far more common. It is a disease which was completely incurable. It is no mere skin infection, as some ignorantly suppose. It is a radical disease of the whole man. It attacks not merely the skin but the blood, the flesh and the bones, until the unhappy patient begins to lose his extremities and to rot by inches. Let us remember besides this that, amongst the Jews, the leper was reckoned unclean, and was cut off from the congregation of Israel and the ordinances of religion. He had to live in a separate house. No one was allowed to touch him or serve him. Let us remember all this, and then we may have some idea of the remarkable wretchedness of a person with leprosy. To use the words of Aaron when he interceded for Miriam, the leper was "like a stillborn infant coming from its mother's womb with its flesh half eaten away" (Numbers 12:12).

But is there nothing like leprosy among ourselves? Yes, indeed there is. There is a foul soul-disease which is engrained in our very nature, and clings to our bones and marrow with deadly force. That disease is the plague of sin. Like leprosy, it is a deep-seated disease, infecting every part of our human nature, heart, will, conscience, understanding, memory and affections. Like leprosy, it makes us loathsome and abominable, unfit for the company of God and for the glory of heaven. Like leprosy, it is incurable by any earthly physician, and is slowly but surely dragging us down to the second death. And worst of all, far worse than leprosy, it is a disease from which no mortal is exempt. "All of us have become" in God's sight "like one who is unclean" (Isaiah 64:6).

Do we know these things? Have we found them out? Have we discovered our own sinfulness, guilt and corruption? Happy indeed are those who have been really taught to feel that they are "miserable sinners," and that there is "no health in them"! Blessed indeed are those who have learned that they are spiritual lepers, bad, wicked and sinful creatures! To know our disease is one step towards a cure. It is the misery and the ruin of many souls that they never yet saw their sins and their need.

2. Christ's power

Second, let us learn from these verses the wondrous and almighty power of the Lord Jesus Christ.

We are told that the unhappy leper came to our Lord "and begged him on his knees, 'If you are willing, you can make me clean'" (verse 40). We are told that "filled with compassion, Jesus reached out his hand and touched the man. 'I am willing,' he said. 'Be clean!'" (verse 41). At once the cure was effected. That very instant the deadly plague left the poor sufferer, and he was healed. It is but a word, and a touch, and there stands before our Lord not a leper but a sound and healthy man.

Who can conceive the greatness of the change in the feelings of this leper when he found himself healed? The morning sun rose upon him, a miserable being, more dead than alive, his whole frame a mass of sores and corruption, his very existence a burden. The evening sun saw him full of hope and joy, free from pain and fit for the society of his fellows. Surely the change must have been like life from the dead.

Let us bless God that the Saviour with whom we have to do is almighty. It is a cheering and comforting thought that with Christ nothing is impossible. There is no heart-disease so deep-seated that he is unable to cure it. No plague of soul is so virulent that our great physician cannot heal it. Let us never despair of anyone's salvation, so long as he lives. The worst of spiritual lepers may yet be cleansed. No cases of spiritual leprosy could be worse than those of Manasseh, Saul and Zacchaeus, yet they were all cured. Jesus Christ made them well. The chief of sinners may yet be brought near to God by the blood and Spirit of Christ. People are not lost because they are too bad to be saved, but because they will not come to Christ so that he may save them.

3. A time to be silent about Christ's work

Third, let us learn from these verses that there is a time to be silent about the work of Christ, as well as a time to speak.

This is a truth which is taught us in a remarkable way. We find our Lord strictly telling this man to tell no one of his cure: "See that you don't tell this to anyone" (verse 44). We find this man in the warmth of his zeal disobeying this injunction, and "spreading the news" of his cure freely. And we are told that the result was that Jesus "could no longer enter a town openly but stayed outside in lonely places" (verse 45).

There is a lesson in all this of deep importance, however difficult it may be to apply it properly. It is clear that there are times when our Lord would have us work for him quietly and silently, rather than attract public attention by a noisy zeal. There is a zeal which is "not based on knowledge," as well as a zeal which is righteous and praiseworthy. Everything is beautiful in its season. Our Master's cause may on some occasions be more advanced by quietness and patience than in any other way. We are not to "give dogs what is sacred," nor "throw your pearls to pigs" (Matthew 7:6). By forgetting this we may even do more harm than good, and retard the very cause we want to assist.

The subject is a delicate and difficult one, without doubt. Unquestionably the majority of Christians are far more inclined to be silent about their glorious Master than to confess him before other people, and they do not need the bridle so much as the spur. But still it is undeniable that there is a time for all things; and to know the time should be one great aim of a Christian. There are good people who have more zeal than discretion, and even help the enemy of truth by unseasonable acts and words.

[It would not be wise for a speaker at an English public meeting to proclaim the names of the families in Italy where the Bible is read, and to point out the streets and houses where these families resided. Such a speaker might be well-meaning, and full of zeal. He might really desire to glorify Christ, and spread the news of the triumphs of his grace. But he would be guilty of a sad indiscretion, and show great ignorance of the very lesson which the verses before us contain. The words of Petter on this subject deserve notice:

In that our Saviour forbids this leper to publish this miracle at this unseasonable time, we learn that all truths are not fit to be professed or uttered at all times. Though we must never deny any truth, being demanded of it, or lawfully enjoined to profess it, yet there is a wise concealment of the truth, which is sometimes to be used (Ecclesiastes 3:7).

When are we to conceal the truth? 1. When the case stands so, that the uttering of it may bring hurt to the truth itself, as here, the publishing of this miracle was like to stop Christ's ministry. 2. When we are in the company of such persons as are more likely to cavil and scoff at the truth, than to make any good use of it. 3. When we are in the company of malicious enemies of the truth.]

Let us all pray for the Spirit of wisdom and of a sound mind. Let us seek daily to know the path of duty, and ask daily for discretion nd good sense. Let us be bold as a lion in confessing Christ, and not be afraid to "speak of him before princes" if need be. But let us never forget that "wisdom is profitable to direct" (Ecclesiastes 10:10, KJV) and let us beware of doing harm by an ill-directed zeal.

Mark
Chapter 2

Privileges of Capernaum; a paralytic healed *(2:1–12)*

This passage shows our Lord once more at Capernaum. Once more we find him doing his accustomed work, preaching the Word and healing those who were sick.

1. Spiritual privileges and their neglect
First, we see in these verses what great spiritual privileges some people enjoy, and yet make no use of them.

This is a truth which is strikingly illustrated by the history of Capernaum. No city in Palestine appears to have enjoyed so much of our Lord's presence during his earthly ministry as did this city. It was the place where he lived after he left Nazareth (Matthew 4:13). It was the place where many of his miracles were worked, and many of his sermons delivered. But nothing that Jesus said or did seems to have had any effect on the hearts of the inhabitants. They crowded to hear him, as we read in this passage – "there was no room left, not even outside the door" (verse 2). They were amazed. They were astonished. They were filled with wonder at his mighty works. But they were not converted. They lived in the full noon-tide blaze of the Sun of Righteousness and yet their hearts remained hard. And they drew from our Lord the heaviest condemnation that he ever pronounced against any place, except Jerusalem: "You, Capernaum, will you be lifted up to the skies? No, you will go down to the depths. If the miracles that were performed in you had been performed in Sodom, it would have remained to this day. But I tell you that it will be more bearable for Sodom on the day of judgment than for you" (Matthew 11:23–24).

It is good for us all to take good note of this case of Capernaum. We are all too apt to suppose that it needs nothing but the powerful preaching of the Gospel to convert people's souls, and that if the Gospel is only brought into a place everybody *must* believe. We forget the amazing power of unbelief, and the depth of man's enmity against God. We forget that the Capernaites heard the most faultless preaching, and saw it confirmed by the most surprising miracles, and yet remained dead in their transgressions and sins. We need reminding that the same Gospel which is the savor of life to some is the savor of death to others, and that the same fire which softens the wax will also harden the clay. Nothing, in fact, seems to harden people's hearts so much as to hear the Gospel regularly, and yet deliberately prefer the service of sin and the world. Never were people so favored as the people of Capernaum, and never did people appear to become so hard. Let us beware of walking in their steps. We ought often to use the prayer of the Litany: "From hardness of heart, Good Lord, deliver us."

2. Affliction may be a blessing to the soul

Second, we see from these verses how great a blessing affliction may prove to the soul.

We are told that a paralytic was brought to our Lord at Capernaum in order to be healed. Helpless and impotent, he was carried on his mat by four kind friends, and let down into the midst of the place where Jesus was preaching. At once the object of the man's desire was gained. The great Physician of soul and body saw him, and gave him speedy relief. He restored him to health and strength. He granted him the far greater blessing of forgiveness of sins. In short, the man who had been carried from his house that morning weak, dependent and bowed down both in body and soul, returned to his own house rejoicing.

Who can doubt that to the end of his days this man would thank God for this paralysis? Without it he would probably have lived and died in ignorance, and never seen Christ at all. Without it, he might have kept his sheep on the green hills of Galilee all his life long, and never been brought to Christ, and never heard the blessed words, "your sins are forgiven." That paralysis was indeed a blessing. Who can tell but it was the beginning of eternal life to his soul?

How many in every age can testify that this paralytic's experience has been their own! They have learned wisdom by affliction. Bereavements have proved mercies. Losses have proved real gains. Sicknesses have led them to the great Physician of souls, sent them to the Bible, shut out the world, shown them their own foolishness, taught them to pray. Thousands can say like David, "It was good for me to be afflicted so that I might learn your decrees" (Psalm 119:71).

Let us beware of grumbling under affliction. We may be sure there is a reason for every cross, and a wise purpose in every trial. Every sickness and sorrow is a gracious message from God, and is meant to call us nearer to him. Let us pray that we may learn the lesson that each affliction is appointed to convey. Let us see that we do not "refuse him who speaks" (Hebrews 12:25).

3. Christ's priestly power of forgiveness

Third, we see in these verses the priestly power of forgiving sins which is possessed by our Lord Jesus Christ.

We read that our Lord said to the paralytic, "Son, your sins are forgiven" (verse 5). He said these words with a meaning. He knew the hearts of the teachers of the law by whom he was surrounded. He intended to show them that he laid claim to be the true High Priest, and to have the power of absolving sinners, though at present the claim was seldom put forward. But he expressly told them that he had the power. He says, "the Son of Man has authority on earth to forgive sins" (verse 10). In saying "your sins are forgiven," he had only exercised his rightful office.

Let us consider how great must be the authority of him who has the power to forgive sins! This is the thing that no one but God can do. No angel in heaven, no person on earth, no church in council, no minister of any denomination, can take away from the sinner's conscience the load of guilt, and give him peace with God. They may point to the fountain open for all sin. They may declare with authority whose sins God is willing to forgive. But they cannot absolve by their own authority. They cannot put away transgressions. This is God's prerogative, and he has put it in the hands of his Son Jesus Christ.

Let us think for a moment how great a blessing it is that Jesus is our great High Priest, and that we know where to go for absolution. We must have a priest and a sacrifice between ourselves and God.

Conscience demands an atonement for our many sins. God's holiness makes it absolutely necessary. Without an atoning priest there can be no peace of soul. Jesus Christ is the very priest that we need, powerful to forgive and pardon, tender-hearted and willing to save.

And now let us ask ourselves whether we have yet known the Lord Jesus as our High Priest. Have we asked him? Have we sought absolution? If not, we are still in our sins. May we never rest till the Spirit witnesses with our spirit that we have sat at the feet of Jesus and heard his voice saying, "Son, your sins are forgiven."

The calling of Levi; Christ the physician; new wine *(2:13–22)*

The person who is called Levi at the beginning of this passage is the same person who is called Matthew in the first of the four Gospels. Let us not forget this. It is no less than an apostle and an evangelist whose early history is now before our eyes.

1. Christ's power to call people to be his disciples
First, we learn from these verses the power of Christ to call people out from the world and make them his disciples. We read that he said to Levi, when "sitting at the tax collector's booth" (verse 14), "Follow me." And at once he "got up and followed him." From a tax collector he became an apostle, and a writer of the first book in the New Testament, which is now known all over the world.

This is a truth of deep importance. Without a divine call no one can be saved. We are all so sunk in sin, and so wedded to the world, that we should never turn to God and seek salvation unless he first called us by his grace. God must speak to our hearts by his Spirit before we ever speak to him. Those who are children of God, says the 17th Article [of the *Thirty-Nine Articles*], are "called according to God's purpose by his Spirit working in due season." Now how blessed is the thought that this calling of sinners is committed to so gracious a Saviour as Christ!

When the Lord Jesus calls a sinner to be his servant, he acts as a Sovereign; but he acts with infinite mercy. He often chooses those who seem most unlikely to do his will, and furthest off from his kingdom. He draws them to himself with almighty power, breaks the chains of old habits and customs, and makes them new creatures. As the lode-stone attracts the iron, and the south wind softens the frozen ground, so does Christ's calling draw sinners out from the world, and melt the hardest heart. "The voice of the Lord is mighty in operation." Blessed are they who, when they hear it, do not harden their hearts!

We ought never to despair entirely of anyone's salvation when we read this passage of Scripture. He who called Levi still lives and still works. The age of miracles is not yet past. The love of money is a powerful principle, but the call of Christ is even more powerful. Let us not despair even about those who sit "at the tax collector's booth" and enjoy abundance of this world's good things. The voice which said to Levi, "Follow me," may yet reach their hearts. We may yet see them get up and take up the cross and follow Christ. Let us hope continually, and pray for others. Who can tell what God may be going to do for anyone around us? No one is too bad for Christ to call. Let us pray for all.

2. Christ as Physician

Second, we learn from these verses that one of Christ's principal roles is that of a Physician. The teachers of the law and Pharisees found fault with him for eating and drinking with tax collectors and "sinners." But "on hearing this, Jesus said to them, 'It is not the healthy who need a doctor, but the sick'" (verse 17).

The Lord Jesus did not come into the world, as some suppose, to be nothing more than a law-giver, a king, a teacher, and an example. Had this been all the purpose of his coming, there would have been small comfort for us. Diet sheets and rules of living are all very well for the convalescent, but not suitable to the person laboring under a mortal disease. A teacher and an example might be sufficient for an unfallen being like Adam in the Garden of Eden. But fallen sinners like ourselves want healing first, before we can value rules.

The Lord Jesus came into the world to be a physician as well as a teacher. He knew the needs of human nature. He saw us all sick of a mortal disease, stricken with the plague of sin, and dying daily. He pitied us, and came down to bring divine medicine for our relief. He came to give health and cure to the dying, to heal the broken-hearted, and to offer strength to the weak. No sin-sick soul is too far gone for him. It is his glory to heal and restore to life the most desperate cases. For unfailing skill, for unwearied tenderness, for long experience of people's spiritual ailments, the great Physician of souls stands alone. There is none like him.

But what do we know ourselves of this special role of Christ's? Have we ever felt our spiritual sickness and applied to him for relief? We are never right in the sight of God until we do. We have got nothing right in religion if we think the sense of sin should keep us back from Christ. To feel our sins and know our sickness is the beginning of real Christianity. To be aware of our corruption and abhor our own transgressions is the first symptom of spiritual health. Happy indeed are those who have found out their soul's disease! Let them know that Christ is the very Physician they require, and let them consult him without delay.

3. Mixing different things in religion is worse than useless

Third, we learn from these verses that in religion it is worse than useless to attempt to mix things which essentially differ. "No one," he tells the Pharisees, "sews a patch of unshrunk cloth on an old garment" (verse 21). "No one pours new wine into old wineskins" (verse 22).

These words, we must of course see, were a parable. They were spoken with special reference to the question which the Pharisees had just raised: "How is it that John's disciples . . . are fasting, but yours are not?" (verse 18). Our Lord's reply evidently means that to enforce fasting among his disciples would be inexpedient and unseasonable. His little flock was as yet young in grace, and weak in faith, knowledge and experience. They must be led on softly, and not burdened at this early stage with requirements which they were not able to bear. Fasting, moreover, might be suitable to the disciples of someone who was only the Bridegroom's friend, who lived in the wilderness, preached the baptism of repentance, was clothed in camel's hair, and ate locusts and wild honey. But fasting was not so suitable for the disciples of the Bridegroom himself, who brought glad news to sinners, and came living like other people. In short, to require fasting of his disciples at present would be putting "new wine into old wineskins." It would be trying to mingle and amalgamate things that essentially differed.

The principle laid down in these little parables is one of great importance. It is a kind of proverbial saying, and can be applied widely.

Forgetting it has frequently done great harm in the church. The evils that have arisen from trying to sew the new patch on the old garment and put the new wine into old wineskins have been neither few nor small.

How was it with the Galatian church? It is recorded in St. Paul's letter. People wished in that church to reconcile Judaism with Christianity, and to circumcise as well as baptize. They endeavored to keep alive the law of ceremonies and ordinances, and to place it side by side with the Gospel of Christ. In fact they would have put the "new wine into old wineskins." And in so doing they made a great mistake.

How was it with the early Christian church, after the apostles were dead? We have it recorded in the pages of church history. Some tried to make the Gospel more acceptable by mingling it with Platonic philosophy. Some labored to recommend it to the heathen by borrowing rituals, processions and vestments from the temples of the heathen gods. In short, they "sewed the new patch on the old garment." And in so doing they paved the way for the whole Roman apostasy.

How is it with many professing Christians in the present day? We have only to look around us and see. There are thousands who are trying to reconcile the service of Christ and the service of the world, to have the name of Christian and yet live the life of the ungodly – to keep in with the servants of pleasure and sin, and yet be the followers of the crucified Jesus at the same time. In a word, they are tyring to enjoy the "new wine" and yet cling to the "old wineskins." They will find one day that they have attempted what cannot be done.

Let us leave the passage in a spirit of serious self-inquiry. It is one that ought to raise great searchings of heart in the prsent day. Have we never read what the Scripture says? "No one can serve two masters. . . . You cannot serve both God and Money" (Matthew 6:24). Let us place side by side with this text the concluding words of our Lord in this passage, "new wine into new wineskins."

The right view of the Sabbath day *(2:23–28)*

These verses set before us a remarkable scene in our Lord Jesus Christ's earthly ministry. We see our blessed Master and his disciples going "through the grain fields" on the Sabbath day (verse 23). We are told that "as his disciples walked along, they began to pick some heads of grain." At once we hear the Pharisees accusing them to our Lord, as if they had committed some great moral offense. "Why are they doing what is unlawful on the Sabbath?" (verse 24). They received an answer full of deep wisdom, which all should study well if they desire to understand the subject of Sabbath observance.

1. Excessive importance attached to trifles
First, we see from these verses what excessive importance is attached to trifles by those who merely observe the external forms of religion.

The Pharisees were such people, if ever there were any in the world. They seem to have thought exclusively of the outward part, the husk, the shell, and the ceremonies of religion. They even added to these externals by traditions of their own. Their godliness was made up of washings, fastings, peculiarities in dress, and worship of the will, while repentance, faith and holiness were comparatively overlooked.

The Pharisees would probably have found no fault if the disciples had been guilty of some offense against the moral law. They would have winked at covetousness, or perjury, or extortion, or excess, because they were sins to which they themselves were inclined. But no sooner did they see an infringement of their human traditions about the right way of keeping the Sabbath, than they raised an outcry, and found fault.

Let us watch and pray lest we fall into the error of the Pharisees. There are never lacking Christians who walk in their steps. There are thousands at the present time who plainly think more of the mere outward ceremonies of religion than of its doctrines. They make more ado about keeping saints' days and turning to the east in the creed and bowing at the name of Jesus, than about repentance, faith or separation from the world. Let us always be on our guard against this spirit. It cannot comfort, satisfy or save.

It ought to be a settled principle in our minds that someone's soul is in a bad state when they begin to regard human rites and ceremonies as things of superior importance, and exalt them above the preaching of the Gospel. It is a symptom of spiritual disease. There is mischief within. It is too often the resource of an uneasy conscience. The first steps of apostasy from Protestantism to Romanism have often been in this direction. No wonder St. Paul said to the Galatians, "You are observing special days and months and seasons and years! I fear for you, that somehow I have wasted my efforts on you" (Galatians 4:10–11).

2. The value of a knowledge of holy Scripture

Second, we see from these verses the value of a knowledge of holy Scripture.

Our Lord replies to the accusation of the Pharisees by a reference to holy Scripture. He reminds his enemies of the conduct of David, when "he and his companions were hungry and in need" (verse 25). "Have you never read what David did?" They could not deny that the writer of the book of Psalms, a man after God's own heart, was not likely to set a bad example. They knew in fact that he had not failed to keep any of the Lord's commands all the days of his life, "except in the case of Uriah the Hittite" (1 Kings 15:5). Yet what had David done? He had gone into the house of God, when pressed by hunger, and eaten "the consecrated bread, which is lawful only for priests to eat" (verse 26). He had thus shown that some requirements of God's laws might be relaxed when necessary. To this Scripture our Lord refers his adversaries. They found nothing to reply to it. The sword of the Spirit was a weapon which they could not resist. They were silenced, and put to shame.

[There is some difficulty in this passage in the mention of Abiathar as "the high priest" (verse 26). In the book of Samuel it appears that Abimelech was the high priest when the incident referred to took place (1 Samuel 21:6).

The explanations of this difficulty are various. They are as follows:

1. Beza says that both Abiathar and Abimelech had each two names, and that Abiathar was frequently called Abimelech, and Abimelech Abiathar. (See in proof of this 2 Samuel 8:17 and 1 Chronicles 18:16 and 24:3.)

2. Lightfoot would translate the words "in the days of Abiathar, the son of the high priest," and says he is named rather than his father because he brought the ephod to David, and by him inquiry was made by Urim and Thummim. He also says that the Jews understood

"Abiathar" to mean the Urim and Thummim, and to say that the thing was done "under Abiathar" would show that it was done by divine direction.

3. Whitby thinks that by "the high priest" here we are not to understand the man who was strictly so called, but only one who was an eminent man of the order. He quotes as examples Matthew 2:4, 26:3 and 27:62; John 11:47 and Mark 14:10 and 43.

4. Some think that both Abimelech and Abiathar officiated as high priests at the same time. That there was nothing altogether unusual in there being two chief priests at once is shown by 2 Samuel 8:17, where two names are given as "the priests."

5. Some think that there has been a mistake made in transcribing the original words of St. Mark in this place, and some words have been inserted, or wrongly written. Beza's manuscript omits the words translated "in the time of Abiathar the high priest" altogether. The St. Gall manuscript and the Gothic version have the word "priest" simply, and not "high priest." The Persian version has "Abimelech" instead of "Abiathar." However, it is only fair to say that the evidence of the great majority of manuscripts and versions is in favor of the text as it stands.

Some of these solutions of the difficulty are evidently more probable than others. But any one of them is far more rasonable and deserving of belief than to suppose, as some have asserted, that St. Mark made a blunder! Such a theory destroys the whole principle of the inspiration of Scripture. Transcribers of the Bible have possibly made occasional mistakes. The original writers were inspired in the writing of every word, and therefore could not err.]

Now the conduct of our Lord on this occasion ought to be a pattern to all his people. Our grand reason for our faith and practice should always be, "This is what is written in the Bible." "What does Scripture say?" We should endeavor to have the Word of God on our side in all debatable questions. We should seekto be able to give a scriptural answer for our behavior in all matters of dispute. We should refer our enemies to the Bible as our rule of conduct. We will always find a plain text the most powerful argument we can use. In a world like this we must expect our opinions to be attacked, if we serve Christ, and we may be sure that nothing silences adversaries so soon as a quotation from Scripture.

Let us however remember that if we are to use the Bible as our Lord did, we must know it well, and be acquainted with its contents. We must read it diligently, humbly, perseveringly, prayerfully, or we shall never find its texts coming to our aid in the time of need. To use the sword of the Spirit effectually, we must be familiar with it, and have it often in our hands. There is no royal road to the knowledge of the Bible. It does not come to people by intuition. The book must be studied, pondered, prayed over, searched into, and not left always lying on a shelf or carelessly looked at now and then. It is the students of the Bible, and they only, who will find it a weapon ready to hand in the day of battle.

3. The principle for deciding questions about the Sabbath

Third, we see from these verses the true principle by which all questions about the observance of the Sabbath ought to be decided. "The Sabbath," says our Lord, "was made for man, not man for the Sabbath" (verse 27).

There is a mine of deep wisdom in those words. They deserve close attention, and the more so because they are not recorded in any Gospel but that of St. Mark. Let us see what they contain.

"The Sabbath was made for man." God made it for Adam in paradise, and renewed it to Israel on Mount Sinai. It was made for all mankind, not for the Jew only, but for the whole family of Adam. It was made for human benefit and happiness. It was for the good of their bodies, the good of their minds, and the good of their souls. It was given as a boon and a blessing, and not as a burden. This was the original institution.

But "man was not made for the Sabbath." The observance of the day of God was never meant to be so enforced as to be an injury to health, or to interfere with necessities. The original command to "remember the Sabbath day by keeping it holy" (Exodus 20:8) was not intended to be so interpreted as to do harm to people's bodies, or prevent acts of mercy to fellow-creatures. This was the point that the Pharisees had forgotten, or buried under their traditions.

There is nothing in all this to warrant the rash assertion of some people that our Lord has done away with the fourth commandment. On the contrary, he clearly speaks of the Sabbath day as a privilege and a gift, and only regulates the extent to which its observance should be enforced. He shows that works of necessity and mercy may be done on the Sabbath day, but he says not a word to justify the notion that Christians need not "remember the Sabbath day by keeping it holy."

Let us be jealous over our own conduct in the matter of observing the Sabbath. There is little danger of the day being kep too strictly in the present age. There is far more danger of its being profaned and forgotten entirely. Let us contend earnestly for its preservation among us in all its integrity. We may rest assured that national prosperity and personal growth in grace are intimately bound up in the maintenance of a holy Sabbath.

[The concluding words of this passage now expounded are remarkable: "the Son of Man is Lord even of the Sabbath" (verse 28). They have received some rather strange interpretations, which it may be well to notice.

1. Chrysostom, Grotius, Calovius and others think that the "Son of Man" in this place means "any man," anyone naturally born of the family of Adam, and not Christ himself. To say nothing of the objections that might be brought against the doctrines involved in such a sense, it is an unanswerable objection that the expression "Son of Man" is never used in this way in the New Testament. Whitby says that it occurs eighty-eight times, and always applies to Christ.

2. Others say that our Lord's meaning is to assert his own right to dispense with the observance of the fourth commandment. This, however, seems a very unsatisfactory interpretation. Our Lord declares publicly in one place that he came not to destroy the law but to fulfill it (Matthew 5:17). He challenges the Jews in another place to convict him of any breach of the law: "can any of you prove me guilty of sin?" (John 8:46). His enemies, when they brought him at last before Caiaphas, did not charge him with breaking the fourth commandment. No doubt they would have done so had he given them occasion, either by his teaching or practice.

The true meaning appears to be that our Lord claims the right to dispense with all the traditional rules, and human laws about the Sabbath, with which the Pharisees had overloaded the day of rest. As Son of Man, who came not to destroy but to save, he asserts his power to set free the blessed Sabbath from the false and superstitious notions with which the Rabbis had clogged and poisoned it, and to restore it to its proper meaning and use. He declares that the Sabbath is his day – his by creation and institution, since he first gave it in paradise and at Sinai – and proclaims his determination to defend and purify his day from Jewish imposition, and to give it to his disciples as a day of blessing, comfort and benefit according to its original intention.

Two things are implied in our Lord's words. One is his own divinity. The "Lord of the Sabbath" could be no less than God himself. It is like the expression, "one greater than the temple is here" (Matthew 12:6). The other is his intention of altering the day of rest from the seventh day of the week to the first. At the time that he spoke, neither of these things doubtless were apparent to the Jews, and probably not to his disciples. After his ascension they "remembered his words."

A passage in Mayer's commentary of 1631 is worth reading.

It is certain that Christ being a perfect pattern of doctrine in all things, did not transgress, or maintain any transgression against any law of God. Wherefore it is to be held that all his speech here tendeth to nothing else but to convince the Pharisees of blindness and ignorance, touching the right keeping of the Sabbath according to the commandment, it being never required to rest so strictly as they thought.]

Mark
Chapter 3

The man with a shriveled hand; Christ watched by his enemies and distressed *(3:1–12)*

These verses show us our Lord again working a miracle. In the synagogue he heals "a man with a shriveled hand" (verse 1). Always about his Father's business – always doing good – doing it in the sight of enemies as well as of friends – such was the daily tenor of our Lord's earthly ministry, "leaving you an example, that you should follow in his steps" (1 Peter 2:21). Blessed indeed are those Christians who strive, however feebly, to imitate their Master!

1. Christ watched by his enemies
First, let us observe in these verses how our Lord Jesus Christ was watched by his enemies. We read that "they watched him closely to see if he would heal him on the Sabbath" (verse 2).

What a sad proof we have here of the wickedness of human nature! It was the Sabbath day when these things happened. It was in the synagogue, where people were assembled to hear the Word and worship God. Yet even on the day of God, and at the time of worshiping God, these wretched hypocrites were plotting mischief against our Lord. The very men who claimed to be so strict and holy in little things were full of malicious and angry thoughts in the midst of the whole assembly (Proverbs 5:14).

Christ's people must not expect to fare better than their master. They are always watched by an ill-natured and spiteful world. Their conduct is scanned with a keen and jealous eye. Their ways are noted and diligently observed. They are marked men. They can do nothing

32

without the world noticing it. Their dress, their expenditure, their employment of time, their conduct in all the relations of life, are all rigidly and closely noted. Their adversaries wait for their halting, and if at any time they fall into an error, the ungodly rejoice.

It is good for all Christians to keep this before their minds. Wherever we go, and whatever we do, let us remember that, like our Master, we are "watched." The thought should make us exercise a holy jealousy over all our conduct, that we may do nothing to cause the enemy to blaspheme. It should make us diligent to avoid even the "appearance of evil" (1 Thessalonians 5:22, KJV). Above all, it should make us pray much to be kept in our tempers, tongues and daily public demeanor. The Saviour who was "watched closely" himself knows how to sympathize with his people, and to supply grace to help in time of need.

2. The principle of Sabbath observance

Second, let us observe the great principle that our Lord lays down about Sabbath observance. He teaches that it is lawful "to do good" on the Sabbath (verse 4).

This principle is taught by a remarkable question. He asks those around him which was "lawful on the Sabbath: to do good or to do evil, to save life or to kill?" (verse 4). Was it better to heal this poor sufferer before him with the shriveled hand, or to leave him alone? Was it more sinful to restore a person to health on the Sabbath than to plot murder and nourish hatred against an innocent person, as they were doing at that moment against himself? Was he to be blamed for saving life on the Sabbath? Were they blameless when they wanted to kill? No wonder that before such a question as this, our Lord's enemies "remained silent" (verse 4).

It is plain from these words of our Lord that no Christian need ever hesitate to do a really good work on a Sunday. A real work of mercy, such as ministering to the sick or relieving pain, may always be done without scruple. The holiness with which the fourth commandment invests the Sabbath day is not in the least invaded by anything of this kind.

But we must take care that the principle here laid down by our Lord is not abused and turned to bad account. We must not allow ourselves to suppose that the permission to "do good" implies that everyone may seek his own pleasure on the Sabbath. The permission to "do good" was never meant to open the door to amusements, worldly festivities, traveling, journeying and sensual gratification. It was never intended to license the Sunday railway train or the Sunday steam boat, or the Sunday exhibition. These things do good to no one, and do certain harm to many. They rob many a servant of his seventh day's rest. They turn the Sunday of thousands into a day of hard toil. Let us beware of perverting our Lord's words from their proper meaning. Let us remember what kind of "doing good" on the Sabbath was sanctioned by his blessed example. Let us ask ourselves whether there is the slightest likeness between our Lord's works on the Sabbath and those ways of spending the Sabbath which many people argue for and still dare to appeal to our Lord's example. Let us fall back on the plain meaning of our Lord's words, and take our stand on them. He gives us liberty to "do good" on Sunday, but he gives no liberty at all for feasting, sightseeing, party-giving and excursions.

3. The feelings of Christ for his enemies

Third, let us observe the feelings which the conduct of our Lord's enemies called up in his heart. We are told that "he looked round at them in anger" and was "deeply distressed at their stubborn hearts" (verse 5).

This expression is very remarkable, and demands special attention. It is meant to remind us that our Lord Jesus Christ was a man like ourselves in every way, yet was without sin. Whatever sinless feelings belong to the human constitution, our Lord shared them and knew them by experience. We read that he "marveled," that he "rejoiced," that he "wept," that he "loved," and here we read that he felt "anger" (verse 5).

It is plain from these words that there is an "anger" which is lawful, right and not sinful. There is an indignation which is justifiable, and on some occasons may properly be displayed. The words of Solomon and St. Paul both seem to teach the same lesson. "As a north wind brings rain, so a sly tongue brings angry looks" (Proverbs 25:23). "In your anger do not sin" (Ephesians 4:26).

Yet it must be confessed that the subject is full of difficulty. Of all the feelings that man's heart experiences, there is none perhaps which so soon runs into sin as the feeling of anger. There is none which leads on to so much evil. The length to which ill-temper, irritability and passion will carry even godly people, everybody must know. The story of the "sharp disagreement" between Paul and Barnabas at Antioch, and the story of Moses being provoked till "rash words came from Moses' lips" (Psalm 106:33) are familiar to every Bible reader. The awful fact that passionate words are a breach of the sixth commandment is plainly taught in the Sermon on the Mount. And yet here we see that there is an anger which is lawful.

Let us leave this subject with an earnest prayer that we may all be enabled to watch our spirit in the matter of anger. We may rest assured that there is no human feeling which needs so much cautious guarding as this. A sinless wrath is a very rare thing. Human wrath is seldom for the glory of God. In every case a righteous indignation should be mingled with grief and sorrow for those who cause it, even as it was in the case of our Lord. And this, at all events, we may be sure of: it is better never to be angry than to be angry and sin.

[In connection with this subject, Bishoop Butler's Sermon on Resentment deserves to be looked at. He says at the conclusion of it:

That passion, from whence men take occasion to run into the dreadful sins of malice and revenge, even that passion, as implanted in our nature by God, is not only innocent but a generous movement of mind. It is in itself, and in its original, no more than indignation against injury and wickedness – that which is the only deformity in the creation, and the only reasonable object of abhorrence and dislike.]

The appointing of the twelve apostles; Christ's zeal misunderstood by his friends (3:13–21)

The beginning of this passage describes the appointment of the twelve apostles. It is an event in our Lord's earthly mnistry which should always be read with deep interest. What a vast amount of benefit these few men have conferred on the world! The names of a few Jewish fishermen are known and loved by millions all over the globe, while the names of many kings and rich men are lost and forgotten. People who do good to souls are the ones who are "remembered forever" (Psalm 112:6).

1. Called to be disciples before becoming apostles
First, let us notice in these verses how many of the twelve who are here named had been called to be disciples before they were ordained apostles.

There are six, at least, out of the number whose first call to follow Christ is specially recorded. These six are Peter and Andrew, James and John, Philip and Matthew. In short, there can be little doubt that eleven of our Lord's apostles were converted before they were ordained.

It ought to be the same with all ministers of the Gospel. They ought to be people who have been first called by the Spirit, before they are set apart for the great work of teaching others. The rule should be the same with them as with the apostles – "first converted, then ordained."

It is impossible to overrate the importance of this to the interests of true religion. Bishops and presbyteries can never be too strict and particular in the inquiries they make about the spiritual character of candidates for orders. An unconverted minister is utterly unfit for his job. How can he speak from an experience of grace which he has never tasted himself? How can he commend the Saviour to his people if he himself only knows him by name? How can he urge on souls the need of that conversion and new birth which he himself has not experienced?

Parents who persuade their sons to become clergymen in order to obtain a good living or follow a respectable profession are miserably mistaken! What is it but persuading them to say what is not true, and to take the Lord's name in vain? There is no one who does such injury to the cause of Christianity as unconverted, worldly ministers. They are a support to the unbeliever, a joy to the devil and an offense to God.

2. The nature of the apostles' ministry
Second, let us notice the nature of the ministry to which the apostles were ordained. They were to "be with" Christ. They were to be sent out "to preach." They were to have "authority to drive out demons."

These three points deserve attention. They contain much instruction.

Our Lord's twelve apostles, beyond doubt, were a distinct order of men. They had no successors when they died. Strictly and literally speaking, there is no such thing as apostolic succession. No one can really be called a "successor of the apostles" unless he can work miracles and teach infallibly, as they did. But still, in saying this, we must not forget that in many things the apostles were intended to be patterns and models for all ministers of the Gospel. Bearing this in mind, we may draw most useful lessons from this passage concerning the duties of a faithful minister.

Like the apostles, the faithful minister ought to keep up close communion with Christ. He should be "with him" a lot. His fellowship should be with the Son (1 John 1:3). He should remain in him. He should be separate from the world, and sit each day, like Mary, at Jesus' feet, and hear his Word. He should study him, copy him, drink in his Spirit, and walk in his steps. He should strive to be able to say, when he enters the pulpit, "we proclaim to you what we have seen and heard" (1 John 1:3).

Like the apostles, the faithful minister ought to be a preacher. This must always be his principal work, and receive the greatest part of his thought. He must place it above the administration of the sacraments (1 Corinthians 1:17). He must exalt it above the reading of services. An unpreaching minister is of little use to the church of Christ. He is a lampless lighthouse, a silent trumpeter, a sleeping watchman, a painted fire.

Like the apostles, the faithful minister must labor to do good in every way. Though he cannot heal the sick, he must seek to alleviate sorrow, and to increase happiness among everyone he has to do with. He must strive to be known as the comforter, the counselor, the peacemaker, the helper and the friend of all. People should know him not as one who rules and domineers, but as one who is their servant for Jesus' sake (2 Corinthians 4:5).

Like the apostles, the faithful minister must oppose every work of the devil. Though not called to drive out evil spirits from the body, he must always be ready to resist the devil's devices and to denounce his snares for the soul. He must expose the tendency of races, theaters, balls, gambling, drunkenness, Sabbath-profanation and sensual gratifications. Every age has its own particular temptations. Many are the devices of Satan. But wherever the devil is most busy, the minister ought to be there, ready to confront and withstand him.

How great is the responsibility of ministers! How heavy their work, if they do their duty! How much they need the prayers of all praying people in order to support and strengthen their hands! No wonder St. Paul says so often to the churches, "Pray for us."

3. Christ's zeal misunderstood

Third, let us notice how our Lord Jesus Christ's zeal was misunderstood by his enemies. We are told that they "went to take charge of him, for they said, 'He is out of his mind'" (verse 21).

There is nothing in this fact that need surprise us. The prophet who came to anoint Jehu was called a "madman" (2 Kings 9:11). Festus told Paul that he was out of his mind (Acts 26:24). Few things show the corruption of human nature more clearly than people's inability to understand zeal in religion. Zeal about money, science, war, commerce or business is intelligible to the world. But zeal about religion is too often reckoned foolishness, fanaticism and the sign of a weak mind.

If someone injures his health by study, or excessive attention to business, no fault is found – "he is a hard worker." But if he wears himself out with preaching, or spends his whole time in doing good to souls, the cry is raised, "He is too enthusiastic and too righteous." The world has not changed. The "things that come from the Spirit of God" are always "foolishness" to people without the Spirit (1 Corinthians 2:14).

Let it not shake our faith if we have to drink of the same cup as our blessed Lord. Hard as it may be to flesh and blood to be misunderstood by our relations, we must recollect it is no new thing. Let us call to mind our Lord's words, "Anyone who loves his father or mother more than me is not worthy of me" (Matthew 10:37). Jesus knows the bitterness of our trials. Jesus feels for us. Jesus will give us help.

Let us bear patiently the unreasonableness of unconverted people, just as our Lord did. Let us pity their blindness and lack of knowledge, and not love them one whit the less. Above all, let us pray that God would change their hearts. Who can tell but the very people who now try to turn us away from Christ may one day become new creatures, see all things differently and follow Christ themselves?

CHAPTER 3

Warning against divisions; forgiveness; damnation *(3:22–30)*

We all know how painful it is to have our conduct misunderstood and misrepresented when we are doing right. It is a trial which our Lord Jesus Christ had to endure continually, all through his earthly ministry. We have an instance in the passage before us. The "teachers of the law who came down from Jerusalem" saw the miracles which he worked. They could not deny their reality. What then did they do? They accused our blessed Saviour of being in league and union with the devil. They said, "He is possessed by Beelzebub! By the prince of demons he is driving out demons!" (verse 22).

In our Lord's solemn answer to this wicked accusation, there are expressions which deserve special attention. Let us see what lessons they contain for our use.

1. The evil of dissension and division
First, we ought to notice how great is the evil of dissension and division.

This is a lesson which is strongly brought out in the beginning of our Lord's reply to the teachers of the law. He shows the absurdity of supposing that Satan would "drive out Satan" and so help to destroy his own power (verses 23–24). He appeals to the notorious fact, which even his enemies must admit, that there can be no strength where there is division: "If a kingdom is divided against itself, that kingdom cannot stand."

This truth is one which does not receive sufficient consideration. On no point has the abuse of the right of private judgment produced so much evil. The divisions of Christians are one great cause of the weakness of the visible church. They often absorb energy, time and power which might have been well bestowed on better things. They furnish the unbeliever with a prime argument against the truth of Christianity. They help the devil. Satan indeed is the chief promoter of religious divisions. If he cannot extinguish Christianity, he labors to make Christians quarrel with one another, and to set everyone against each other. No one knows better than the devil that "to divide is to conquer."

Let us resolve, so far as in us lies, to avoid all differences, dissensions and disputes in religion. Let us loathe and abhor them as the plague of

39

the churches. We cannot be too jealous about all saving truths. But it is easy to mistake dead scruples for conscientiousness, and zeal about mere trifles for zeal about the truth. Nothing justifies separation from a church but the separation of that church from the gospel. Let us be ready to concede much, and make many sacrifices for the sake of unity and peace.

2. Christ's declaration about the forgiveness of sins

Second, we ought to notice what a glorious declaration our Lord makes in these verses about the forgiveness of sins. He says, "all the sins and blasphemies of men will be forgiven them" (verse 28).

These words fall lightly on the ears of many people. They see no particular beauty in them. But to the person who is alive to his own sinfulness and is deeply aware of his need of mercy, these words are sweet and precious. "All sins will be forgiven." The sins of youth and age – the sins of head, hand, tongue and imagination – the sins against all God's commandments – the sins of persecutors, like Saul – the sins of idolaters, like Manasseh – the sins of open enemies of Christ, like the Jews who crucified him – the sins of backsliders from Christ, like Peter – all may be forgiven. The blood of Christ can cleanse all away. The righteousness of Christ can cover all, and hide all from God's eyes.

The doctrine here laid down is the crown and glory of the Gospel. The very first thing it proposes to man is free pardon, full forgiveness, complete remission, without money and without price. "Through him everyone who believes is justified from everything you could not be justified from by the law of Moses" (Acts 13:39).

Let us take hold of this doctrine without delay, if we never received it before. It is for us, as well as for others. We too, this very day, if we come to Christ, may be completely forgiven. "Though your sins are like scarlet, they shall be white as snow" (Isaiah 1:18).

Let us cling firmly to this doctrine, if we have received it already. We may sometimes feel faint, and unworthy, and cast down. But if we have really come to Jesus by faith, our sins are completely forgiven. They have been thrown behind God's back – blotted out of the book of life – sunk into the depths of the sea. Let us believe and not be afraid.

3. A soul can be lost forever in hell

Third, we ought to notice that it is possible for a soul to be lost forever in hell. The words of our Lord are distinct and explicit. He speaks of someone who is "guilty of an eternal sin" (verse 29).

This is an awful truth, beyond doubt. But it is a truth, and we must not shut our eyes against it. We find it asserted over and over in Scripture. Imagery of all kinds is multiplied, and language of every sort is employed, in order to make it plain and unmistakable. In short, if there is no such thing as "eternal damnation" (verse 29, KJV) we may throw the Bible aside, and say that words have no meaning at all.

We greatly need to keep this awful truth steadily in view in these days. Teachers have risen up who are openly attacking the doctrine of the eternity of punishment, or laboring hard to explain it away. People's ears are being tickled with plausible sayings about "the love of God" and the impossibility of a loving God permitting an everlasting hell. The eternity of punishment is spoken of as a mere "speculative question," about which men may believe anything they please. In the midst of all this flood of false doctrine, let us hold firmly the old truths. Let us not be ashamed to believe that there is an eternal God – an eternal heaven – and an eternal hell. Let us remember that sin is an infinite evil. It needed an atonement of infinite value to deliver the believer from its consequences – and it entails an infinite loss on the unbeliever who rejects the remedy provided for it. Above all, let us fall back onto plain scriptural statements like that before us today. One plain text is worth a thousand abstruse arguments.

Finally, if it is true that there is an "eternal damnation," let us work hard to make sure that we ourselves do not fall into it. Let us escape for our lives and not linger (Genesis 19:16–17). Let us flee for refuge to the hope set before us in the Gospel, and never rest till we know and feel that we are safe. And never, never let us be ashamed of seeking to be delivered from an eternal hell.

[There is an expression in the passage now expounded which appears to demand special notice. It is confessedly one of the hard things of Scripture, and has often troubled the hearts of Bible readers. I refer to the saying of our Lord, "whoever blasphemes against the Holy Spirit will never be forgiven" (verse 29). It seems that there is such a thing as an *unpardonable sin*.

Some interpreters have endeavored to cut the knot of the difficulty, by maintaining that the sin here referred to was entirely confined to the time when our Lord was on earth. They say that when the teachers of the law and the Pharisees saw the evidence of our Lord's miracles, and yet refused to believe in him as the Messiah, they committed the unpardonable sin. Their assertion that our Lord worked miracles through Beelzebub was blasphemy against the Holy Spirit.

There might be something in this view, if the passage under consideration stood entirely alone – though even then he would be a bold man who would assert that there were no hardened teachers of the law and Pharisees among the 3000 converted and forgiven on the day of Pentecost. But unfortunately for this theory, the doctrine here laid down is to be found in other places of Scripture beside this. I allude of course to the well-known passages Hebrews 6:4–6, Hebrews 10:26 and 1 John 5:17. In all these places there seems a reference to a sin which is not forgiven.

What then is the unpardonable sin? It must be frankly confessed that its precise nature is nowhere defined in holy Scripture. The most probable view is that it is a combination of clear intellectual knowledge of the Gospel, with deliberate rejection of it and willful choice of sin. It is a union of light in the head and hatred in the heart. Such was the case of Judas Iscariot. We must not flatter ourselves that no one has walked in his steps. In the absence of any definition in Scripture, we shall probably not get much nearer to the mark than this. Yet even this view must be treated carefully. The limits which knowledge combined with unbelief must pass, in order to become the unpardonable sin, are graciously withheld from us. God has mercifully ordered that we can never decide positively about any person that they have committed a sin which cannot be forgiven.

But although it is difficult to define what the unpardonable sin is, it is far less difficult to point out what it is not. A few words on this point may possibly help to relieve tender consciences.

We may lay it down as nearly certain that those who are troubled with fears that they have sinned the unpardonable sin are the very people who have not sinned it. The very fact that they are afraid and anxious about it is the strongest possible evidence in their favor. A troubled conscience – an anxiety about salvation and a dread of being cast away – a concern about the next world and a desire to escape from the wrath of God – these will probably never be found in the hearts of people who have sinned the sin for which there is no forgiveness. It is far more probable that the general marks of such a person will be utter hardness of conscience, a seared heart, an absence of any feeling, a thorough lack of spiritual feeling. The subject may safely be left there. There is such a thing as a sin which is never forgiven. But those who are troubled about it are most unlikely to have committed it.

The following quotation from Thomas Fuller's *Cause and Cure of a Wounded Conscience* deserves attention:

> The sin against the Holy Ghost is ever attended with these two symptoms – an absence of all contrition, and of all desire of forgiveness. Now, if thou canst truly say that thy sins are a burden to thee, that thou dost desire forgiveness and wouldst give anything to attain it, be of good comfort; thou hast not yet, and by God's grace never shall commit that unpardonable offense. I will not define how near thou hast been unto it. As David said to Jonathan, "there is but a step between me and death" (1 Samuel 20:3) – so maybe thou hast missed it very narrowly; but assure thyself thou art not as yet guilty thereof.]

Christ's brother and sister and mother *(3:31–35)*

In the verses immediately preceding this passage, we see our blessed Lord accused by the teachers of the law of being in league with the devil. They said, "He is possessed by Beelzebub! By the prince of demons he is driving out demons" (verse 22).

Now in this next passage we find that this absurd charge of the teachers of the law was not all that Jesus had to endure at this time. We are told that "Jesus' mother and brothers arrived. Standing outside, they sent someone in to call him" (verse 31). They could not yet understand the beauty and usefulness of the life that our Lord was living. Though they doubtless loved him well, they wanted to persuade him to cease from his work and "spare himself." Little did they know what they were doing! Little had they observed or understood our Lord's words when he was only twelve years old, "Didn't you know I had to be in my Father's house?" (Luke 2:49).

[The remarks of Scott on the conduct of our Lord's mother on this occasion are worth quoting:

It is plain that many of these intimations were suited, and doubtless prophetically intended, to be a Scriptural protest againbst the idolatrous honor, to this day, by vast multitudes, rendered to Mary the mother of Jesus. She was an excellent and honorable character, but evidently not perfect. She is entitled to great estimation, and high veneration, but surely not to religious confidence and worship.

It is difficult to mention any doctrine more completely destitute of Scriptural foundation than the Roman Catholic doctrine of the efficacy of the Virgin Mary's intercession, or the usefulness of addressing our prayers to her. As to the doctrine of the immaculate conception of the Virgin Mary, which has recently been accredited by the Roman Catholic church, it is a mere human figment without a single word of Scripture to support it. Holy and full of grace as the Virgin Mary was, it is plain that she regarded herself as one "born in sin" and needing a Saviour. We have her own remarkable words on this last point: "My spirit rejoices in God my Saviour" (Luke 1:47).

As to the opinion of the Fathers on the conduct of the mother of our Lord in this place, Whitby has collected come curious expressions: "Theophylact taxes her with vainglory and guilt, in endeavoring to draw Jesus from teaching the word. Tertullian pronounces her guilty of incredulity, Chrysostom of vainglory, infirmity and madness, for this very thing."]

It is interesting to note the quiet, firm perseverance of our Lord in the face of all discouragements. The slanderous suggestions of enemies and the well-meant remonstrances of ignorant friends were alike powerless to turn him from his course. He had set his face as a flint towards the cross and the crown. He knew the work he had come into the world to do. He had a baptism to undergo, and was distressed until it was completed (Luke 12:50).

So let it be with all true servants of Christ. Let nothing turn them for a moment out of the narrow way, or make them stop and look back. Let them take no notice of the ill-natured remarks of enemies. Let them not give way to the well-intentioned but mistaken entreaties of unconverted relations and friends. Let them reply in the words of Nehemiah, "I am carrying on a great project and cannot go down" (Nehemiah 6:3). Let them say, "I have taken up the cross, and I will not throw it down."

Jesus Christ's relations

We learn from these verses one mighty lesson. We learn who are regarded as the relations of Jesus Christ. It is "whoever does God's will" (verse 35). Such people the great head of the church regards as his "brother and sister and mother."

How much there is in this single expression! What a rich mine of consolation it opens to all true believers! Who can conceive the depth of our Lord's love towards Mary the mother who bore him, and at whose breast he had been nursed? Who can imagine the breadth of his love towards his blood brothers, with whom the tender years of his childhood had been spent? Doubtless no heart ever had within it such deep well-springs of affection as the heart of Christ. Yet he says of "whoever does God's will" that they are his "brother and sister and mother."

Let all true Christians drink comfort out of these words. Let them know that there is one at least who knows them, loves them, cares for them and counts them as his own family. What does it matter if they are poor in this world? They have no cause to be ashamed when they remember that they are the brothers and sisters of the Son of God. What does it matter if they are persecuted and ill-treated in their own homes because of their religion? They may remember the words of David, and apply them to their own case: "Though my mother and father forsake me, the LORD will receive me" (Psalm 27:10).

Finally, let all who persecute and ridicule others because of their religion be warned by these words, and repent! Who are they persecuting and ridiculing? The relations of Jesus the Son of God! The family of the King of kings and Lord of lords! Surely they would be wise to hold their peace and think carefully about what they are doing. Those they persecute have a powerful Friend: "their Defender is strong; he will take up their case against you" (Proverbs 23:11).

Mark
Chapter 4

The parable of the sower *(4:1–20)*

These verses contain the parable of the sower. Of all the parables spoken by our Lord, probably none is so well known as this. There is none which is so easily understood by all, from the gracious familiarity of the images which it contains. There is none which is of such universal application. So long as there is a church of Christ and a congregation of Christians, so long there will be a use for this parable.

[Thomas Taylor in his book on the parable of the sower (1634) writes:

> Our Saviour borroweth his comparisons from easy and familiar things, such as the sower, the seed, the ground, the growth, the withering, the answering or failing of the sower's expectations, all of them things well known, and by all these would teach us some spiritual instruction. For there is no earthly thing which is not fitted to put us in mind of some heavenly. Christ cannot look upon the sun, the wind, fire, water, a hen, a little grain of mustard seed – nor upon ordinary occasions, as the penny given for the day's work, the wedding garment and ceremonies of the Jews about it, nor the waiting of servants at their master's table, of children asking bread and fish at their father's table, but he applies all to some special use of edification in grace.

> Earthly things must remind us of heavenly. We must translate the book of nature into the book of grace.]

The language of the parable requires no explanation. To use the words of an ancient writer, "it needs application, not exposition." Let us now see what it teaches.

1. The path

First, we are taught that there are some hearers of the Gospel whose hearts are like the path in a field.

These are people who hear sermons but pay no attention to them. They go to a place of worship for form's sake, or because it is fashionable, or to appear respectable before other people. But they take no interest whatever in the preaching. It seems to them a mere matter of words, names and unintelligible talk. It is neither money nor meat nor drink nor clothes nor company, and as they sit with the sound of it going on around them they are taken up with thinking of other things. It does not matter at all whether it is law or Gospel. It produces no more effect on them than water on a stone. And at the end they go away knowing no more than when they came in.

There are myriads of people who claim to be Christians but are in this state of soul. There is hardly a church or chapel where scores of them are not to be found. Sunday after Sunday they allow the devil to snatch away the good seed that is sown on the face of their hearts. Week after week they live on without faith, fear, knowledge or grace, feeling nothing, caring nothing, taking no more interest in religion than if Christ had never died on the cross at all. And in this state they often die and are buried, and are lost forever in hell. This is a sad picture, but only too true.

2. The rocky places

Second, we are taught that there are some hearers of the Gospel whose hearts are like the rocky places in a field.

These are people on whom preaching produces temporary impressions, but no deep, lasting and abiding effect. They take pleasure in hearing sermons in which the truth is faithfully displayed. They can speak with apparent joy and enthusiasm about the sweetness of the Gospel and the happiness which they experience in listening to it. They can be moved to tears by the appeals of preachers, and talk with apparent earnestness of their own inner conflicts, hopes, struggles, desires and fears. But unhappily there is no stability about their religion.

"Since they have no root, they last only a short time" (verse 17). There is no real work of the Holy Spirit in their hearts. Their impressions are like Jonah's gourd which came up in a night and perished in a night. They fade as rapidly as they grow. "When trouble or persecution comes because of the word," they fall away (verse 17). Their goodness proves as "the morning mist, like the early dew that disappears" (Hosea 6:4). Their religion has no more life in it than the cut flower. It has no root, and soon withers way.

There are many in every congregation which hears the Gospel, who are just in this state of soul. They are not careless and inattentive hearers, like many round them, and are therefore tempted to think well of their own condition. They feel a pleasure in the preaching to which they listen, and therefore flatter themselves they must have grace in their hearts. And yet they are thoroughly deceived. Old things have not yet passed away. There is no real work of conversion in their inner being. With all their feelings, affections, joys, hopes and desires, they are actually on the high road to destruction.

[Anyone who wishes to understand the character of the "rocky places heart" should study Jonathan Edwards' *Treatise concerning Religious Affections*. Few Christians who have not looked into the subject have any idea of the lengths to which a person may go in religious feeling while at the same time being utterly destitute of the grace of God.]

3. The thorny ground

Third, we are taught that there are some hearers of the Gospel whose hearts are like the thorny ground in a field.

These are peope who attend to the preaching of Christ's truth and to a certain extent obey it. Their understanding assents to it. Their judgment approves of it. Their conscience is affected by it. Their affections are in favor of it. They acknowledge that it is all right, good and worth receiving. They even abstain from many things which the Gospel condemns, and adopt many habits which the Gospel requires. But here unhappily they stop short. Something appears to chain them fast, and they never get beyond a certain point in their religion. And the grand secret of their condition is the world. "The worries of this life, the deceitfulness of wealth and the desires for other things" prevent the word having its full effect on their souls (verse 19). With everything apparently that is promising and favorable in their spiritual state, they stand still. They never come up to the full standard of New Testament Christianity. They bring no fruit to perfection.

There are few faithful ministers of Christ who could not point to cases like these. Of all cases they are the most melancholy. To go so far and yet go no further – to see so much and yet not see all – to approve so much and yet not give Christ the heart, this is indeed most deplorable! And there is but one verdict that can be given about such people. Without a decided change they will never enter the kingdom of heaven. Christ wants our whole heart. "Friendship with the world is hatred towards God" (James 4:4).

4. The good soil

Fourth, we are taught that there are some hearers of the Gospel whose hearts are like the good soil in a field.

These are the people who really receive Christ's truth into the bottom of their hearts, believe it implicitly and obey it thoroughly. In these the fruits of that truth will be seen – uniform, plain and unmistakable results in heart and life. Sin will be truly hated, mourned over, resisted and renounced. Christ will be truly loved, trusted in, followed, loved and obeyed. Holiness will show itself in all their conversation, in humility, spiritual-mindedness, patience, meekness and love. There will be something that can be seen. The true work of the Holy Spirit cannot be hidden.

There will always be some persons in this state of soul wherever the Gospel is faithfully preached. Their numbers may very likely be few compared with the worldly people around them. Their experience and degree of spiritual attainment may differ widely, some producing thirty, some sixty and some a hundred times what was sown. But the crop of the seed falling into good ground will always be of the same kind. There will always be visible repentance, visible faith in Christ and visible holiness of life. Without these things, there is no saving religion.

And now let us ask ourselves, What are we? Under which class of hearers ought we to be ranked? With what kind of hearts do we hear the word? Never, never may we forget that there is only one infallible mark of being a right-hearted hearer! That mark is to bear fruit. To be without fruit is to be on the way to hell.

A lamp on a stand; the importance of hearing *(4:21–25)*

These verses seem to be intended to enforce the parable of the sower on the attention of those who heard it. They are remarkable for the succession of short, pithy, proverbial sayings which they contain. Such sayings are eminently calculated to arrest an ignorant hearer. They often strike, and stick in the memory when the main subject of the sermon is forgotten.

[The passage under consideration is one among many proofs that our Lord used the same words and the same ideas on many different occasions. The proverbial saying about the light under a bowl (verse 21) will be found in the Sermon on the Mount. So also the saying that "whatever is concealed is meant to be brought out into the open" (verse 22) and the saying "With the measure you use, it will be measured to you" (verse 24) are both to be found in the Gospel of St. Matthew, but in both cases in an entirely different context from the passage in St. Mark now before us (Matthew 10:26 and 7:2).

The subject is one that deserves attention. The needless difficulties that have been created by attempting to harmonize the Gospels and to make out that our Lord never said the same thing more than once, are neither few nor small.]

1. We ought to pass our knowledge on to others

First, we learn from these verses that we ought not only to receive knowledge, but impart it to others.

A lamp is not lit in order to be hidden and concealed, but to be put on a lampstand and used. Religious light is not given to us for ourselves alone, but for the benefit of others. We are to try to spread and diffuse our knowledge. We are to display to others the precious treasure that we have found, and persuade them to seek it for themselves. We are to tell them of the good news that we have heard, and endeavor to make them believe it and value it themselves.

We shall all have to give account of our use of knowledge one day. The books of God in the day of judgment will show what we have done. If we have buried our talent in the earth – if we have been content with a lazy, idle, do-nothing Christianity, and cared nothing what happened to others so long as we went to heaven ourselves – there will be a fearful exposure at last: "whatever is concealed is meant to be brought out into the open."

It becomes all Christians to lay these things to heart. It is high time that the old tradition that the clergy alone ought to teach and spread religious knowledge is exploded and cast aside forever. To do good and diffuse light is a duty for which all members of Christ's church are responsible, whether ministers or laity. Neighbors ought to tell neighbors if they have found an unfailing remedy in time of plague. Christians ought to tell others that they have found medicine for their souls, if they see them ignorant and dying for lack of it. What does St. Peter say? "Each one should use whatever gift he has received to serve others" (1 Peter 4:10). They will be happy days for the church when that text is obeyed.

2. The importance of thinking about what we hear

Second, we learn from these verses the importance of hearing, and of thinking carefully about what we hear.

This is a point to which our Lord evidently attaches great weight. We have seen it already brought out in the parable of the sower. We see it here enforced in two remarkable expressions. "If anyone has ears to hear, let him hear" (verse 23). "Consider carefully what you hear" (verse 24).

Hearing the truth is one principal avenue through which grace is conveyed to the human soul. "Faith comes from hearing the message" (Romans 10:17). One of the first steps towards conversion is to receive from the Spirit a hearing ear. People are seldom brought to repentance and faith in Christ without "hearing." The general rule is that of which St. Paul reminded the Ephesians: "You also were included in Christ when you heard the word of truth" (Ephesians 1:13).

Let us bear this in mind when we hear preaching decried as a means of grace. There is never any lack of people who seek to cast it down from the high place which the Bible gives it. There are many people who proclaim loudly that it is of far more importance to the soul to hear liturgical forms read, and to receive the Lord's Supper, than to hear God's Word expounded. Let us beware of all such ideas. Let it be a settled principle with us that "hearing the Word" is one of the foremost means of grace that God has given to us. Let us give every other means and ordinance its proper value and importance. But never let us forget the words of St. Paul: "Do not treat prophecies with contempt" (1 Thessalonians 5:20), and his dying charge to Timothy: "Preach the Word" (2 Timothy 4:2).

[Archbishop Grindal in his letter to Queen Elizabeth wrote:

> Public and continual preaching of God's Word is the ordinary means and instrument of the salvation of mankind. St. Paul calleth it the ministry of reconciliation of man unto God. By preaching of God's Word, the glory of God is enlarged, faith is nourished and charity increased. By it the ignorant is instructed, the negligent exhorted and invited, the stubborn rebuked, the weak conscience comforted, and to all those that sin of malicious wickedness, the wrath of God is threatened. By preaching, due obedience to Christian princes and magistrates is planted in the hearts of subjects; for obedience proceedeth of conscience, conscience is grounded upon the Word of God, the Word of God worketh his effect by preaching. So as generally when preaching wanteth obedience faileth.]

3. Using religious privileges

Third, we learn from these verses the importance of a diligent use of religious privileges. What does our Lord say? "Whoever has will be given more; whoever does not have, even what he has will be taken from him" (verse 25).

This is a principle which we find continually brought forward in Scripture. All that believers have is undoubtedly of grace. Their repentance, faith and holiness are all the gift of God. But the degree to which a believer attains in grace is always set before us as closely connected with his own hard work in the use of means of grace, and his own faithfulness in living fully up to the light and knowledge which he possesses. Indolence and laziness are always discouraged in God's Word. Labor and pains in hearing, reading and prayer are always represented as bringing their own reward. "The desires of the diligent are fully satisfied" (Proverbs 13:4). "The shiftless man goes hungry" (Proverbs 19:14).

Attention to this great principle is the main secret of spiritual prosperity. Those who make rapid progress in spiritual attainments – who grow visibly in grace, knowledge, strength and usefulness – will always be found to be hard workers. They leave no stone unturned to promote their souls' well-doing. They work hard at the Bible, in private devotions, in hearing sermons, in attending the Lord's table. And they reap according to what they sow. Just as the muscles of the body are strengthened by regular exercise, so are the graces of the soul increased by diligence in using them.

Do we wish to grow in grace? Do we desire to have stronger faith, brighter hope and clearer knowledge? Beyond doubt we do, if we are true Christians. Then let us live fully up to our light, and take advantage of every opportunity. Let us never forget our Lord's words in this passage. "With the measure you use, it will be measured to you – and even more." The more we do for our souls, the more shall we find God does for them.

The parable of the growing seed *(4:26–29)*

The parable contained in these verses is short, and only recorded in St. Mark's Gospel. But it is one that ought to be deeply interesting to all who have reason to hope that they are true Christians. It sets before us the story of the work of grace in an individual soul. It summons us to an examination of our own experience in divine things.

There are some expressions in the parable which we must not press too far. Such are the farmer's sleeping and getting up, and the "night and day" (verse 27). In this, as in many of our Lord's parables, we must carefully keep in view the main scope and object of the whole story, and not lay too much stress on lesser points. In the case before us the main thing taught is the close resemblance between some familiar operations in the cultivation of grain, and the work of grace in the heart. Let us rigidly confine our attention to this.

1. There must be a sower
First, we are taught that, as in the growth of grain so in the work of grace, there must be a sower.

The earth, as we all know, never produces grain by itself. It is a mother of weeds, but not of wheat. Human hands must plow it and scatter the seed, or else there would never be a harvest.

The human heart, similarly, will never of itself turn to God, repent, believe and obey. It is utterly barren of grace. It is entirely dead towards God, and unable to give itself spiritual life. The Son of Man must break it up by his Spirit, and give it a new nature. He must scatter over it by the hand of his laboring ministers the good seed of the Word.

Let us take good note of this truth. Grace in the human heart is an exotic. It is a new principle from outside, sent down from heaven and implanted in the soul. Left to themselves, no living person would ever seek God. And yet in communicating grace, God usually works through intermediaries. To despise the instrumentality of teachers and preachers is to expect grain where no seed has been sown.

2. Much is beyond us

Second, we are taught that, as in the growth of grain so in the work of grace, there is much that is beyond our comprehension and control.

The wisest farmer on earth can never explain all that takes place in a grain of wheat, when he has sown it. He knows the broad fact that unless he puts it into the ground and covers it up, there will not be an ear of wheat at harvest-time. But he cannot command the prosperity of each grain. He cannot explain why some grains come up and others die. He cannot specify the hour or the minute when life begins to show itself. He cannot define what that life is. These are matters he must leave alone. He sows his seed, and leaves the growth to God. It is "God who makes things grow" (1 Corinthians 3:7).

[Greswell in his book on the parables (Vol. 2, p. 132) writes:

A grain of corn, committed to the ground by the hand of man, will sprout and shoot; the shoot will disclose the stem, the stem the ear, and the ear the fruit: and were the most illiterate and unphilosophical person to be asked why all this should necessarily follow from the mere act of burying a seed in the earth, he might be disposed to laugh at the apparent simplicity of the question. Yet no human wisdom was ever able to return the answer to this question – no human sagacity ever yet could penetrate into the true causes of this effect; and no human knowledge, upon such subjects, has ever gone further than the mere discovery, by a regular and constant experience, that such and such consequences will uniformly follow from such and such previous acts.]

The workings of grace in the heart, similarly, are utterly mysterious and unsearchable. We cannot explain why the Word produces effects on one person in a congregation and not upon another. We cannot explain why, in some cases – with every possible advantage, and in spite of every entreaty – people reject the Word, and continue dead in transgressions and sins. We cannot explain why in other cases – with every possible difficulty, and with no encouragement – people are born again, and become committed Christians. We cannot define the manner in which the Spirit of God conveys life to a soul, and the exact process by which a believers receives a new nature. All these are hidden things to us. We see certain results, but we can go no further. "The wind blows wherever it pleases. You hear its sound, but you cannot tell where it comes from or where it is going. So it is with everyone born of the Spirit" (John 3:8).

Let us note this truth also, for it is deeply instructive. It is humbling no doubt to ministers, and teachers of others. The highest abilities, the most powerful preaching, the hardest work, cannot command success. God alone can give life. But it is a truth at the same time which supplies an admirable antidote to worry and despondency. Our principal work is to sow the seed. That done, we may wait with faith and patience for the result. We may go to sleep and get up night and day and leave our work with the Lord. He alone can, and if he thinks fit he will, give success.

3. Life appears gradually

Third, we are taught that, as in the growth of grain so in the work of grace, life appears gradually.

There is a true proverb which says, "Nature does nothing at a bound." The ripe ear of wheat does not appear at once, as soon as the seed bursts forth into life. The plant goes through many stages before it arrives at perfection – "first the stalk, then the ear, then the full grain in the ear" (verse 28). But in all these stages one great thing is true about it: even at its weakest, it is a living plant.

The work of grace, similarly, goes on in the heart by degrees. The children of God are not born perfect in faith, hope, knowledge or experience. Their beginning is generally a "day of small things." They see in part their own sinfulness, and Christ's fullness, and the beauty of holiness. But for all that, the weakest child in God's family is a true child of God. With all his weakness and infirmity he is alive. The seed of grace has really come up in his heart, though at present it be only in the stalk. He is "alive from the dead." And the wise man says, "even a live dog is better off than a dead lion!" (Ecclesiastes 9:4).

Let us notice this truth also, for it is full of consolation. Let us not despise grace because it is weak, or think people are not converted because they are not yet as strong in the faith as St. Paul. Let us remember that grace, like everything else, must have a beginning. The mightiest oak was once an acorn. The strongest man was once a baby. Better a thousand times have grace in the stalk than no grace at all.

4. No harvest till the seed is ripe

Fourth, we are taught that, as in the growth of grain so in the work of grace, there is no harvest till the seed is ripe.

No farmer thinks of cutting his wheat when it is green. He waits till the sun and rain, heat and cold, have done their appointed work, and the golden ears hang down. Then, and not till then, he puts in the sickle and gathers the wheat into his barn.

God deals with his work of grace exactly in the same way. He never removes his people from this world till they are ripe and ready. He never takes them away till their work is done. They never die at the wrong time, however mysterious their deaths appear sometimes to us. Josiah, and James the brother of John were both cut off in the midst of usefulness. King Edward VI of England was not allowed to reach manhood. But we shall find on the resurrection morning that there was a reason. All was done well about their deaths, as well as about their births. The Great Farmer never cuts his corn till it is ripe.

Let us leave the parable with this truth on our minds, and take comfort about the death of every believer. Let us rest satisfied that there is no chance, no accident, no mistake about the decease of any of

God's children. They are all "God's husbandry," and God knows best when they are ready for the harvest.

The parable of the mustard seed *(4:30–34)*

The parable of the mustard seed is one of those parables which have some of the characteristics of history and some of prophecy. It seems to be intended to illustrate the history of Christ's visible church on earth from the time of the first advent down to the judgment day. The seed scattered on the ground in the preceding parable showed us the work of grace in a heart. The mustard seed shows us the progress of Christianity in the world.

1. Small and weak beginnings

First, we learn that, like the grain of mustard seed, Christ's visible church was to be small and weak in its beginnings.

A grain of mustard seed was a proverbial expression among the Jews for something very small and insignificant. Our Lord calls it "the smallest seed you plant in the ground" (verse 31). Twice in the Gospels we find our Lord using the image as a word of comparison when speaking of a weak faith (Matthew 17:20 and Luke 17:6). The idea was doubtless familiar to a Jewish mind, however strange it may sound to us. Here, as in other places, the Son of God shows us the wisdom of using language familiar to the minds of the people we are speaking to.

It would be difficult to find a picture which more faithfully represents the history of the visible church of Christ than this grain of mustard seed.

Weakness and apparent insignificance were undoubtedly the characteristics of its beginning. How did its head and King come into the world? He came as a feeble infant, born in a manger at Bethlehem, without riches, armies, attendants or power. Who were the men that the head of the church gathered round himself and appointed his apostles? They were poor and unlearned persons: fishermen, tax collectors and men of similar occupations, to all appearance the most unlikely people to shake the world. What was the last public act of the earthly ministry of the great head of the church? He was crucified like a criminal, between two thieves, after having been deserted by nearly all his disciples, betrayed by one and denied by another. What was the doctrine which the first builders of the church went out to preach to mankind from the upstairs room in Jerusalem? It was a doctrine which was a stumbling-block to Jews and foolishness to Gentiles. It was a proclamation that the great head of their new religion had been put to death on a cross, and that despite this they offered life through his death to the world! In all this the human mind can perceive nothing but weakness and feebleness. Truly the picture of the grain of mustard seed was confirmed and fulfilled to the very letter. To human eyes the beginning of the visible church was contemptible, insignificant, powerless and small.

2. Great increase

Second, we learn that, like the mustard seed, the visible church, once planted, was to grow and greatly increase.

"When it is planted," says our Lord, the grain of mustard seed "grows and becomes the largest of all garden plants" (verse 32). Those words may sound startling to an English ear. We are not accustomed to such a growth in our cold northern climate. But to those who know eastern countries there is nothing surprising in it. The testimony of well-informed and experienced travelers is clear, that such growth is both possible and probable.

[To show the size to which the mustard plants will grow in eastern countries, Lightfoot quotes the following passage from Rabbinical writers:

There was a stalk of mustard in Sichim, from which sprang out three boughs, one of which was broken off and covered the tent of a potter, and produced three cabs of mustard." Rabbi Simeon ben Chalaphta said: "A stalk of mustard seed was in my field, into which I was wont to climb as men are wont to climb into a fig-tree."

The enormous size to which the rhododendron, heather and fern will grow in some climates which suit them better than ours, should be remembered by an English reader of this parable.]

No imagery could be chosen more strikingly applicable to the growth and increase of Christ's visible church in the world. It began to grow from the day of Pentecost, and grew with a rapidity which nothing can account for but the finger of God. It grew wonderfully when three thousand souls were converted at once, and five thousand more in a few days afterwards. It grew wonderfully when at Antioch, Ephesus, Philippi, Corinth and Rome congregations were gathered together and Christianity was firmly established. It grew wonderfully when at last the despised religion of Christ spread over the greater part of Europe, Asia Minor and North Africa, and, in spite of fierce persecution and oppression, supplanted heathen idolatry and became the professed creed of the whole Roman empire. Such growth must have been marvelous in the eyes of many. But it was only what our Lord foretold in the parable before us. "The kingdom of God is like . . . a mustard seed."

The visible church of Christ has not yet finished growing. Despite the sad apostasy of some of its branches and the deplorable weakness of others, it is still extending and expanding over the world. New branches have continually been springing up in America, India, Australia, Africa, China and the South Sea islands. There are undoubtedly many evils. False professions of belief, and corruption, abound. But still, on the whole, heathenism is waning, wearing out and melting away. In spite of all the predictions of Voltaire and Paine, in spite of foes without and treachery within, the visible church progresses – the mustard seed is still growing.

And the prophecy, we may rest assured, is not yet exhausted. A day will yet come when the great head of the church will take up his power and reign, and put down every enemy under his feet. The earth will yet be filled with the knowledge of the Lord as the waters cover the sea (Isaiah 11:9). Satan will yet be bound. The heathen will yet be our Lord's inheritance, and the utmost parts of the earth his possession. And then this parable will be competely fulfilled. The little seed will become a "great tree" and fill the whole earth (Daniel 3:35).

Let us leave the parable with a resolution never to despise any movement or instrumentality in the church of Christ, because at first it is weak and small. Let us remember the manger of Bethlehem and learn wisdom. The name of the helpless infant who lay there is now known all over the globe. The little seed which was planted on the day when Jesus was born has become a great tree, and we ourselves are rejoicing under its shadow. Let it be a settled principle in our religion never to despise "the day of small things" (Zechariah 4:10). One child may be the beginning of a flourishing school, one conversion the beginning of a mighty church, one word the beginning of some blessed Christian enterprise, one seed the beginning of a rich harvest of saved souls.

[It is fair to say that the view which I have adopted of the meaning of this parable is not the view which is held by some interpreters.

Some think that the parable is intended to show the progress of the work of grace in the heart of an individual believer. I am not prepared to say that this may not have been in our Lord's mind when he told the parable. I think it quite possible that the parable admits of a double interpretation, for the experience of a believer and the experience of the whole church are much the same. My principal objection to this view is that it does not appear to suit the language of the parable so well as the one I have maintained.

Some few interpreters think that the mustard seed denotes the principle of evil and corruption, and that the main object of the parable is to show how insidiously apostasy would begin in the church, and how completely it would at last overgrow and fill the whole body. I confess that I cannot for a moment see the soundness of this interpretation. To say nothing of other reasons, there seems an excessive harshness in this sense when we consider the opening words of the parable, "What shall we say the kingdom of God is like?" (verse 30). One would rather expect the question to have been "What shall we say the kingdom of the devil is like?" if the whole parable is occupied with describing the progress of evil.

I confess that I think the meaning of "the birds of the air" is a point which is doubtful. Many think that it denotes the number of converts to Christianity who, as the church increased, joined themselves to it and came "like doves to their nests" (Isaiah 60:8). Some think that it denotes the number of worldly and false believers who joined the church from mere worldly motives when it began to be great and prosperous, as in the days of Constantine. When we remember that the "birds of the air" in the parable of the sower (Mark 4:4, 15) are declared by our Lord himself to mean "Satan," we must admit that there is considerable force in this interpretation.]

The storm on the Sea of Galilee miraculously calmed *(4:35–41)*

These verses describe a storm on the Sea of Galilee, when our Lord and his disciples were crossing it, and a miracle performed by our Lord in calming the storm in a moment. Few miracles recorded in the Gospel were so likely to strike the minds of the disciples as this. Four of them at least were fishermen. Peter, Andrew, James and John had probably known the Sea of Galilee and its storms from their youth. Few events in our Lord's journeyings on earth contain more rich instruction than the one related in this passage.

1. Christ's servants not exempt from storms

First, let us learn that Christ's service does not exempt his servants from storms. Here were the twelve disciples in the path of duty. They were obediently following Jesus wherever he went. They were daily attending on his ministry and listening to his word. They were daily testifying to the world that, whatever the teachers of the law and Pharisees might think, they believed in Jesus, loved Jesus and were not ashamed to give up everything for his sake. Yet here we see these men in trouble, tossed up and down by a tempest and in danger of being drowned.

Let us note this lesson well. If we are true Christians, we must not expect everything smooth in our journey to heaven. We must count it no strange thing if we have to endure sicknesses, losses, bereavements and disappointments just like other people. Free pardon and full forgiveness, grace on the way and glory at the end – all this our Saviour has promised to give. But he has never promised that we shall have no afflictions. He loves us too well to promise that. By affliction he teaches us many precious lessons which without it we should never learn. By affliction he shows us our emptiness and weakness, draws us to the throne of grace, purifies our affections, weans us from the world, makes us long for heaven. On the resurrection morning we will all say, "it was good for me to be afflicted" (Psalm 119:71). We will thank God for every storm.

2. Christ was really and truly man

Second, let us learn that our Lord Jesus Christ was really and truly

61

man. We are told in these verses that when the storm began and the waves were breaking over the ship he was in the stern "sleeping" (verse 38). He had a body exactly like our own, a body that could hunger and thirst and feel pain and be weary and need rest. No wonder his body needed rest at this time. He had been working hard at his Father's business all the day. He had been preaching to a great crowd in the open air. No wonder that "when evening came" and his work finished, he fell asleep.

Let us note this lesson attentively too. The Saviour in whom we are told to trust is as really man as he is God. He knows the trials of a man, for he has experienced them. He knows the bodily weaknesses of a man, for he has felt them. He can well understand what we mean when we cry to him for help in this world of need. He is just the very Saviour that men and women with weary bodies and aching heads in a weary world require for their comfort every morning and night. "We do not have a high priest who is unable to sympathize with our weaknesses" (Hebrews 4:15).

3. Christ has almighty power

Third, let us learn that our Lord Jesus Christ, as God, has almghty power. We see him in these verses dong what is proverbially impossible. He speaks to the winds, and they obey him. He speaks to the waves, and they submit to his command. He turns the raging storm into a calm with a few words – "Quiet! Be still!" (verse 39). Those words were the words of him who first created all things. The elements knew the voice of their Master, and like obedient seravnts were quiet at once.

Let us note this lesson too, and lay it up in our minds. With the Lord Jesus Christ nothing is impossible. No stormy passions are so strong that he cannot tame them. No temper is so rough and violent that he cannot speak peace to it and make it calm. No one need ever despair if he will only bow down his pride and come as a humbled sinner to Christ. Christ can do miracles with his heart. No one need ever despair of reaching their journey's end if they have once committed their soul to Christ's keeping. Christ will carry them through every danger. Christ will make them conqueror over every foe. What if our relations oppose us? What if our neighbors laugh us to scorn? What if our job is hard? What is our temptations are great? It is all nothing if Christ is on our side and we are in the ship with him. He who is for us is greater than all those who are against us.

4. Christ is patient and compassionate in dealing with his people

Fourth, we learn from this passage that our Lord Jesus Christ is exceedingly patient and compassionate in dealing with his own people. We see the disciples on this occasion showing great lack of faith, and giving way to the most unseemly fears. They forgot their Master's miracles and care for them in days gone by. They thought of nothing but their present peril. They woke our Lord hastily, and cried, "Don't you care if we drown?" (verse 38). We see our Lord dealing most gently and tenderly with them. He does not sharply reprove them. He does not threaten to cast them off because of their unbelief. He simply asks the touching question, "Why are you so afraid? Do you still have no faith?" (verse 40).

Let us take good note of this lesson. The Lord Jesus is very compassionate and of tender mercy. "As a father has compassion on his children, so the LORD has compassion on those who fear him" (Psalm 103:13). He does not deal with believers according to their sins, nor reward them according to their iniquities. He sees their weakness. He is aware of their shortcomings. He knows all the defects of their faith, hope, love and courage. And yet he will not cast them off. He bears with them continually. He loves them right to the end. He raises them when they fall. He restores them when they go wrong. His patience, like his love, is a patience that passes knowledge. When he sees a heart right, it is his glory to pass over many a shortcoming.

Let us leave these verses with the comforting recollection that Jesus has not changed. His heart is still the same as it was when he crossed the Sea of Galilee and stilled the storm. High in heaven at the right hand of God, Jesus is still sympathizing – still almighty – still compassionate and patient towards his people. Let us be more loving and patient towards our brothers and sisters in the faith. They may go wrong in many things, but if Jesus has received them and can bear with them, surely we may bear with them too. Let us be more hopeful about ourselves. We may be very weak, frail and unstable; but if we can truly say that we do come to Christ and believe in him, we may take comfort.

The question for conscience to answer is not, "Are we like the angels? Are we perfect as we shall be in heaven?" The question is, "Are we real and true in our approaches to Christ? Do we truly repent and believe?"

[The Sea of Galilee, or Tiberias, on which the incident recorded in this passage took place, is an inland lake through which the River Jordan flows, about fifteen miles long and six broad. It lies in a deep valley well below sea level – its surface being 652 feet below that of the Mediterranean – and is surrounded on most sides by steep hills. Because of these, sudden squalls or storms are reported by all travelers to be very common on the lake.

The Sea of Galilee and the country srrounding it were favored with more of our blessed Lord's presence during his earthly ministry than any other part of Palestine. Capernaum, Tiberias, Bethsaida and the region of the Gadarenes were all on its shores or in the immediate neighborhood of this lake. It was on the Sea of Galilee that our Lord walked. It was on its shore that he appreared to his disciples after his resurrection. Sitting in a boat on its waters and in a house hard by, he delivered the seven parables recorded in Matthew 13. On its banks, he called Peter, Andrew, James and John. From it he commanded his disciples to draw the miraculous catch of fishes. Within sight of it he twice fed the crowds with a few loaves and fishes. On its shore he healed the man possessed by demons; and into it the two thousand pigs plunged headlong after that miracle had been worked.

Few localities in the Holy Land were so closely connected with our Lord's ministry as the Sea of Galilee and the country round it.]

Mark
Chapter 5

Demons cast out in the region of the Gerasenes *(5:1–17)*

These verses describe one of those mysterious miracles which the Gospels frequently record, the driving out of a demon. Of all the cases of this kind in the New Testament, none is so fully described as this one. Of all the three evangelists who relate the story, none gives it so fully and minutely as St. Mark.

1. Demon possession was a real thing in our Lord's time
First, we see in these verses that the possession of a person's body by the devil was a real and true thing in the time of our Lord's earthly ministry.

It is a painful fact that there is never any lack of people who claim to be Christians, yet try to explain away our Lord's miracles. They endeavor to account for them by natural causes, and to show that they were not worked by any extraordinary power. Of all miracles, there are none which they assault so strenuously as the driving out of demons. They do not scruple to deny Satanic possession entirely. They tell us that it was nothing more than lunacy, frenzy or epilepsy, and that the idea of a demon inhabiting someone's body is absurd.

The best and simplest answer to such skeptical objections is a reference to the plain narratives of the Gospels, and especially to the one before us at this moment. The facts here detailed are utterly inexplicable if we do not believe in demonic possession. It is well known that lunacy and frenzy and epilepsy are not infectious complaints, and at any rate cannot be communicated to a herd of pigs! Yet people ask us to believe that as soon as this man was healed, two thousand pigs ran violently down a steep place into the lake, by a sudden impulse, without any apparent cause to account for their so doing! Such reasoning is the height of credulity. When people can satisfy themselves with such explanations, they are in a pitiable state of mind.

Let us beware of a skeptical and incredulous spirit in all matters relating to the devil. No doubt there is much in the subject of demonic possession which we do not understand, and cannot explain. But let us not therefore refuse to believe it. The eastern king who would not believe in the possibility of ice because he lived in a hot country and had never seen it, was not more foolish than the person who refuses to believe in demonic possession because he never saw a case himself and cannot understand it. We may be sure that, on the subject of the devil and his power, we are far more likely to believe too little than too much. Unbelief about the existence and personality of Satan has often proved the first step to unbelief about God.

2. Satan is cruel, powerful and malicious

Second, we see in these verses what an awfully cruel, powerful and malicious being Satan is. On all these three points, the passage before us is full of instruction.

The *cruelty* of Satan appears in the miserable condition of the unhappy man whose body was possessed by the demons. We read that he lived "in the tombs," that "no one could bind him any more, not even with a chain" (verse 3), that "no one was strong enough to subdue him" (verse 4) and that, naked, "night and day among the tombs and in the hills he would cry out and cut himself with stones" (verse 5). Such is the state to which the devil would bring us all, if he only had the power. He would rejoice to inflict upon us the utmost misery, both of body and mind. Cases like this are faint types of the miseries of hell.

The *power* of Satan appears in the awful words which the evil spirit used when our Lord asked, "What is your name?" (verse 9). He answered, saying, "My name is Legion, for we are many." We probably have not the faintest idea of the number, subtlety and activity of Satan's agents. We forget that he is king over an enormous host of subordinate spirits who do his will. We would probably find, if our eyes were opened to see spirits, they they are about our path and about our bed and observing all our ways, to an extent of which we have no conception. In private and in public, in church and in the world, there are busy enemies always near us, of whose presence we are not aware.

The *malice* of Satan appears in the strange request, "Send us among the pigs" (verse 12). Driven out of the man whose body they had so long inhabited and possessed, they still thirsted to do mischief. Unable to injure an immortal soul any more, they asked permission to injure the dumb animals which were feeding nearby. Such is the true character of Satan. It is the bent of his nature to do harm, to kill and to destroy. No wonder he is called Apollyon, the destroyer.

Let us beware of giving way to the senseless habit of joking about the devil. It is a habit which gives awful evidence of the blindness and corruption of human nature, and one which is far too common. When it is seemly in the mind of a condemned criminal to joke about his executioner, then, and not till then, it will be seemly for mortals to talk lightly about Satan. It would be good for us all if we strove more to realize the power and presence of our great spiritual enemy, and prayed more to be delivered from him. It was a true saying of an eminent Christian, now gone to rest, that "no prayer is complete which does not contain a petition to be kept from the devil."

3. Christ's complete authority over the devil

Third, we see from these verses how complete is our Lord's power and authority over the devil. We see it in the cry of the evil spirit, "Swear to God that you won't torture me!" (verse 7). We see it in the command, "Come out of this man, you evil spirit!" (verse 8), and the immediate obedience which followed. We see it in the blessed change that at once took place in the man who had been possessed: he was found "sitting there, dressed and in his right mind" (verse 15). We see it in the request of all the demons, "Send us among the pigs" (verse 12), admitting that they were aware they could do nothing without permission. All these things show that someone more powerful than Satan was there. Strong as the great enemy of mankind was, he was in the presence of someone stronger still. Numerous as his hosts were, he was confronted with someone who could command more than twelve legions of angels. "A king's word is supreme" (Ecclesiastes 8:4).

The truth here taught is full of strong consolation for all true Christians. We live in a world full of difficulties and snares. We are ourselves beset with weakness. The awful thought that we have a powerful spiritual enemy always near us, subtle, powerful and malicious as Satan is, might well disturb and depress us. But, thanks be to God, we have in Jesus an almighty Friend who is "able to save us completely." He has already triumphed over Satan on the cross. He will always triumph over him in the hearts of believers, and pray that their faith does not fail. And he will finally triumph over Satan completely, when he comes again, and will bind him in the bottomless pit.

And now, are we ourselves delivered from Satan's power? This after all is the grand question that concerns our souls. He still reigns and rules in the hearts of all who are disobedient (Ephesians 2:2). He is still a king over the ungodly. Have we, by grace, broken his bonds and escaped his hand? Have we really renounced him and all his works? Do we daily resist him and make him flee? Do we put on the whole armour of God and stand against him? May we never rest till we can give satisfactory answers to these questions.

[The whole subject of the demoniacs, or cases of Satanic possession recorded in the New Testament, is unquestionably full of deep mystery. The miserable sufferings of the unhappy people possessed – their clear knowledge that our Lord was the Son of God – their double consciousness, sometimes the spirit speaking, sometimes the person – all these are deep mysteries. And it can hardly be otherwise. We know little of beings that we cannot see and touch. We know nothing of the manner in which a spirit operates on the mind of a creature with flesh and bones like ourselves. We can see plainly that there were many people possessed by demons during our Lord's earthly ministry. We can see plainly that bodily possession was something different from possession of heart and soul. We can conjecture the reason of their permitted possession – to make it plain that our Lord came to destroy the works of the devil. But we must stop here. We can go no further.

Let us, however, beware of supposing that demonic possession was entirely confined to our Lord's time, and that there is no such thing in our own days. This would be a rash and unwarrantable conclusion. Awful as the thought is, there are sometimes cases in mental hospitals which, if they are not cases of Satanic possession, approach as nearly to it as possible. In short I believe the opinion of not a few

eminent physicians is clear and decided that Satanic possession still
continues, though cases are exceedingly rare.

Of course it would be presumption to handle so fearful a doctrine
lightly, and to pronounce positively of any particular person that they
had a demon. But if such things have been – and the New Testament
puts this beyond question – no good reason can be assigned why they
should not be again. Human nature has not changed since our Lord
was on earth. Satan is not yet bound. Satanic possession is therefore
niether impossible nor improbable, though limits may be set to the fre-
quency of it, through the mercy of God.]

The man who had been possessed by demons sent home to his friends (5:18–20)

The conduct of those whom our Lord Jesus Christ healed and cured
when on earth, after their healing, is something not often related in the
Gospels. The story often describes the miraculous cure, and then leaves
the subsequent history of the person cured in obscurity, and passes on
to other things.

But there there are some deeply interesting cases in which the later
conduct of people who had been cured is described; and the man from
whom the demons were driven out in the region of the Gerasenes is
one. The verses before us tell the story. Few as they are, they are full of
precious instruction.

1. Jesus knows better than his people, what is the best place for them
First, we learn from these verses that the Lord Jesus knows better than
his people what is the right position for them to be in. We are told that
when our Lord was on the point of leaving the country of the
Gerasenes, "the man who had been demon-possessed begged to go
with him" (verse 18). We can well understand that request. He felt
grateful for the blessed change that had taken place in himself. He felt
full of love towards his deliverer. He thought he could not do better
than follow our Lord and go with him as his companion and disciple.
He was ready to give up home and country and go after Christ. And
yet, strange as it appears at first sight, the request was refused. "Jesus

did not let him" (verse 19). Our Lord had other work for him to do. Our Lord saw better than he did in what way he could glorify God most. "Go home to your family and tell them how much the Lord has done for you," he says (verse 19).

There are lessons of profound wisdom in these words. The place that Christians wish to be in is not always the place which is best for their souls. The position that they would choose if they could have their own way is not always the one Jesus wants them to occupy.

There are none who need this lesson so much as believers newly converted to God. Such people are often very poor judges of what is really for their good. Full of the new views which they have been graciously taught, excited with the novelty of their present position, seeing everything around them in a new light, knowing little yet of the depths of Satan and the weakness of their own hearts – knowing only that a little time ago they were blind, and now, through mercy, they see – of all people they are in the greatest danger of making mistakes. With the best intentions, they are apt to fall into mistakes about their plans in life, their choices, their moves, their professions. They forget that what we like best is not always best for our souls, and that the seed of grace needs winter as well as summer, cold as well as heat, to ripen it for glory.

Let us pray that God will guide us in all our ways after conversion, and not allow us to go wrong in our choices, or to make hasty decisions. The place and position which is most healthy for us is the one in which we are kept most humble – most taught our own sinfulness – drawn most to the Bible and prayer – led most to live by faith and not by sight. It may not be quite what we like. But if Christ by his providence has placed us in it, let us not be in a hurry to leave it. Let us stay there with God. The great thing is to have no will of our own, and to be where Jesus would have us be.

[I cannot help remarking, in connection with our Lord's words in this passage, that it is questionable whether people do not *sometimes* act unadvisedly in giving up a secular calling in order to enter the ministry of the Gospel. In plain words, I doubt whether men who have been suddenly converted to God in the army, the navy, the law or the merchant's office do not *sometimes* desert their professions with undue haste in order to become clergymen.

It seems to be forgotten that conversion alone is no proof that we are called and qualified to become teachers of others. God may be glorified as really and truly in the secular calling as in the pulpit. Converted people can be eminently useful as landlords, magistrates, soldiers, sailors, barristers or merchants. We want witnesses for Christ in all these professions. Colonel Gardiner and Captain Vicars probably did more for the cause of Christ as military men than they would ever have done if they had left the army and become clergymen.

In steering our course through life, we should carefully look for the call of providence as well as the call of inclination. The position that we choose for ourselves is often that which is the worst for our souls. When two conflicting paths of duty lie before a believer, the path which has least of the cross and is most agreeable to his own taste is seldom the right one.

I write all this with a due recollection of many eminent Christians who began in a secular profesion, and left it for the office of the minister. John Newton and Edward Bickersteth are instances. But I sense that such cases are exceptions. I sense moreover that in every such case there would be found to have been a remarkable call of providence as well as an inward call of the Holy Spirit. As a general rule, I believe that the rule of St. Paul ought to be carefully observed: "Each man, as responsible to God, should remain in the situation God called him to" (1 Corinthians 7:24).]

2. A believer's home has the first claim on his attention

Second, we learn from these verses that a believer's own home has the first claims on his attention. We are taught that in the striking words which our Lord addresses to the man who had been possessed with demons. "Go home to your family," he says, "and tell them how much the Lord has done for you" (verse 19). The friends of this man had probably not seen him for some years, except under the influence of Satan. Most likely it was to them as though he was dead, or worse than dead, and a constant cause of trouble, anxiety and sorrow. Here then was the path of duty. Here was the way by which he could most glorify God. Let him go home and tell his friends what Jesus had done for him. Let him be a living witness before their eyes of the compassion of Christ. Let him deny himself the pleasure of being in Christ's bodily presence, in order to do the higher work of being useful to others.

How much there is in these simple words of our Lord! What thoughts they ought to stir up in the hearts of all true Christians! "Go home to your family and tell them." Home is the place above all others where the child of God ought to make his first endeavors to do good. Home is the place where he is most continually seen, and where the reality of his grace ought most truly to appear. Home is the place where his best affections ought to be concentrated. Home is the place where he should strive daily to be a witness for Christ. Home is the place where he was daily doing harm by his example while he served the world. Home is the place where he is specially bound to be a living letter of Christ, as soon as he has been mercifully taught to serve God. May we all remember these things daily! May it never be said of us that we are saints everywhere else but wicked by our own fireside, talkers about religion elsewhere but worldly and ungodly at home!

But after all, have we anything to tell others? Can we testify to any work of grace in our hearts? Have we experienced any deliverance from the power of the world, the flesh and the devil? Have we ever tasted the graciousness of Christ? These are indeed serious questions. If we have never yet been born again and made new creatures, we of course have nothing to "tell."

If we have anything to tell others about Christ, let us resolve to tell it. Let us not be silent, if we have found peace and rest in the Gospel. Let us speak to our relations and friends and families and neighbors, according as we have opportunity, and tell them what the Lord has done for our souls. All are not called to be ministers. All are not intended to preach. But all can walk in the steps of the man of whom we have been reading, and in the steps of Andrew (John 1:41) and Philip (John 1:45) and the Samaritan woman (John 4:29). Happy the person who is not ashamed to say to others, "let me tell you what he has done for me" (Psalm 66:16).

A woman's bleeding healed (5:21–34)

The main subject of these verses is the miraculous healing of a sick woman. Great is our Lord's experience in cases of disease! Great is his sympathy with his sick and ailing members! The gods of the heathen are generally represented as terrible and mighty in battle, delighting in bloodshed, the strong man's patrons, and the warrior's friends. The Saviour of the Christian is always set before us as gentle, and easy to call on, the healer of the broken-hearted, the refuge of the weak and helpless, the comforter of the distressed, the sick person's best friend. And is not this just the Saviour that human nature needs? The world is full of pain and trouble. The weak on earth are far more numerous than the strong.

1. The misery brought by sin

First, let us notice in these verses what misery sin has brought into the world. We read of someone who had had a most painful disease "for twelve years" (verse 25). She had "suffered a great deal under the care of many doctors and had spent all she had, yet instead of getting better she grew worse" (verse 26). Every kind of remedy had been tried in vain. Medical skill had proved unable to cure. Twelve long weary years had been spent in battling with disease, and relief seemed no nearer than at first. "Hope deferred" might well make her "heart sick" (Proverbs 13:12).

How astonishing it is that we do not hate sin more than we do! Sin is the cause of all the pain and disease in the world. God did not create us to be ailing and suffering creatures. It was sin, and nothing but sin, which brought in all the ills that flesh is heir to. It was sin to which we owe every racking pain, and every loathsome illness, and every humbling weakness to which our poor bodies are liable. Let us always bear this in mind. Let us hate sin with a godly hatred.

2. People's different feelings in coming to Christ

Second, let us note how different are the feelings with which people draw near to Christ. We are told in these verses that "a large crowd followed" our Lord "and pressed around him" (verse 24). But we are only told of one person who "came up behind him in the crowd" and touched him with faith and was healed. Many followed Jesus from curiosity, and derived no benefit from him. One, and only one, followed under a deep sense of her need, and of our Saviour's power to relieve her, and that one received a mighty blessing.

We see the same thing going on continually in the church of Christ at the present day. Crowds go to our places of worship and fill our pews. Hundreds come up to the Lord's table and reeceive the bread and wine. But of all these worshipers and communicants, how few really obtain anything from Christ! Fashion, custom, form, habit, the love of excitement, or an itching ear are the true motives of the vast majority. There are just a few here and there who touch Christ by faith and go home "in peace" (verse 34). These may seem hard sayings, but they are sadly too true!

3. An instantaneous cure

Third, let us note how immediate and instantaneous was the cure which this woman received. No sooner did she touch our Lord's clothes than she was healed. The thing that she had sought in vain for twelve years was done in a moment. The cure that many physicians could not effect was wrought in an instant of time. "She felt in her body that she was freed from her suffering" (verse 29).

We need not doubt that we are meant to see here a picture of the relief that the Gospel confers on souls. The experience of many a weary conscience has been exactly like that of this woman with her disease. Many people have spent sorrowful years in search of peace with God, and failed to find it. They have gone to earthly remedies and obtained no relief. They have wearied themselves in going from place to place, and church to church, and have felt after all that "instead of getting better" they have grown "worse." But at last they have found rest. And where have they found it? They have found it where this woman found hers, in Jesus Christ. They have stopped their own works. They have given over looking to their own efforts and doings for relief. They have come to Christ himself, as humble sinners, and committed themselves to his mercy. At once the burden has fallen from their shoulders. Heaviness is turned to joy, and anxiety to peace. One touch of real faith can do more for the soul than a hundred self-imposed austerities. One look at Jesus is more efficacious than years of sack-cloth and ashes. May we never forget this to our dying day! Personally going to Christ is the real secret of peace with God.

4. Telling others what benefits we have received from Christ

Fourth, let us note how right it is for Christians to tell other people the benefits they receive from Christ. We see that this woman was not allowed to go home, when cured, without her cure being noticed. Our Lord asked who had touched him, and "kept looking round to see who had done it" (verse 32). No doubt he knew perfectly well the name and history of the woman. He did not need anyone to tell him. But he wanted to teach her, and all around him, that healed souls should make public acknowledgment of mercies received.

There is a lesson here which all true Christians would do well to remember. We are not to be ashamed to confess Christ before other people, and to let others know what he has done for our souls. If we have found peace through his blood, and been renewed by his Spirit, we must not shrink from avowing it on every proper occasion. It is not necessary to blow a trumpet in the streets and force our experience on everybody's notice. All that is required is a willingness to acknowledge Christ as our Master, without flinching from the ridicule or persecution which doing so may bring on us. More than this is not required; but less than this ought not to content us. If we are ashamed of Jesus in front of other people, he will one day be ashamed of us in front of his Father and the angels.

5. Faith is a precious grace

Fifth, let us note how precious a grace is faith. "Daughter," says our Lord to the woman who was healed, "your faith has healed you. Go in peace" (verse 34).

Of all the Christian graces, none is so frequently mentioned in the New Testament as faith, and none is so highly commended. No grace brings such glory to Christ. Hope brings an eager expectation of good things to come. Love brings a warm and willing heart. Faith brings an empty hand, receives everything, and can give nothing in return. No grace is so important to the Christian's own soul. By faith we begin. By faith we live. By faith we stand. We walk by faith and not by sight. By faith we overcome. By faith we have peace. By faith we enter into rest. No grace should be the subject of so much self-inquiry. We should often ask ourselves, "Do I really believe? Is my faith true, genuine and the gift of God?"

May we never rest till we can give a satisfactory answer to these questions! Christ has not changed since the day when this woman was healed. He is still generous and still powerful to save. There is only one thing needed if we want salvation. That one thing is the hand of faith. Let us only "touch" Jesus, and we shall be made whole.

[Some remarks of Melanchthon's on this woman's case are worth reading. We are doubtless to be careful that we do not hastily attach an allegorical and mystical sense to the words of Scripture. Yet we must not forget the depth of meaning which lies in all the acts of our Lord's earthly ministry; and at any rate there is much beauty in the thoughts which the good Reformer expresses. He says:

> This woman aptly represents the Jewish synagogue for long troubled with many mischiefs and miseries, especially tortured with dreadful rulers and incompetent priests, or soul doctors, the Pharisees and Sadducees, on whom she had spent all she had, and yet she was not a bit better, but grew worse, till the blessed Lord of Israel in his own person came and redeemed her.]

The ruler's daughter raised to life (5:35–43)

A great miracle is recorded in these verses. A dead girl is restored to life. Mighty as the "King of terrors" is, there is one more powerful still. The keys of death are in our Lord Jesus Christ's hands. He will one day "swallow up death forever" (Isaiah 25:8).

1. Rank places no one beyond the reach of sorrow

First, let us learn from these verses that rank places no one beyond the reach of sorrow. Jairus was a "ruler" (verse 35), yet sickness and trouble came to his house. Jairus probably had wealth, and all the medical help that wealth can command; yet money could not keep death away from his child. The daughters of rulers are liable to sickness just as much as the daughters of poor people. The daughters of rulers must die.

It is good for us all to remember this. We are too apt to forget it. We often think and talk as if the possession of riches were the great antidote to sorrow, and as if money could secure us against sickness and death.

But it is the very extreme of blindness to think so. We have only to look around us and see a hundred proofs to the contrary. Death comes to halls and palaces, as well as to cottages – to landlords as well as to tenants – to rich as well as to poor. It stands on no ceremony. It waits for no one's leisure or convenience. It will not be kept out by locks and bars. "Man is destined to die once, and after that to face judgment" (Hebrews 9:27). Everyone is going to one place, the grave.

We may be sure there is far more equality in the lots appointed to people than at first sight appears. Sickness is a great leveller. It makes no distinction. Heaven is the only place where no one living will say, "I am ill" (Isaiah 33:24). Happy are those who set their affections on things above! They, and only they, have a treasure which is incorruptible. A little while longer, and they wll be where they will hear no more bad news. All tears will be wiped from their faces. They will put on mourning no more. Never again will they hear those sorrowful words, "your daughter/your son/your wife/your husband is dead." The old things will have passed away.

2. Christ's power is almighty

Second, let us learn how almighty is the power of our Lord Jesus Christ. That message which pierced the ruler's heart, telling him that his child was dead, did not stop our Lord for a moment. At once he cheered the father's fainting spirits with these gracious words, "Don't be afraid; just believe" (verse 36). He comes to the house where many are crying and wailing loudly, and enters the room where the child is lying. He takes her by the hand, and says, "Little girl, I say to you, get up!" (verse 41). At once the heart begins to beat again, and the breath returns to the lifeless body. "The girl stood up and walked around" (verse 42). No wonder we read that "they were completely astonished."

Let us think for a moment how wonderful was the change which took place in that house. From crying to rejoicing – from mourning to congratulation – from death to life – how great and marvelous must have been the transition! Only people who have faced death and had the light of their households put out and felt the iron entering into their own souls can tell what it was like. Only they can conceive what the family of Jairus must have felt, when they saw their beloved one given back once more into their bosom by the power of Christ. There must have been a happy family gathering that night!

Let us see in this glorious miracle a proof of what Jesus can do for dead souls. He can raise our children from death of trangressions and sins, and make them walk before him in newness of life. He can take our sons and daughters by the hand and say to them, "Get up," and tell them to live not for themselves but for him who died for them and rose again. Have we a dead soul in our family? Let us call on the Lord to come and bring him to life (Ephesians 2:1, 5). Let us send to him message after message, and beg him to help. He who came to the help of Jairus is still full of mercy, and powerful.

Finally, let us see in this miracle a blessed pledge of what our Lord will do on the day of his second coming. He will call his believing people from their graves. He will give them a better, more glorious and more beautiful body than they had in the days of their pilgrimage. He will gather his elect from north and south and east and west, to part no more, and die no more. Believing parents will once more see believing children. Believing husbands will once more see believing wives. Let us beware of sorrowing like those who have no hope, over friends who fall asleep in Christ. The youngest and loveliest believer can never die before the right time. Let us look forwrd. There is a glorious resurrection morning yet to come. "God will bring with Jesus those who have fallen asleep in him" (1 Thessalonians 4:14). Those words will one day be completely fulfilled: "I will ransom them from the power of the grave; I will redeem them from death. Where, O death, are your plagues? Where, O grave, is your destruction?" (Hosea 13:14). He who raised the daughter of Jairus is still alive. When he gathers his flock on the last day, not one lamb will be found missing.

Mark
Chapter 6

Christ in his own town; the sin of unbelief *(6:1–6)*

This passage shows us our Lord Jesus Christ in "his own town," Nazareth. It is a sad illustration of the wickedness of the human heart, and deserves special attention.

1. Undervaluing the familiar
First, we see how apt people are to undervalue things with which they are familiar. The people of Nazareth "took offense" at our Lord. They could not think it possible that someone who had lived among them for so many years, and whose brothers and sisters they knew, could deserve to be followed as a public teacher.

Nowhere on earth ever had the privileges Nazareth had. For thirty years the Son of God lived in this town, and went about its streets. For thirty years he walked with God under the eyes of its inhabitants, living a blameless, perfect life. But it was all lost on them. They were not ready to believe the Gospel when the Lord came among them and taught in their synagogue. They would not believe that someone whose face they knew so well and who had lived such a long time eating, drinking and dressing like one of themselves, had any right to claim their attention. They "took offense at him" (verse 5).

There is nothing in all this that need surprise us. The same thing is going on around us every day, in our own country. The holy Scriptures, the preaching of the Gospel, the public ordinances of religion, the abundant means of grace that we enjoy, are continually undervalued by people. They are so accustomed to them they do not know their privileges. It is an awful truth that in religion more than in anything else familiarity breeds contempt.

There is comfort in this part of our Lord's experience for some of the Lord's people. There is comfort for faithful ministers of the Gospel who are depressed by the unbelief of their parishioners or regular hearers. There is comfort for true Christians who stand alone in their families, and see all around them clinging to the world. Let both remember that they are drinking the same cup as their beloved Master. Let them remember that he too was despised most by those who knew him best. Let them learn that the utmost consistency of conduct will not make others adopt their views and opinions, any more than it did the people of Nazareth. Let them know that the sorrowful words of their Lord will generally be fulfilled in the experience of his servants, "Only in his own town, among his relatives and in his own house is a prophet without honor" (verse 4).

2. The lowliness of Christ's life before he began his ministry

Second, we see how humble was the rank of life which our Lord stooped to occupy, before he began his public ministry. The people of Nazareth said of him, in contempt, "Isn't this the carpenter?" (verse 3).

This is a remarkable expression, and is only found in the Gospel of St. Mark. It shows us plainly that for the first thirty years of his life, our Lord was not ashamed to work with his own hands. There is something marvelous and overwhelming in the thought! He who made heaven and earth and sea and all that is in them – he without whom nothing was made that has been made – the Son of God himself, took the very nature of a servant, and by the sweat of his brow ate his food (Genesis 3:19), as a working man. This is indeed that "love that surpasses knowledge" (Ephesians 3:19). Though he was rich, yet for our sakes he became poor. Both in life and in death he humbled himself, so that sinners might live and reign forevermore through him.

Let us remember when we read this passage that there is no sin in poverty. We never need be ashamed of poverty, unless our own sins have brought it upon us. We never ought to despise others because they are poor. It is disgraceful to be a gambler, or a drunkard, or covetous, or a liar; but it is no disgrace to work with our own hands and earn our own bread by our own labor. The thought of the carpenter's shop at

Nazareth should cast down the high thoughts of all who make an idol of riches. It cannot be dishonorable to occupy the same position as the Son of God and Saviour of the world.

3. The sinfulness of unbelief

Third, we see how exceedingly sinful is the sin of unbelief. Two remarkable expressions are used in teaching this lesson. One is that our Lord "could not do any miracles there" because of the hardness of the people's hearts (verse 5). The other is that "he was amazed at their lack of faith" (verse 6). The one shows us that unbelief has the power to rob people of the highest blessings. The other shows that it is so suicidal and unreasonable a sin that even the Son of God regards it with surprise.

We can never be too much on our guard against unbelief. It is the oldest sin in the world. It began in the Garden of Eden, when Eve listened to the devil's promises instead of believing God's words, "you will die." It is the most ruinous of all sins in its consequences. It brought death into the world. It kept Israel out of Canaan for forty years. It is the sin that especially fills hell. "Whoever does not believe will be condemned" (Mark 16:16). It is the most foolish and inconsistent of all sins. It makes people refuse the plainest evidence, shut their eyes against the clearest testimony, and yet believe lies. Worst of all, it is the commonest sin in the world. Thousands are guilty of it on every side. They claim they are Christians. They know nothing of Paine and Voltaire. But in practice they are really unbelievers. They do not implicitly believe the Bible and receive Christ as their Saviour.

Let us watch our own hearts carefully in the matter of unbelief. The heart, and not the head, is the seat of its mysterious power. It is neither the lack of evidence nor the difficulties of Christian doctrine that make people unbelievers. It is lack of will to believe. They love sin. They are wedded to the world. In this state of mind they never lack specious reasons to confirm their will. The humble, childlike heart is the heart that believes.

Let us go on watching our hearts, even after we have believed. The root of unbelief is never entirely destroyed. We have only to leave off watching and praying, and a rank crop of unbelief will soon spring up. No prayer is so important as that of the disciples, "Lord, increase our faith."

[There is a peculiar expression in this passage which deserves notice. I refer to the words which say that our Lord "*could not* do any miracles there," because of their unbelief.

This expression of course cannot mean that it was "impossible" for our Lord to do a miracle there, and that although he had the will to do miracles he was stopped and prevented by a power greater than his own. Such a view would be dishonoring to our Lord, and in fact would be a practical denial of his divinity. With Jesus nothing is impossible. If he had willed to do miracles, he had the power.

The meaning evidently must be that our Lord *would* not do any miracle there, because of the unbelief that he saw. He was prevented by what he perceived was the state of the people's hearts. He would not waste signs and wonders on an unbelieving and hardened generation. He "could not" do any miracles there without departing from his rule, "according to your faith will it be done to you" (Matthew 9:29). He had the power in his hands, but he did not will to use it.

The distinction I have attempted to draw is doubly useful because of the light it throws on another scriptural expression which is often girevously misunderstood. I refer to the expression "No one can come to me unless the Father who sent me draws him" (John 6:44). The words "no one *can* come" are often much misunderstood.

The text is a plain declaration of humanity's natural corruption and helpless impotence. We are dead in sin. We cannot come to Christ, unless the Father draws us. In a word, we are *unable* to come. But what is the precise nature of this inability? This is the very point on which misunderstanding exists.

Once for all, let us clearly understand that our inability to come to Christ is not physical. It is utterly untrue to say that a person can have a strong decided will to come to Christ and yet be stopped by some mysterious physical obstacle – that we can really and honestly have a will to come, and yet have no power. Such a doctrine entirely overthrows human responsibility, and leads in many cases to wicked continuance in sin. Thousands of ignorant people will tell you that "they wish to believe, and wish to come to Christ, and wish to be saved" and yet say that "though they have the will, they have not the power." It is a fatal delusion, and ruinous to many souls.

The truth is that such inability to come to Christ, and impotence to do what is good, is *moral*, and not physical. It is not true that a person like this has the will to come to Christ but is unable. He is unable, doubtless, and has no power; but it is simply *because* he has no will. His will is the principal cause of his unconverted state, and until his will is changed by the Holy Spirit he will never alter. He may not like this. But it is true. The fault of his condition is his own will. Say what he pleases, the blame lies there. He may pretend to have many good wishes, but in reality he has no honest, sincere WILL to be better. He "will not come to Christ that he may have life."]

The first sending out of the apostles to preach *(6:7–13)*

These verses describe the first sending out of the apostles to preach. The great head of the church tested his ministers before he left them alone in the world. He taught them to try their own powers of teaching, and to find out their own weaknesses, while he was still with them. Thus, on the one hand, he was enabled to correct their mistakes. One the other, they were trained for the work they were one day to do, and were not novices when finally left to themselves. It would be good for the church if all ministers of the Gospel were prepared for their duty in like manner, and did not so often take up their office untried, untested and inexperienced.

1. Sent out "two by two"
First, let us observe in these verses how our Lord Jesus Christ sent out his apostles "two by two" (verse 7). St. Mark is the only evangelist who mentions this fact. It is one that deserves special notice.

There can be no doubt that this fact is meant to teach us the advantages of Christian company to all who work for Christ. The wise man had good reason for saying "two are better than one" (Ecclesiastes 4:9). Two men together will do more work than two men singly. They will help one another in judgment, and commit fewer mistakes. They will aid one another in difficulties, and less often fail to succeed. They will stir one another up when tempted to idleness, and less often relapse into indolence and indifference. They will comfort one another in times of trial, and be less often cast down. "Pity the man who falls and has no one to help him up!" (Ecclesiastes 4:10).

It is probable that this principle is not sufficiently remembered in the church of Christ in these latter days. The harvest is undoubtedly great all over the world, both at home and abroad. The laborers are unquestionably few, and the supply of faithful people far less than the demand. The arguments for sending people out "one by one," under existing circumstances, are undeniably strong and weighty. But still the conduct of our Lord in this place is a striking fact. The fact that there is hardly a single case in the Acts where we find Paul or any other apostle working entirely alone is another remarkable circumstance. It is difficult to avoid the conclusion that if the rule of going out "two by two" had been more strictly observed, the missionary field would have yielded larger results than it has.

One thing at all events is clear, and that is the duty of all workers for Christ to work together and help one another whenever they can. "As iron sharpens iron, so one man sharpens another" (Proverbs 27:17). Ministers and missionaries and district visitors and Sunday school teachers should make opportunities for meeting and helping one another. The words of the letter to the Hebrews contain a truth which is too much forgotten: "Let us consider how we may spur one another on towards love and good deeds. Let us not give up meeting together" (Hebrews 10:24–25).

2. Those who will not receive Christ's ministers

Second, let us observe what solemn words our Lord uses about those who will not receive or hear his ministers. He says, "It will be more bearable for Sodom and Gomorrah on the day of judgment than for that town" (Matthew 10:15; also included in Mark 4:11 by KJV).

This is a truth which we find very frequently laid down in the Gospels. It is painful to think how entirely it is overlooked by many. Thousands appear to suppose that so long as they go to church and do not murder, steal, cheat or openly break any of God's commandments, they are in no great danger. They forget that it needs something more than mere abstinence from outward irregularities to save one's soul. They do not see that one of the greatest sins a person can commit in the sight of God is to hear the Gospel of Christ and not believe it – to be invited to repent and believe, and yet remain careless and unbelieving.

In short, to reject the Gospel will sink a person to the lowest place in hell.

Let us never turn away from a passage like this without asking ourselves what we are doing with the Gospel. We live in a Christian country. We have the Bible in our houses. We hear of the salvation of the Gospel frequently every year. But have we received it into our hearts? Have we really obeyed it in our lives? Have we, in short, laid hold on the hope set before us, taken up the cross, and followed Christ? If not, we are far worse than the heathen who bow down to stocks and stones. We are far more guilty than the people of Sodom and Gomorrah. They never heard the Gospel, and therefore never rejected it. But as for us, we hear the Gospel and yet will not believe. May we search our own hearts, and take care that we do not ruin our own souls!

3. The doctrine preached by the apostles

Third, let us observe what was the doctrine which our Lord's apostles preached. We read that "they went out and preached that people should repent" (verse 12).

The necessity of repentance may seem at first sight a very simple and elementary truth. And yet volumes might be written to show the fullness of the doctrine and its suitableness to every age and time, and to every rank and class of mankind. It is inseparably connected with right views of God, of human nature, of sin, of Christ, of holiness and of heaven. All have sinned and fall short of the glory of God. All need to be brought to a sense of their sins – to a sorrow for them – to a willingness to give them up – and to a hunger and thirst after pardon. All, in a word, need to be born again and to flee to Christ. This is repentance unto life. Nothing less than this is required for anyone's salvation. Nothing less than this ought to be pressed on people by everyone who claims to teach Bible religion. We must call people to repent if we want to walk in the steps of the apostles, and when they have repented we must call them to repent more and more to their last day.

Have we ourselves repented? This after all is the question that concerns us most. It is good to know what the apostles taught. It is good to be familiar with the whole system of Christian doctrine. But it is far better to know repentance by experience and to feel it inwardly in our own hearts. May we never rest till we know and feel that we have repented! There are no impenitent people in the kingdom of heaven. All who enter in there have felt, mourned over, forsaken and sought pardon for sin. This must be our experience if we hope to be saved.

[The concluding verse in this passage, together with one in the letter of James (James 5:14), is generally quoted by Roman Catholics in support of their so-called sacrament of extreme unction. A moment's reflection will show that neither this text nor the other referred to is any proof at all.

In both cases, the anointing with oil is expressly connected with the *healing* of those anointed. Extreme unction on the contrary is an anointing administered to a *dying* person, when there is no hope of their recovery.

This discrepancy between the anointing of the apostolic times and the anointing practiced by the Church of Rome is so glaring that some of the ablest Roman controversialists have been obliged to acknowledge that "extreme unction" is founded on church authority and not on the authority of Scripture. Lombard, Bonaventura, Bellarmine, Jansen, and Tirinus are all mentioned by Calovius as being of this opinion.]

John the Baptist put to death by Herod *(6:14–29)*

These verses describe the death of one of the most eminent saints of God. They relate to the murder of John the Baptist. Of all the evangelists none tells this sad story so fully as St. Mark. Let us see what practical lessons the passage contains for our own souls.

1. The power of truth over the conscience
First, we see the amazing power of truth over the conscience. Herod "feared" John (verse 20) while he was alive, and was troubled about him after he died. A friendless, solitary preacher, with no other weapon than God's truth, disturbs and terrifies a king.

Everybody has a conscience. Here lies the secret of a faithful minister's power. This is the reason why Felix "was afraid" (Acts 24:25) and Agrippa was "almost persuaded" (Acts 24:28, KJV) when Paul spoke before them. God has not left himself without witness in the hearts of unconverted people. Fallen and corrupt as they are, there are thoughts within them accusing or defending, according as they live – thoughts that will not be shut out – thoughts that can make even kings, like Herod, restless and afraid.

No one ought to remember this so much as ministers and teachers. If they preach and teach Christ's truth, they may rest assured that their work is not in vain. Children may seem inattentive in schools. Hearers may seem indifferent in congregations. But in both cases there is often far more going on in the conscience than our eyes see. Seeds often spring up and bear fruit when the sower, like John the Baptist, is dead or gone.

2. People may go a long way and still miss salvation because of one master-sin

Second, we see how far people may go in religion, and yet miss salvation by yielding to one master-sin.

King Herod went further than many. He "feared John." He knew him to be "a righteous and holy man" (verse 20). He even "liked to listen to him" (verse 20). But there was one thing Herod would not do. He would not cease from adultery. He would not give up Herodias. And so he ruined his soul forevermore.

Let us take warning from Herod's case. Let us keep back nothing – cling to no favorite vice – spare nothing that stands between us and salvation. Let us often look within, and make sure that there is no darling lust or pet transgression which, Herodias-like, is murdering our souls. Let us rather cut off the right hand, and pluck out the right eye, than go into hell fire. Let us not be content with admiring favorite preachers, and gladly hearing evangelical sermons. Let us not rest till we can say with David, "because I consider all your precepts right, I hate every wrong path" (Psalm 119:128).

3. A faithful minister should rebuke sin boldly

Third, we see how boldly a faithful minister of God ought to rebuke sin. John the Baptist spoke faithfully to Herod about the wickedness of his life. He did not excuse hismelf on the grounds that it was not prudent, or not politic, or not timely, or useless to speak out. He did not say smooth things and palliate the king's ungodliness by using soft words to describe his offense. He told his royal hearer the plain truth, regardless of all consequences – "It is not lawful for you to have your brother's wife" (verse 18).

Here is a pattern that all ministers ought to follow. Publicly and privately, from the pulpit and in private visits, they ought to rebuke all open sin, and deliver a faithful warning to all who are living in it. It may give offense. It may entail immense unpopularity. They have nothing to do with any of this. Duties are duties. Results are God's.

No doubt it requires great grace and courage to do this. No doubt a reprover like John the Baptist must go to work wisely and lovingly in carrying out his master's commission, and rebuking the wicked. But it is a matter in which his reputation for faithfulness and love are clearly at stake. If he believes someone is injuring his soul, he surely ought to tell him so. If he loves him truly and tenderly, he ought not to let him ruin himself unwarned. Great as the present offense may be, in the long run the faithful reprover will generally be respected. "He who rebukes a man will in the end gain more favor than he who has a flattering tongue" (Proverbs 28:23).

4. Hatred of the reprover by those who want to keep their sins

Fourth, we see how bitterly people hate a reprover when they are determined to keep their sins. Herodias, the king's unhappy partner in iniquity, seems to have sunk even deeper in sin than Herod. Hardened and scarred in conscience by her wickedness, she hated John the Baptist for his faithful testimony, and never rested till she had procured his death.

We need not wonder at this. When men and women have chosen their line and resolved to have their own wicked way, they dislike anyone who tries to turn them. They would rather be left alone. They are irritated by opposition. They are angry when they are told the truth. The prophet Elijah was called a "troubler of Israel" (1 Kings 18:17). The prophet Micaiah was hated by Ahab, "because he never prophesies anything good about me, but always bad" (2 Chronicles 18:7). The prophets and faithful preachers of every age have been treated similarly. They have been hated by some people, as well as not believed.

Let it never surprise us when we hear of faithful ministers of the Gospel being spoken against, hated and reviled. Let us rather remember that they are ordained to bear witness against sin, the world and the devil, and that if they are faithful they cannot help giving offense. It is no disgrace to a minister's character to be disliked by the wicked and ungodly. It is no real honor to a minister to be thought well of by everybody. Those words of our Lord are not considered enough – "Woe to you when all men speak well of you" (Luke 6:26).

5. Sin may follow from feasting and reveling

Fifth, we see how much sin may sometimes follow from feasting and reveling. Herod keeps his birthday with a splendid banquet. Company, drinking, dancing fill up the day. In a moment of excitement he grants a wicked girl's request to have the head of John the Baptist cut off. Next day, in all probability, he repented bitterly of his conduct. But the deed was done. It was too late.

This is a faithful picture of what often results from feasting and merry-making. People do things at such times from heated feelings, which they afterwards deeply repent. Happy are those who keep clear of temptations, and avoid giving opportunity to the devil! People never know what they may do when they once venture off safe ground. Late hours, crowded rooms, splendid entertainments, mixed company, music and dancing may seem harmless to many people. But the Christian should never forget that to take part in these things is to open a wide door to temptation.

6. Little worldly reward for some of God's best servants

Sixth, we see in these verses how little reward some of God's best servants receive in this world. An unjust imprisonment and a violent death were the last fruit that John the Baptist reaped in return for his labor. Like Stephen and James and others of whom the world was not worthy, he was called to seal his testimony with his blood.

Stories like these are meant to remind us that the true Christians' best things are yet to come. Their rest, their crown, their wages, their reward are all on the other side of the grave. Here in this world they must walk by faith and not by sight; and if they look for human praise they will be disappointed. Here in this life they must sow, and labor, and fight, and endure persecution; and if they expect a great earthly reward, they expect what they will not find. But this life is not all.

There is to be a day of retribution. There is a glorious harvest yet to come. Heaven will make amends for everything. No eye has seen, no ear has heard the glorious things that God has prepared for those who love him. The value of real religion is not to be measured by the things seen, but by the unseen things. "Our present sufferings are not worth comparing with the glory that will be revealed in us" (Romans 8:18). "Our light and momentary troubles are achieving for us an eternal glory that far outweighs them all" (2 Corinthians 4:17).

The apostles' return; the importance of rest; Christ's compassion (6:30–34)

1. The apostles' conduct when they returned

First, let us note in this passage the conduct of the apostles when they returned from their first mission as preachers. They "gathered round Jesus and reported to him all that they had done and taught" (verse 30).

These words are deeply instructive. They are a bright example to all ministers of the Gospel, and to all laborers in the great work of doing good to souls. All such people should daily do as the apostles did on this occasion. They should tell all their proceedings to the great head of the church. They should spread all their work before Christ, and ask him for advice, guidance, strength and help.

Prayer is the main secret of success in spiritual business. It moves him who can move heaven and earth. It brings down the promised aid of the Holy Spirit, without whom the finest sermons, the clearest teaching and hardest work are all alike in vain. It is not always those who have the most eminent gifts who are most successful laborers for God. It is generally those who keep up closest communion with Christ and are most instant in prayer. It is those who cry with the prophet Ezekiel, "Come from the four winds, O breath, and breathe into these slain, that they may live" (Ezekiel 37:9). It is those who follow most exactly the apostolic model, and give their "attention to prayer and the ministry of the word" (Acts 6:4). Happy is the church that has a praying as well as a preaching ministry! The question we should ask about new ministers is not merely "Can they preach well?" but "Do they pray much for their people and their work?"

2. What Christ said to the returned apostles

Second, let us note the words of our Lord to the apostles when they returned from their first public ministry. "He said to them, 'Come with me by yourselves to a quiet place and get some rest'" (verse 31).

These words are full of tender consideration. Our Lord knows well that his servants are flesh as well as spirit, and have bodies as well as souls. He knows that at best they have a treasure in earthen vessels, and are themselves subject to many weaknesses. He shows them that he does not expect from them more than their bodily strength can do. He asks for what we can do, and not for what we cannot do. "Come to a quiet place," he says, "and get some rest."

These words are full of deep wisdom. Our Lord knows well that his servants must attend to their own souls as well as the souls of others. He knows that a constant attention to public work is apt to make us forget our own private soul-business, and that while we are taking care of the vineyards of others we are in danger of neglecting our own (Song of Songs 1:6). He reminds us that it is good for ministers to withdraw occasionally from public work and look within. "Come to a quiet place," he says.

Sadly, there are few in the church of Christ who need these admonitions. There are but few in danger of overworking themselves and injuring their own bodies and souls by excessive attention to others. The vast majority of professing Christians are indolent and slothful, and do nothing for the world around them.

There are few comparatively who need the bridle nearly so much as the spur. Yet these few ought to take to heart the lessons of this passage. They should husband their health as a talent, and not squander it like gamblers. They should be content with spending their daily income of strength, and should not draw recklesly on their capital. They should remember that to do a little, and do it well, is often the way to do most in the long run. Above all they should never forget to watch their own hearts jealously, and to make time for regular self-examination, and calm meditation. The prosperity of their ministry and public work is ultimately bound up with the prosperity of their own soul. Occasional retirement is one of the most useful practices.

3. Christ's feelings for the people who came to him

Third, let us note the feelings of our Lord Jesus Christ towards the people who came together to him. We read that he "had compassion on them, because they were like sheep without a shepherd" (verse 34). They were destitute of teachers. They had no guides but the blind teachers of the law and the Pharisees. They had no spiritual food but human traditions. Thousands of immortal souls stood before our Lord, ignorant, helpless and on the high road to ruin. It touched the gracious heart of our Lord Jesus Christ. He "had compassion on them. . . . So he began teaching them many things" (verse 34).

Let us never forget that our Lord is the same yesterday, today and forever. He never changes. High in heaven, at God's right hand, he still looks with compassion on us – on the ignorant and those that have gone astray. He is still willing to teach us many things. Special as his love is towards his own sheep who hear his voice, he still has a mighty general love towards all mankind – a love of real pity and compassion. We must not overlook this. It is a poor theology which teaches that Christ cares only for believers. There is warrant in Scripture for telling the chief of sinners that Jesus pities them, and cares for their souls, that Jesus is willing to save them, and invites them to believe and be saved.

Let us ask ourselves, as we leave the passage, whether we know anything of the mind of Christ. Are we like him, tenderly concerned about the souls of the unconverted? Do we, like him, feel deep compassion for all who are still like sheep without a shepherd? Do we care about the impenitent and ungodly near our own doors? Do we care about the heathen, the Jew, the Muslim and the Roman Catholic in foreign lands? Do we use every means and give our money willingly to spread the Gospel in the world? These are serious questions and demand a serious reply. The man who cares nothing for the souls of other people is not like Jesus Christ. It may well be doubted whether he is converted himself, and knows the value of his own soul.

The crowd fed with five loaves and two fishes (6:35–46)

Of all our Lord Jesus Christ's miracles, none is so frequently described in the Gospels as this. Each of the four Evangelists was inspired to record it. It is evident that it demands a more than ordinary attention from every reader of God's word.

1. An example of Christ's power

First, let us observe what an example this miracle affords of our Lord Jesus Christ's almighty power. We are told that he fed five thousand men with five loaves and two fishes. We are clearely told that this crowd had nothing to eat. We are no less clearly told that the whole provision for their sustenance consisted of only five loaves and two fishes. And yet we read that our Lord took these loaves and fishes, blessed, broke, and gave them to his disciples to put before the people. And the conclusion of the narrative tells us that "twelve basketfuls of broken pieces" were picked up (verse 43).

Here was creative power, beyond all question. Something real, solid and substantial must plainly have been called into being, which did not exist before. There is no room left for the theory that the people were under the influence of an optical illusion, or a heated imagination. Five thousand hungry people would never have been satisfied if they had not received into their mouths material bread. Twelve basketfuls of broken pieces would never have been taken up if the five loaves had not been miraculously mulitiplied. In short, it is plain that the hand of him who made the world out of nothing was present on this occasion. None but he who at the first created all things, and sent down manna in the desert, could thus have "spread a table in the desert" (Psalm 78:19).

All true Christians should store up facts like these in their minds, and remember them in time of need. We live in the midst of an evil world, and see few with us, and many against us. We carry within us a weak heart, too ready at any moment to turn aside from the right way. We have near us, at every moment, a busy devil, watching continually for our hesitation and seeking to lead us into temptation. Where shall we turn for comfort? What will keep faith alive and preserve us from sinking into despair? There is only one answer. We must look to Jesus. We must think of his almighty power, and his wonders of old. We must recall how he can create food for his people out of nothing, and meet the needs of those who follow him, even in the desert. And as we think these thoughts, we must remember that this Jesus still lives, never changes, and is on our side.

2. Christ's conduct when the miracle had been performed

Secod, let us observe in this passage our Lord Jesus Christ's conduct when the miracle of feeding the crowd had been performed. We read that "after leaving them, he went up on a mountainside to pray" (verse 46).

There is something deeply instructive in this detail. Our Lord was not looking for human praise. After one of his great miracles, we find him immediately seeking solitude and spending his time in prayer. He practiced what he had taught elsewhere, when he said, "go into your room, close the door and pray to your Father, who is unseen" (Matthew 6:6). No one ever performed such miracles as he did. No one ever spoke such words. No one was ever so instant in prayer.

Let our Lord's conduct in this respect be our example. We cannot work miracles as he did; in this he stands alone. But we can walk in his steps in the matter of private devotion. If we have the Spirit of sonship, we can pray. Let us resolve to pray more than we have done hitherto. Let us strive to make time, and place, and opportunity for being alone with God. Above all, let us not only pray before we attempt to work for God, but pray also after our work is done.

It would be good for all of us to examine ourselves more frequently as to our habits about private prayer. What time do we give to it in the twenty-four hours of the day? What progress can we mark, from one year to another, in the fervency, fullness and earnestness of our prayers? What do we know by experience of "wrestling in prayer" (Colossians 4:12)? These are humbling inquiries, but they are useful for our souls. There are few things, it may be feared, in which Christians come so far short of Christ's example as they do in the matter of prayer. Our Master's strong crying and tears, his continuing all night in prayer to God and his frequent withdrawal to private places to hold close communion with the Father, are things more talked of and admired than imitated. We live in an age of hurry, bustle and so-called activity. People are tempted continually to cut short their private devotions and abridge their prayers. When this is the case, we need not wonder that the church of Christ does little in proportion to its machinery. The church must learn to copy its head more closely. Its members must be in their rooms more. We have little because we do not ask God (James 4:2).

Christ walking on the water *(6:47–56)*

The event first recorded in these verses is a beautiful picture of the position of all believers between the first and second comings of Jesus Christ. Like the disciples, we are now tossed to and fro by storms, and do not enjoy the visible presence of our Lord. Like the disciples, we shall see our Lord face to face again, though it may be a time of great extremity when he returns. Like the disciples, we will see everything change for the better when our Master comes to us. We will no longer be buffeted by storms. There will be a great calm.

There is nothing fanciful in such an application of the passage. We need not doubt that there is a deep meaning in every step of his life who "appeared in the body" (1 Timothy 3:16). For the present, however, let us confine ourselves to the plain, practical lessons which these verses contain.

1. Christ sees our troubles and will help us
First, let us notice how our Lord sees the troubles of his believing people, and in due time will help them. We read that when "the boat was in the middle of the lake, and he was alone on land" he "saw the disciples straining at the oars," came to them walking on the lake, cheered them with the gracious words "It is I. Don't be afraid," and changed the storm into a calm.

There are thoughts of comfort here for all true believers. Wherever they may be, or whatever their circumstances, the Lord Jesus sees them. Alone or in company, in sickness or in health, by sea or by land, in perils in the city or in perils in the desert, the same eye which saw the disciples tossed on the lake is always looking at us. We are never beyond the reach of his care. Our way is never hidden from him. He knows the path that we take, and is still able to help. He may not come to our aid at the time we like best, but he will never allow us utterly to fail. He who walked on the water never changes. He will always come at the right time to hold his people up. Though he delays, let us wait patiently. Jesus sees us, and will not desert us.

2. The disciples' fears when they saw Jesus walking on the lake
Second, let us notice the fears of the disciples when they first saw our

Lord walking on the lake. We are told that "they thought he was a ghost. They cried out, because they all saw him and were terrified" (verses 49–50).

What a true picture of human nature we have in these words! How many thousands today, if they had seen what the disciples saw, would have behaved in the same way! How few, if they were on board a ship in a storm at midnight and suddenly saw someone walking on the water and coming near to the ship – how few would preserve their composure and be altogether free from fear! Let people laugh, if they want to, at the superstitious fears of these uneducated disciples. Let them boast, if they like, of the march of intellect and the spread of knowledge in our time. We may confidently state that there are few who, in the same position as the apostles, would have shown more courage than they did. The boldest skeptics have sometimes proved the greatest cowards when appearances have been seen at night which they could not explain.

The truth is, there is an instinctive feeling in us all which makes us shrink from anything which seems to belong to another world. There is a consciousness which many try in vain to conceal by pretending to be indifferent – a consciousness that there are unseen beings as well as those we can see, and that the life which we now live in the body is not the only life in which we have a share. The common stories about ghosts and apparitions are undoubtedly foolish and superstitious. They are almost always traceable to the fears and imaginations of weak-minded people. Yet the universal currency which such stories obtain, all over the world, is a fact that deserves notice. It is an indirect evidence of latent belief in unseen things, just as counterfeit coin is evidence that there is true money. It forms a unique testimony which the unbeliever would find it hard to explain away. It proves that there is something within people which testifies of a world beyond the grave, and that when they feel it, they are afraid.

The plain duty of the true Christian is to live with an antidote against all fears of the great unseen world. That antidote is faith in an unseen Saviour, and constant communion with him. Armed with that antidote, and seeing him who is invisible, nothing need make us afraid. We travel on towards a world of spirits. We are surrounded even now by many dangers. But with Jesus for our shepherd we have no cause for alarm. With him for our shield, we are safe.

3. An example of duty to one another

Third, let us notice at the end of the chapter what a bright example we have of our duty to one another. We are told that when our Lord came to Gennesaret the people "ran throughout that whole region" and "carried the sick on mats" to him. We read that "wherever he went – into villages, towns or countryside – they placed the sick in the market-places. They begged him to let them touch even the edge of his cloak."

Let us see here a pattern for ourselves. Let us go and do likewise. Let us strive to bring all around us who are in need of spiritual medicine, to Jesus the great Physician, that they may be healed. Souls are dying every day. Time is short. Opportunities are rapidly passing away. The night is coming when no one can work. Let us spare no pains in laboring to bring men and women to the knowledge of Jesus Christ, that they may be saved. It is a comforting thought that "all who touch him will healed."

Mark
Chapter 7

The religion of the Pharisees *(7:1–13)*

This passage contains a humbling picture of what human nature is capable of doing in religion. It is one of those Scriptures which ought to be studied frequently and diligently by all who desire the prosperity of the church of Christ.

1. The degraded state of Jewish religion when Christ was on earth
The first thing which demands our attention in these verses is the low and degraded condition of Jewish religion when our Lord was on earth. What can be more deplorable than the statement here? We find the principal teachers of the Jewish nation finding fault because our Lord's disciples were "eating food with hands that were 'unclean,' that is, unwashed" (verse 2). We are told that they attached great importance to the "washing of cups, pitchers and kettles" (verse 4). In short, the man who paid most rigid attention to mere external observances of human invention was reckoned the holiest man!

Remember that the nation in which this state of things existed was the most highly favored in the world. To it was given the law on Mount Sinai, the service of God, the priesthood, the covenants and the promises. Moses, Samuel, David and the prophets lived and died among its people. No nation on earth ever had so many spiritual privileges. No nation ever misused its privileges so fearfully, and so thoroughly deserted its own mercies. Never did fine gold become so dim! From the religion of the books of Deuteronomy and Psalms, to the religion of washing hands and cups and pitchers, how great was the fall! No wonder our Lord, in the time of his earthly ministry, found the people like sheep without a shepherd. External observances alone feed no consciences and sanctify no hearts.

Let the history of the Jewish church be a warning to us never to trifle with false doctrine. If we once tolerate it we never know how far it may go, or into what degraded state of religion we may fall in the end. Once leave the King's highway of truth, and we may end with washing cups and pitchers like the Pharisees and teachers of the law. There is nothing too small, trifling or irrational for people once they turn their back on God's Word. There are branches of the church of Christ today in which the Scriptures are never read, and the Gospel never preached – branches in which the only religion now remaining consists in using a few unmeaning forms and keeping certain human fasts and feasts – branches which began well, like the Jewish church, and like the Jewish church have now fallen into utter barrenness and decay. We can never be too jealous about false doctrine. A little yeast works through the whole batch of dough. Let us earnestly contend for the faith that was once for all entrusted to the saints.

[Absurd and ridiculous as the customs and traditions of the Pharisees appear at first sight, it is a humbling fact that the Pharisees have never lacked imitators and successors. Zeal about washing cups, pitchers and kettles may seem almost ludicrous, and childish; but we need not look far to find an exact parallel near home. What can we say to the gravity and seriousness with which people argue on behalf of chasubles, albs, tunicles, piscinas, sedilia, credence tables, rood screens and the like, in the present day? What can we say to the exaggerated attention paid by many to ceremonies, ornaments, gestures and postures in the worship of God, about which it is enough to say that Scripture is totally silent? What is it all but Pharisaism over again? What is it but a sad repetition of disproportioned zeal about people's traditional usages? What single argument can be used in defense of these things that the Pharisees might not have used with equal force? Nineteen hundred years have passed away, and yet the generation that made so much ado about washing cups, pitchers and kettles is still amongst us. The succession of the Pharisees has never ceased.]

2. The uselessness of lip-service in worshiping God
The second thing that demands our attention is the uselessness of mere

lip-service in the worship of God. Our Lord enforces this lesson by a quotation from the Old Testament: "Isaiah was right when he prophesied about you hypocrites; as it is written: 'These people honor me with their lips, but their hearts are far from me'" (verse 6).

The heart is the part which God chiefly notices in religion. The bowed head and the bended knee, the serious face and the rigid posture, the regular response and the formal amen, all these together do not make up a spiritual worshiper. The eyes of God look further and deeper. He requires the worship of the heart. "My son," he says to every one of us, "give me your heart."

Let us remember this in the public congregation. It must not content us take our bodies to church if we leave our hearts at home. The human eye may detect no flaw in our service. Our minister may look at us with approval. Our neighbors may think us patterns of what a Christian ought to be. Our voice may be heard foremost in the praise and prayer. But it is all worse than nothing in God's sight if our hearts are far away. It is only wood, hay and stubble before him who discerns thoughts and reads the secrets of our inner being.

Let us remember this in our private devotions. It must not satisfy us to say good words if our heart and our lips do not go together. What does it profit us to be fluent and lengthy if our imaginations are roving far away while we are on our knees? It does us no good at all. God sees what we are about, and rejects our offering. Heart-prayers are the prayers he loves to hear. Heart-prayers are the only prayers that he will answer. Our petitions may be weak, stammering and mean in our eyes. They may be presented with no fine words or well-chosen language, and might seem almost unintelligible if they were written down, but if they come from a right heart God understands them. Such prayers are his delight.

3. The tendency for human invention to supplant God's Word

The last thing that demands our atttention in these verses is the tendency of human inventions in religion to supplant God's Word. Three times we find this charge brought forward by our Lord against the Pharisees. "You have let go of the commands of God and are holding on to the traditions of men" (verse 8). "You have a fine way of setting aside the commands of God in order to observe your own traditions" (verse 9). "You nullify the Word of God by your tradition that you have handed down" (verse 13). The first step of the Pharisees was to add their traditions to the Scriptures as useful supplements. The second was to place them on a level with the Word of God, and give them equal authority. The last was to honor them above the Scriptures, and to degrade Scripture from its lawful position. This was the state of things which our Lord found when he was on earth. Practically, the human traditions were everything, and the Word of God was nothing at all. Obedience to the traditions constituted true religion. Obedience to the Scriptures was lost sight of altogether.

It is a sad fact that Christians have far too often walked in the steps of Pharisees in this matter. The very same consequences have resulted. Religious observances of human invention have been pressed on the acceptance of Christians – observances to all appearance useful, and at all events well-meant, but observances nowhere commanded in the Word of God. These very observances have in time been enjoined with more vigor than God's own commands, and defended with more zeal than the authority of God's own Word. We need not look far for examples. The history of our own church will supply them.

[The persecution of the Puritans in the time of the Stuarts, on account of canons and rubrics, was in too many cases neither more nor less than zeal for traditions. An enormous amount of zeal was expended in enforcing conformity to the Church of England, while drunkenness, swearing and open sin were comparatively let alone. Obedience to human ecclesiastical rules was required on pain of fine or imprisonment, while open disobedience to God's Ten Commandments was overlooked. Experience supplies painful proof that traditions once called into being are first called *useful*. Then they become *necessary*. In the end they are too often made *idols*, and everyone must bow down to them or be punished.]

Let us beware of attempting to add anything to the Word of God as necessary to salvation. It provokes God to give us over to judicial blindness. It is as good as saying that his Bible is not perfect, and that we know better than he does what is necessary for our salvation. It is just as easy to destroy the authority of God's Word by addition as by subtraction, by burying it under human inventions as by denying its truth. The whole Bible, and nothing but the Bible, must be our rule of faith – nothing added and nothing taken away.

Finally, let us draw a broad line of distinction between those things in religion which have been devised by mankind, and those which are plainly commanded in God's Word. What God commands is necessary to salvation. What mankind commands is not. What mankind devises may be useful and expedient for the times; but salvation does not hinge on obedience to it. What God requires is essential to life eternal. Those who willfully disobey it ruin their own soul.

[The subtle way in which the Pharisees evaded the requirements of the fifth commandment, to which our Lord refers in this passage, calls for a few words of explanation. We must remember that the Pharisees did not openly deny the obligation of the fifth commandment. In all probability they professed to attach as much importance to it as anyone. And yet they contrived to nullify it! How did they achieve this?

They taught that a man might dedicate to God's service, as sacred, any part of his property which might be applied to the relief of his parents, and so discharge himself from any further expense on them. He had only to say that all his money was "Corban" – that is, given over to holy purposes – and no further claim could be made upon him for his father's or mother's support. Under the pretense of giving God a prior claim, he set himself free from the burden of maintaining them forever. He did not flatly deny his duty to meet his parents' needs from his worldly goods, but he evaded it by setting up a human tradition and asserting a higher call of duty, namely duty to God.

The similarity between the traditions and sophistries of the Pharisees, nullifying God's Word under the pretense of zeal for God's glory, and those of the Jesuits and other advocates of the Roman Catholic church, is painfully striking. The following passage from Petter's commentary on St. Mark is worth reading:

> The Scriptures teach that there is no difference to be put between meats, in regard of holiness, but that every creature of God is good. This the Papists make void by teaching that it is matter of religion and conscience to abstain from flesh meats at certain seasons. The Scripture teacheth that we should pray to God alone. This they make void by their manifold prayers to saints departed. The Scripture teacheth Christ alone to be our

mediator, both of redemption and intercession. This they make void by making saints intercessors. The Scripture teacheth Christ to be the only head of the church. This they abrogate by their doctrine of the Pope's supremacy. The Scripture teacheth that every soul should be subject to the higher power. This they abrogate by exempting the Pope and popish clergy from subjection to the civil power of princes and magistrates. Lastly, to instance in the same kind as our Saviour here against the Pharisees, whereas the Word of God commands children to honor their parents, the Papists teach that if the child have vowed a monastical life, he is exempted from duty to parents.]

The heart as the true source of impurity *(7:14–23)*

1. People are slow to understand spiritual things
We see in the beginning of this passage how slow people are to understand spiritual things. "Listen," says our Lord to the people, "listen to me, everyone, and understand this" (verse 14). "Are you so dull?" he says to his disciples (verse 18). "Don't you see?"

The corruption of human nature is a universal disease. It affects not only the human heart, will and conscience, but the mind, memory and understanding. The very same person who is quick and clever in worldly things will often completely fail to comprehend the simplest truths of Christianity. He will often be unable to take in the plainest reasonings of the Gospel. He will see no meaning in the clearest statements of evangelical doctrine. They will sound to him either foolish or mysterious. He will listen to them like someone listening to a foreign language, catching a word here and there, but not seeing the drift of the whole. "The world through its wisdom" does not know God (1 Corinthians 1:21). It hears, but does not understand.

We must pray daily for the teaching of the Holy Spirit if we want to make progress in the knowledge of divine things. Without him, the most powerful intellect and the strongest reasoning powers will carry us only a little way. In reading the Bible and hearing sermons, everything depends on the spirit in which we read and hear. A humble, teachable, childlike frame of mind is the grand secret of success. Happy is the person who often says with David, "teach me your decrees" (Psalm 119:64). Such a person will understand as well as hear.

2. The heart is the chief source of defilement

Second, we see from this passage that the heart is the chief source of defilement and impurity in God's sight. Moral purity does not depend on washing or not washing, touching things or not touching them, eating things or not eating them, as the teachers of the law and the Pharisees taught. "Nothing that enters a man from the outside can make him 'unclean,'" said our Lord (verse 18). "What comes out of a man is what makes him 'unclean'" (verse 20).

There is a deep truth in these words which is frequently overlooked. Our original sinfulness and natural inclination to evil are seldom sufficiently considered. Human wickedness is often attributed to bad examples, bad company, unusual temptations or the snares of the devil. It seems forgotten that everyone carries a fountain of wickedness within. We need no bad company to teach us, and no devil to tempt us, in order to run into sin. We have within us the beginning of every sin under heaven.

We ought to remember this in the training and education of children. In all our management we must never forget that the seeds of all mischief and wickedness are in their hearts. It is not enough to keep boys and girls at home and shut out every outward temptation. They carry within them a heart ready for any sin, and until that heart is changed they are not safe, whatever we do. When children do wrong, it is a common practice to lay all the blame on bad companions. But it is mere ignorance, blindness and foolishness to do so. Bad companions are a great evil no doubt, and an evil to be avoided as much as possible, but no bad companion teaches a boy or girl half as much sin as their own hearts will suggest to them, unless they are renewed by the Spirit. The beginning of all wickedness is within. If parents were half as diligent in praying for their children's conversion as they are in keeping them from bad company, their children would turn out far better than they do.

[The common arguments against "public school" education appear to me based on forgetfulness of our Lord's teaching about the heart. Unquestionably there are many evils in "public schools," however carefully run. It must be so. We must expect it. But it is no less true that there are great dangers in private education, and dangers in their kind quite as formidable as any which beset a boy at public school. Of course no universal rule can be laid down. Regard must be had to individual character and temperament. But to suppose, as some people seem to do, that boys educated at public schools must turn out badly, and boys educated at home must turn out well, is surely not wise. It is forgetting our Lord's doctrine that the heart is the principal source of evil. Without a change of heart a boy may be kept at home, and yet learn all manner of sin.]

3. A black catalog of evils in the human heart

Third, we see from this passage what a black catalog of evils the human heart contains. "Out of men's hearts," says our Lord, "come evil thoughts, sexual immorality, theft, murder, adultery, greed, malice, deceit, lewdness, envy, slander, arrogance and folly. All these evils come from inside" (verses 21–23).

Let us clearly understand when we read these words that our Lord is speaking of the human heart generally. He is not speaking only of the notorious profligate or the prisoner in jail. He is speaking of all mankind. All of us, whether high or low, rich or poor, masters or servants, old or young, learned or unlearned – all of us have by nature such a heart as Jesus here describes. The seeds of all the evils here mentioned lie within us all. They may lie dormant all our lives. They may be kept down by the fear of consequences, the restraint of public opinion, the dread of discovery, the desire to be thought respectable and, above all, by the almighty grace of God. But everyone has the root of every sin inside.

How humble we ought to be, when we read these verses! "All of us have become like one who is unclean" (Isaiah 64:6) in God's sight. He sees in each one of us countless evils which the world never sees at all, for he reads our hearts. Surely of all sins to which we are liable, self-righteousness is the most unreasonable and unbecoming.

How thankful we ought to be for the Gospel when we read these verses! That Gospel contains a complete provision for all the needs of our poor defiled natures. The blood of Christ can "cleanse us from all sin." The Holy Spirit can change even our sinful hearts, and keep them clean when they are changed. The person who does not glory in the Gospel can surely know little of the plague that is within.

How watchful we ought to be when we remember these verses!

What a careful guard we ought to keep over our imagination, our tongues and our daily behavior! At the head of the black list of our heart's contents stand "evil thoughts." Let us never forget that. Thoughts are the parents of words and deeds. Let us pray daily for grace to keep our *thoughts* in order, and let us cry earnestly and fervently, "lead us not into temptation."

The Syro-Phoenician woman whose daughter had an evil spirit (7:24–30)

We know nothing about the woman here mentioned beyond the facts that we read here. Her name, her previous history, the way in which she was led to seek our Lord although she was a Gentile and lived in the vicinity of Tyre, all these things are hidden from us. But the few facts that are related about this woman are full of precious instruction. Let us observe them and learn wisdom.

1. Encouragement to pray for others
First, this passage is meant to encourage us to pray for others. The woman who came to our Lord in the story here must doubtless have been in deep affliction. She saw a beloved child possessed by an evil spirit. She saw her in a condition in which no teaching could reach the mind, and no medicine could heal the body – a condition only one degree better than death itself. She hears of Jesus, and beseeches him to "drive the demon out of her daughter" (verse 26). She prays for one who could not pray for herself, and never rests till her prayer is granted. By prayer she obtains the cure which no human means could obtain. Through the prayer of the mother, the daughter is healed. On her own behalf that daughter did not speak a word; but her mother spoke for her to the Lord, and did not speak in vain. Hopeless and desperate as her case appeared, she had a praying mother, and where there is a praying mother there is always hope.

The truth here taught is one of deep importance. The case here recorded is one that does not stand alone. Few duties are so strongly recommended by Scriptural example as the duty of praying for others. There is a long catalog of instances in Scripture which show the benefits that may be conferred on others by praying for them. The nobleman's son at Capernaum, the centurion's servant and the daughter of Jairus are all striking examples. Wonderful as it may seem, God chooses to do great things for souls when friends and relations are moved to pray for them. "The prayer of a righteous man is powerful and effective" (James 5:16).

Fathers and mothers are especially bound to remember the case of this woman. They cannot give their children new hearts. They can give them Christian education, and show them the way of life; but they cannot give them a will to choose Christ's service and a mind to love God. Yet there is one thing they can always do; they can pray for them. They can pray for the conversion of profligate sons, who will have their own way and run greedily into sin. They can pray for the conversion of worldly daughters who set their minds on things below and love pleasure more than God. Such prayers are heard on high. Never, never let us forget that the children for whom many prayers have been offered seldom finally perish. Let us pray more for our sons and daughters. Even when they will not let us speak to them about religion, they cannot prevent us speaking for them to God.

2. Perseverance in praying for others

Second, this passage is meant to teach us to persevere in praying for others. The woman whose story we have here appeared at first to obtain nothing by her coming to the Lord. On the contrary, our Lord's reply was discouraging. Yet she did not give up in despair. She prayed on, and did not faint. She pressed her suit with ingenious arguments. She would take no refusal. She pleaded for a few "crumbs" of mercy rather than none at all. And through this holy importunity she succeeded. She heard at last these joyful words: "For such a reply, you may go; the demon has left your daughter" (verse 29).

Perseverance in prayer is a point of great moment. Our hearts are too apt to become cool and indifferent, and to think that it is no use drawing near to God. Our hands soon hang down and our knees grow weak. Satan is always working to draw us off from our prayers, and filling our minds with reasons why we may give them up. These things are true with repsect to all prayers, but they are especially true with respect to prayers for other people. They are always far more meager than they ought to be. They are often attempted for a little while, and then left off. We see no immediate answer to our prayers. We see the persons for whose souls we pray continuing in sin. We draw the conclusion that it is useless to pray for them, and allow our intercession to come to an end.

In order to arm our minds with arguments for perseverance in prayer for others, let us often study the case of this woman. Let us remember how she prayed on and did not faint in the face of great discouragement. Let us note how at last she went home rejoicing, and let us resolve by God's grace to follow her example.

Do we know what it is to pray for ourselves? This, after all, is the first question for self-enquiry. Those who never speak to God about their own soul can know nothing of prayer for others. They are as yet Godless, Christless and hopeless, and have to learn the very rudiments of religion. Let them awake, and call upon God.

But do we pray for ourselves? Then let us take care that we pray for others too. Let us beware of selfish prayers – prayers which are wholly taken up with our own affairs, and in which there is no place for other souls beside our own. Let us continually name before God all those we love. Let us pray for all – the worst, the hardest and the most unbelieving. Let us continue praying for them year after year, in spite of their continued unbelief. God's time of mercy may be a distant one. Our eyes may not see an answer to our prayers. The answer may not come for ten, fifteen or twenty years. It may not come till we have exchanged prayer for praise, and are far aware from this world. But while we live, let us pray for others. It is the greatest kindness we can do to anyone, to speak for them to our Lord Jesus Christ. The day of judgment will show that one of the greatest links in drawing some souls to God has been the prayer of friends for them.

The healing of a deaf and mute man (7:31–37)

1. A mighty miracle

The first thing that demands our notice in these verses is the mighty miracle which is here recorded. We read that they brought to our Lord "a man who was deaf and could hardly talk, and they begged him to place his hand on the man" (verse 32). At once the request is granted, and the cure is worked. Speech and hearing are instantaneously given to the man by a word and a touch. "The man's ears were opened, his tongue was loosened and he began to speak plainly" (verse 35).

We only see half the teaching of this passage if we only regard it as an example of our Lord's divine power. It is such an example, beyond doubt, but it is something more than that. We must look further, deeper and lower than the surface, and we will find in the passage precious spiritual truths.

Here we are meant to see our Lord's power to heal the spiritually deaf. He can give the chief of sinners a hearing ear. He can make him delight in listening to the very Gospel which he once ridiculed and despised.

Here also we are meant to see our Lord's power to heal the spiritually dumb. He can teach the hardest of transgressors to call to God. He can put a new song in the mouth of someone whose talk was once only of this world. He can make the vilest person speak of spiritual things and testify of the Gospel of the grace of God.

When Jesus pours out his Spirit, nothing is impossible. We must never despair of others. We must never regard our own hearts as too bad to be changed. He who healed the deaf and dumb is still alive. The cases which moral philosophy pronounced hopeless are not incurable if they are brought to Christ.

2. Christ's method

The second thing which demands our notice in these verses is the unusual method by which our Lord thought good to work the miracle here recorded. We are told that "he took him aside, away from the crowd" and "put his fingers into the man's ears. Then he spat and touched the man's tongue. He looked up to heaven and with a deep sigh said to him" – and then, and not till then, came the words of commanding power, "'Ephphatha!' (which means, 'Be opened!')" (verses 33–34).

There is undoubtedly much that is mysterious in these actions. We do not know why they were used. It would have been as easy to our Lord to speak the word and command health to return at once, as to do what he did here. His reasons for the course he adopted are not recorded. We only know that the result was the same as on other occasions: the man was cured.

But there is one simple lesson to be learned from our Lord's conduct on this occasion. That lesson is, that Christ was not tied to the use of

any one means in doing his works among us. Sometimes he thought fit
to work in one way, sometimes in another. His enemies were never
able to say that unless he always used the same method he could not
work at all.

We see the same thing going on still in the church of Christ. We see
continual proof that the Lord is not tied to any one means exclusively
in conveying grace to the soul. Sometimes he chooses to work by the
word preached publicly, sometimes by the word read privately. Sometimes he awakens people by sickness and affliction, sometimes by the
rebukes or advice of friends. Sometimes he uses means of grace to turn
people out of the way of sin. Sometimes he arrests their attention by
some providence, without any means of grace at all. He will not have
any means of grace made an idol and exalted, to the disparagement of
other means. He will not have any means despised as useless, and neglected as of no value. All are good and valuable. All are in their turn
employed for the same great end, the conversion of souls. All are in the
hands of him who "does not answer for any of his actions" (Job 33:13,
footnote), and knows best which means to use, in each separate case
that he heals.

3. The testimony of those who saw the miracle
The last thing which demands our notice in these verses is the remarkable
testimony which was borne by those who saw the miracle here recorded.
They said of our Lord, "He has done everything well" (verse 37).

It is more than probable that those who said these things were hardly
aware of their full meaning when applied to Christ. Like Caiaphas,
they "did not say this on their own" (see John 11:51). But the truth
which they spoke is full of deep and unspeakable comfort, and ought
to be daily remembered by all true Christians.

Let us remember it as we look back over the past days of our lives,
from the hour of our conversion. "Our Lord has done everything
well." In first bringing us out of darkness into wonderful light – in
humbling us and teaching us our weakness, guilt and folly – in strip-
ping us of our idols, and choosing all that comes to us – in placing us
where we are, and giving us what we have – how well everything has
been done! How great the mercy that we have not had our own way!

Let us remember it as we look forward to the days yet to come. We do not know what they may be, bright or dark, many or few. But we know that we are in the hands of him who "does everything well." He will not go wrong in any of his dealings with us. He will take away and give, he will afflict and bereave, he will move and he will settle, with perfect wisdom, at the right time, in the right way. The great shepherd of the sheep makes no mistakes. He leads every lamb of his flock by the right way to the city where they can settle.

We will never see the full beauty of these words till the resurrection morning. We will then look back over our lives and know the meaning of everything that happened from first to last. We will remember all the way by which we were led, and confess that everything was "well done." The why and the wherefore, the causes and the reasons of everything which now perplexes, will be clear and plain as the sun at noon-day. We shall wonder at our own past blindness, and marvel that we could ever have doubted our Lord's love. "Now we see but a poor reflection as in a mirror; then we shall see face to face. Now I know in part; then I shall know fully, even as I am fully known" (1 Corinthians 13:12).

[The reason why our Lord made us of the actions recorded earlier in this miracle – spitting, looking up to heaven and sighing – is a question that has often perplexed comentators. Some observations of Luther, quoted by Stier, are worth reading:

This sigh was not drawn from Christ on account of the single tongue and ear of this poor man; but it is a common sigh over all tongues and ears, indeed over all hearts, bodies and souls, and over all men from Adam to his last descendant. . . .

Our Lord saw well what an amount of suffering and sorrow would be occasioned by tongues and ears. For the greatest mischief which has been inflicted on Christianity has not arisen from tyrants (with persecution, murder and pride against the Word) but from that little bit of flesh which abides between the jaws. It is this that inflicts the greatest injury on the kingdom of God.]

Mark
Chapter 8

The crowd fed with seven loaves; the unbelief of the Pharisees (8:1–13)

Once more we see our Lord feeding a great multitude with a few loaves and fishes. He knew the human heart. He foresaw the rise of cavilers and skeptics who would question the reality of the wonderful works he performed. By repeating the mighty miracle here recorded, he stops the mouth of all who are not willfully blind to evidence. Publicly, and in front of 4000 witnesses, he shows his almighty power a second time.

1. Christ's compassion
First, let us observe in this passage how great is the kindness and compassion of our Lord Jesus Christ. He saw around him a "large crowd" (verse 1) who had nothing to eat. He knew that the great majority were following him from no other motive than idle curiosity, and had no claim whatever to be regarded as his disciples. Yet when he saw them hungry and destitute he had pity on them: "I have compassion for these people; they have already been with me three days and have nothing to eat" (verse 2).

The feeling heart of our Lord Jesus Christ appears in these words. He has compassion even on those who are not his people – the faithless, the graceless, the followers of this world. He feels tenderly for them, though they do not know it. He died for them, though they care little for what he did on the cross. He would receive them graciously and pardon them freely if they would only repent and believe in him. Let us always beware of measuring the love of Christ by any human measure. He has a special love, beyond doubt, for his own believing people.

But he also has a general compassionate love, even for the unthankful and the evil. His love "surpasses knowledge" (Ephesians 3:19).

Let us strive to make Jesus our pattern in this, as well as in everything else. Let us be kind and compassionate and pitiful and courteous to everyone. Let us be ready to do good to everyone, and not only to friends and the family of believers. Let us carry into practice our Lord's injunction, "Love your enemies and pray for those who persecute you" (Matthew 5:44). This is to show the mind of Christ. This is the right way to heap burning coals on an enemy's head, and to melt foes into friends (Romans 12:20).

2. With Christ nothing is impossible

Second, let us observe from this passage that with Christ nothing is impossible. The disciples said, "But where in this remote place can anyone get enough bread to feed them?" (verse 4). They might well say so. Without the hand of him who first made the world out of nothing, the thing could not happen. But in the almighty hands of Jesus seven loaves and a few fishes were made sufficient to satisfy 4000 men. Nothing is too hard for the Lord.

We must never allow ourselves to doubt Christ's power to supply the spiritual needs of all his people. He has "bread enough and to spare" for every soul that trusts in him. Weak, infirm, corrupt, empty as believers feel themselves, let them never despair while Jesus lives. In him a boundless store of mercy and grace is laid up for the use of all his believing members, and ready to be given to all who ask in prayer. "God was pleased to have all his fullness dwell in him" (Colossians 1:19).

Let us never doubt Christ's providential care for the temporal needs of all his people. He knows their circumstances. He is acquainted with all their necessities. He will never allow them to lack anything that is really for their good. His heart has not changed since he ascended and sat at the right hand of God. The one who had compassion on the hungry crowd in the desert and met their need – he is still alive. How much more, may we suppose, will he meet the need of those who trust him? He will supply them without fail. Their faith may occasionally be tried. They may sometimes be kept waiting and be brought very low. But the believer will never be left entirely destitute. "His bread will be supplied, and water will not fail him" (Isaiah 33:16).

3. Christ's sorrow at unbelief

Third, let us observe how much sorrow unbelief occasions to our Lord Jesus Christ. We are told that when "the Pharisees began to question" him, "to test him, they asked him for a sign from heaven. He sighed deeply" (verses 11–12). There was a deep meaning in that sigh! It came from a heart which mourned over the ruin that these wicked men were bringing on their own souls. Enemies as they were, Jesus could not see hardening themselves in unbelief without sorrow.

The feeling which our Lord Jesus Christ here expressed will always be the feeling of all true Christians. Grief over the sins of others is one leading evidence of true grace. The person who is really converted will always regard the unconverted with pity and concern. This was the mind of David: "I beheld the transgressors, and was grieved" (Psalm 119:158, KJV). This was the mind of the godly in the days of Ezekiel: "those who grieve and lament over all the detestable things that are done" in the land (Ezekiel 9:4). This was the mind of Lot: he "was tormented in his righteous soul by the lawless deeds he saw and heard" (2 Peter 2:8). This was the mind of Paul: "I have great sorrow and unceasing anguish in my heart" (Romans 9:2). In all these cases we see something of the mind of Christ. As the great head feels, so feel the members. They all grieve when they see sin.

Let us leave the passage with solemn self-enquiry. Do we know anything of likeness to Christ, and fellow-feeling with him? Do we feel hurt, pained and sorrowful when we see people continuing in sin and unbelief? Do we feel grieved and concerned about the state of the unconverted? These are heart-searching questions, and demand serious consideration. There are few surer marks of an unconverted heart than carelessness and indifference about the souls of other people.

Finally, let us never forget that unbelief and sin are just as great a cause of grief to our Lord now as they were 1900 years ago. Let us strive and pray that we may not add to that grief by any act or deed of ours. The sin of grieving Christ is one which many commit continually without thought or reflection. He who sighed over the unbelief of the Pharisees is still unchanged. Can we doubt that when he sees some people persisting in unbelief today, he is grieved? From such sin may we be delivered!

Warning against false doctrine; the disciples' slowness *(8:14–21)*

1. A solemn warning

First, let us notice the solemn warning which our Lord gives to his disciples at the beginning of this passage. He says, "Be careful. Watch out for the yeast of the Pharisees and that of Herod" (verse 15).

We are not left to conjecture the meaning of this warning. This is made clear by the parallel passage in St. Matthew's Gospel. We there read that Jesus did not mean the yeast of bread, but the yeast of doctrine. The self-righteousness and empty form of religion of the Pharisees and the worldliness and skepticism of Herod's courtiers were the objects of our Lord's caution. Against both he tells his disciples to be on their guard.

Such warnings are of deep importance. It would be good for the church of Christ if they had been remembered more. The assaults of persecution from without have never done half so much harm to the church as the rise of false doctrines within. False prophets and false teachers within the camp have done far more mischief in Christendom than all the bloody persecutions of the emperors of Rome. The sword of the foe has never done such damage to the cause of truth as the tongue and the pen.

The doctrines which our Lord specifies are precisely those which have always been found to inflict most injury on the cause of Christianity. Empty, formal religion on the one hand, and skepticism on the other, have been chronic diseases in the professing church of Christ. In every age many Christians have been infected by them. In every age people need to watch against them and be on their guard.

The expression used by our Lord in speaking of false doctrine is singularly forceful and appropriate. He calls it "yeast." No word more suitable could have been employed. It exactly describes the small beginnings of false doctrine – the subtle quiet way in which it pervades a person's religion unawares – the deadly power with which it changes the whole character of their Christianity. Here, in fact, lies the great danger of false doctrine. If it approached us under its true colors it would do little harm. The great secret of its success is its subtlety and likeness to truth. Every error in religion has been said to be a truth abused.

Let us often "examine ourselves to see whether we are in the faith" (see 2 Corinthians 13:5), and beware of "yeast." Let us no more trifle with a little false doctrine than we would trifle with a little immorality or a little lie. Once admit it into our hearts and we never know how far it may lead us astray. The beginning of departure from the pure truth is like the letting out of waters – first a drop, and at last a torrent. A little yeast works through the whole batch of dough (Galatians 5:9).

2. The dull understanding of the disciples

Second, let us notice the dull understanding of the disciples when our Lord gave the warning of this passage. They thought that the "yeast" of which he spoke must be the yeast of bread. It never struck them that he was speaking of doctrine. They drew from him the sharp reproof: "Do you still not see or understand? Are your hearts hardened? . . . Do you still not understand?" (verses 17–21). Believers, converted, renewed, as the disciples were, they were still slow to understand spiritual things. Their eyes were still dim, and their perception slow in the matters of the kingdom of God.

We will find it useful to ourselves to remember what is here recorded of the disciples. It may help to correct the high thoughts which we are apt to entertain of our own wisdom, and to keep us humble and lowly-minded. We must not imagine that we know everything as soon as we are converted. Our knowledge, like all our graces, is always imperfect, and never so far from perfection as at our first beginning in the service of Christ. There is more ignorance in our hearts than we are at all aware of. "The man who thinks he knows something does not yet know as he ought to know" (1 Corinthians 8:2).

Above all, we will find it useful to remember what is recorded here in dealing with young Christians. We must not expect perfection in new converts. We must not set them down as graceless and godless and false converts because at first they see only half the truth and commit many mistakes. Their hearts may be right in the sight of God, and yet, like the disciples, they may be very slow to understand the things of the Spirit. We must bear with them patiently, and not cast them aside. We must give them time to grow in grace and knowledge, and in the end they may be ripe in wisdom, like Peter and John. It is a blessed thought that Jesus, our Master in heaven, does not despise any of his people.

Their slowness to learn undoubtedly is amazing and blameworthy, but his patience never gives way. He goes on teaching them, "a little here, a little there" (Isaiah 28:13). Let us do likewise. Let it be a rule with us never to despise the weakness and dullness of young Christians. Wherever we see a spark of true grace, however dim and mixed with weakness, let us be helpful and kind. Let us do as we would be done by.

The blind man at Bethsaida healed *(8:22–26)*

We do not know the reason of the unusual method employed by our Lord Jesus Christ in working the miracle recorded in these verses. We see a blind man miraculously healed. We know that a word from our Lord's mouth, or a touch of his hand, would have been sufficient to effect a cure. But we see Jesus taking this blind man by the hand, leading him out of the town, spitting on his eyes, putting his hands on him, and then and not till then restoring his sight. And the meaning of all these actions, the passage before us leave entirely unexplained.

But it is well to remember, in reading passages of this kind, that the Lord is not tied to the use of any one means. In the conversion of souls there are different kinds of operation, but it is the same Spirit which converts. So also in the healing of the body, there were varieties of agency employed by our Lord, but it was the same divine power that effected the cure. In all his works God is a sovereign. He does not answer for any of his actions.

One thing in the message demands our special observation. That is the gradual nature of the cure which our Lord performed on this blind man. He did not deliver him from his blindness at once, but by degrees. He might have done it in a moment, but he chose to do it step by step. First the blind man said that he only saw "people; they look like trees walking around" (verse 24). Afterwards his eyesight was restored completely, and he "saw everything clearly" (verse 25). In this respect the miracle stands entirely alone.

We need hardly doubt that this gradual cure was meant to be a picture of spiritual things. We may be sure that there was a deep meaning

117

in every word and work of our Lord's earthly ministry, and here, as in other places, we shall find a useful lesson.

1. Gradual restoration

First, let us see in this gradual restoration to sight a vivid illustration of the manner in which the Spirit frequently works in the conversion of souls. We are all naturally blind and ignorant in matters which concern our souls. Conversion is an illumination, a change from darkness to light, from blindness to seeing the kingdom of God. Yet few unconverted people see things clearly at first. The nature and proportion of doctrines, practices and ordinances of the Gospel are dimly seen by them, and imperfectly understood. They are like the man before us, who at first saw people like trees walking about. Their vision is dazzled and unaccustomed to the new world into which they have been introduced. It is not till the work of the Spirit has become deeper and their experience has been somewhat matured that they see everything clearly, and give to each part of religion its proper place. This is the history of thousands of God's children. They begin with seeing people like trees walking around; they end by seeing everything clearly. Happy are those who have learned this lesson well, and are humble and distrustful of their own judgment.

2. The church today

Second, let us see in the gradual cure of this blind man a striking picture of the present position of Christ's believieving people in the world, compared with what is to come. We see in part and know in part in the present dispensation. We are like those who travel by night. We do not know the meaning of much that is passing around us. In the providential dealings of God with his children, and in the conduct of many of God's saints, we see much that we cannot understand – and cannot alter. In short, we are like the man seeing people like trees walking around.

But let us look forward and take comfort. The time is coming when we shall see everything clearly. The night is far gone. The day is at hand. Let us be content to wait, watch, work and pray. When the day of the Lord comes, our spiritual eyesight will be perfected. We shall see as we have been seen, and know as we have been known.

Peter's confession of faith; his ignorance of the need for Christ to die *(8:27–33)*

The circumstances here recorded are of great importance. They took place during a journey, and arose out of a conversation "on the way" (verse 27). Happy are those journeys in which time is not wasted on trifles, but redeemed as far as possible for the consideration of serious things.

1. Various opinions about Christ
First, let us observe the variety of opinions about Christ which prevailed among the Jews. Some said that he was John the Baptist, some Elijah, and others one of the prophets. In short every kind of opinion appears to have been current, except the one which was true.

We may see the same thing on everey side at the present day. Christ and his Gospel are just as little understood in reality, and are the subject of just as many different opinions, as they were 1900 years ago. Many know the name of Christ, acknowledge him as one who came into the world to save sinners, and regularly worship in buildings set apart for his service. Few thoroughly realize that he is true God, the one Mediator, the one High Priest, the only source of life and peace, their own Shepherd and their own Friend. Vague ideas about Christ are still very common. Intelligent experience of acquaintance with Christ is still very rare. May we never rest till we can say of Christ, "My lover is mine and I am his" (Song of Songs 2:16). This is saving knowledge. This is life eternal.

2. Peter's good confession of faith
Second, let us observe the good confession of faith which the apostle Peter witnessed. He replied to our Lord's question, "Who do you say I am?" by saying, "You are the Christ" (verse 29).

This was a noble answer, when the circumstances under which it was made are duly considered. It was made when Jesus was poor and without honor, majesty, wealth or power. It was made when the heads of the Jewish nation, both in church and state, refused to receive Jesus as the Messiah. Yet even then Simon Peter says, "You are the Christ." His strong faith was not stumbled by our Lord's poverty and low position in society. His confidence was not shaken by the opposition of teachers of the law and the Pharisees, and the contempt of rulers and priests. None of these things moved Simon Peter. He believed that the man he followed, Jesus of Nazareth, was the promised Saviour, the true Prophet greater than Moses, the long-predicted Messiah. He declared it boldly and unhesitatingly, as the creed of himself and his few companions: "You are the Christ."

There is much that we may profitably learn from Peter's conduct on this occasion. Erring and unstable as he sometimes was, the faith he exhibited in the passage now before us is well worthy of imitation. Such bold confessions as his are the truest evidence of living faith, and are required in every age if people will prove themselves to be Christ's disciples. We too must be ready to confess Christ, even as Peter did. We shall never find our Master and his doctrine popular. We must be prepared to confess him, with few on our side, and many against us. But let us take courage and walk in Peter's steps, and we will not fail to receive Peter's reward. Jesus takes notice of those who acknowledge him before other people, and will one day acknowledge them as his servants before an assembled world.

3. Christ's declaration of his death and resurrection

Third, let us observe the full declaration which our Lord makes of his own coming death and resurrection. We read that "he began to teach them that the Son of Man must suffer many things and be rejected by the elders, chief priests and teachers of the law, and that he must be killed and after three days rise again" (verse 31).

The events here announced must have sounded strange to the disciples. To be told that their beloved Master, after all his mighty works, would soon be put to death, must have been heavy tidings and past their understanding. But the words which convey the announcement are scarcely less than the event – he "*must* suffer . . . *must* be killed and . . . rise again."

Why did our Lord say "must"? Did he mean that he was unable to escape suffering, that he must die by compulsion of a stronger power than his own? Impossible. This could not have been his meaning. Did he mean that he must die to give the world a great example of self-sacrifice and self-denial, and that this, and this alone, made his death necessary? Once more it may be replied, "Impossible." There is a far deeper meaning in the word "must" suffer and be killed. He meant that his death and passion were necessary in order to make atonement for human sin. Without shedding his blood, there could be no remission. Without the sacrifice of his body on the cross, there could be no satisfaction of God's holy law. He "must" suffer to make reconciliation for iniquity. He "must" die, because without his death as a propitiatory offering, sinners could never have life. He "must" suffer, because without his vicarious sufferings our sins could never be taken away. In a word, he "must" be delivered for our offenses, and raised again for our justification.

Here is the central truth of the Bible. Let us never forget that. All other truths compared to this are of secondary importance. Whatever views we hold of religious truth, let us see that we have a firm grasp upon the atoning efficacy of Christ's death. Let the truth so often proclaimed by our Lord to his disciples, and so diligently taught by the disciples to the world, be the foundation truth in our Christianity. In life and in death, in health and in sickness, let us lean all our weight on this mighty fact, that though we ave sinned Christ has died for sinners, and that though we deserve nothing, Christ has suffered on the cross for us, and by that suffering purchased heaven for all who believe in him.

4. Grace and weakness mixed in the Christian

Fourth, let us observe in this passage the strange mixture of grace and infirmity which may be found in the heart of a true Christian. We see that very same Peter who had just witnessed so noble a confession presuming to rebuke his Master because he spoke of suffering and dying. We see him drawing down on himself the sharpest rebuke which ever fell from our Lord's lips during his earthly ministry: "'Get behind me, Satan!' he said. 'You do not have in mind the things of God, but the things of men'" (verse 33).

We have here a humbling proof that the best of saints is a poor fallible creature. Here was *ignorance* in Simon Peter. He did not understand the necessity of our Lord's death, and would have actually prevented his sacrifice on the cross. Here was *self-conceit* in Simon Peter. He thought he knew what was right and fitting for his Master better than his Master himself, and actually undertook to show the Messiah a more excellent way. And last, but not least, Simon Peter did it all with the *best intentions!* He meant well. His motives were pure. But zeal and earnestness are no excuse for error. We may mean well and yet fall into tremendous mistakes.

Let us learn humility from the facts here recorded. Let us beware of being puffed up with our own spiritual attainements, or exalted by the praise of others. Let us never think that we know everything and are not likely to err. We see that it is but a little step from making a good confession to being a "Satan" in Christ's way. Let us pray daily, "Hold me up, keep me, teach me, let me not go wrong."

Lastly, let us learn charity towards others from the facts here recorded. Let us not be in a hurry to cast off our brother as graceless because of errors and mistakes. Let us remember that his heart may be right in the sight of God, like Peter's, though like Peter he may for a time turn aside. Rather let us recall St. Paul's advice and act upon it. "If someone is caught in a sin, you who are spiritual should restore him gently. But watch yourself, or you also may be tempted" (Galatians 6:1).

The necessity of self-denial; the value of the soul; the danger of being ashamed of Christ *(8:34–38)*

The words of our Lord Jesus Christ in this passage are particularly weighty and solemn. They were spoken to correct the mistaken views of his disciples as to the nature of his kingdom. But they contain truths of the deepest importance to Christians in every age of the church. The whole passage is one which should often form the subject of private meditation.

1. The necessity of self-denial
First, we learn from these verses the absolute necessity of self-denial if we would be Christ's disciples and be saved. What does our Lord say? "If anyone would come after me, he must deny himself and take up his cross and follow me" (verse 34).

Salvation is undoubtedly all of grace. It is offered freely in the

Gospel to the chief of sinners, without money and without cost. "It is by grace you have been saved, through faith – and this not from yourselves, it is the gift of God – not by works, so that no one can boast" (Ephesians 2:8–9). But all who accept this great salvation must prove the reality of their faith by carrying the cross after Christ. They must not think to enter heaven without trouble, pain, suffering and conflict on earth. They must be content to take up the cross of doctrine, and the cross of living a life which the world ricidules as too strict and righteous. They must be willing to crucify the flesh, to mortify the deeds of the body, to fight daily with the devil, to come out from the world and to lose their lives if need be for Christ's sake and the Gospel's. These are hard sayings, but they cannot be evaded. The words of our Lord are plain and unmistakable. If we will not carry the cross, we shall never wear the crown.

Let us not be deterred from Christ's service by fear of the cross. Heavy as that cross may seem, Jesus will give us grace to bear it. "I can do everything through him who gives me strength" (Philippians 4:13). Thousands and tens of thousands have borne it before us, and have found Christ's yoke easy, and Christ's burden light. No good thing on earth was ever attained without trouble. We cannot surely expect that we can enter the kingdom of God without trouble. Let us go forward boldly, and allow no difficulty to keep us back. The glory at the end is forevermore.

Let us often ask ourselves whether our Christianity costs us anything. Has it the true stamp of heaven? Does it carry with it any cross? If not, we may well tremble and be afraid. We have everything to learn. A religion which costs nothing is worth nothing. It will do us no good in the life that now is. It will lead to no salvation in the life to come.

2. The value of the soul

Second, we learn from these verses the unspeakable value of the soul. What does our Lord say? "What good is it for a man to gain the whole world, yet forfeit his soul?" (verse 36). These words were meant to stir us up to exertion and self-denial. They ought to ring in our ears like a trumpet every morning when we rise from our beds, and every night when we lie down. May they be deeply graven in our memories, and never effaced by the devil and the world!

We all have souls that will live forevermore. Whether we know it or not, we all carry about with us something which will live on when our bodies are moldering in the grave. We all have souls for which we shall have to give account to God. It is an awful thought, when we consider how little attention most people give to anything except this world. But it is true.

Anyone may lose his own soul. He cannot save it: Christ alone can do that. But he can lose it, and that in many different ways. He may murder it, by loving sin and clinging to the world. He may poison it by choosing a religion of lies, and believing human superstitions. He may starve it, by neglecting all means of grace, and refusing to receive into his heart the Gospel. There are many ways that lead to the pit. Whatever way a man takes, he, and he alone, is accountable for it. Weak, corrupt, fallen, impotent as human nature is, man has a mighty power of destroying, ruining and losing his own soul.

The whole world cannot make up for the loss of the soul. The possession of all the treasures that the world contains would not compensate for eternal ruin. They would not satisfy us and make us happy while we had them. They could only be enjoyed for a few years, at best, and must then be left forevermore. Of all unprofitable and foolish bargains, the worst is that of giving up the soul's salvation for the sake of this present world. It is a bargain of which thousands have repented – but many, like Esau, who sold his birthright for a dish of stew, have repented too late.

Let these sayings of our Lord sink deep into our hearts. Words are inadequate to express their importance. May we remember them in the hour of temptation, when the soul seems a small and unimportant thing, and the world seems very bright and great. May we remember them in the hour of persecution, when we are tried by the fear of other people, and are half-inclined to desert Christ. In times like these, let us call to mind this mighty question of our Lord and repeat it to ourselves, "What good is it for a man to gain the whole world, yet forfeit his soul?"

3. The danger of being ashamed of Christ
Third, we learn from these verses the great danger of being ashamed of Christ. What does our Lord say? "If anyone is ashamed of me and my

words in this adulterous and sinful generation, the Son of Man will be ashamed of him when he comes in his Father's glory with the holy angels" (vese 38).

When can it be said of anyone that he is ashamed of Christ? We are guilty of it when we are ashamed of letting people see that we believe and love the doctrines of Christ, that we desire to live according to the commandment of Christ, and that we wish to be reckoned among the people of Christ. Christ's doctrine, laws and people were never popular, and never will be. Those who boldly acknowledge that they love them are sure to bring on themselves ridicule and persecution. Whoever shrinks from this acknowledgment from fear of this ridicule and persecution is ashamed of Christ and comes under the sentence of the passage before us.

Perhaps there are few of our Lord's sayings which are more condemning than this. "Fear of man" will indeed "prove to be a snare" (Proverbs 29:25). There are thousands of people who would face a lion or storm a breach if duty called them, and fear nothing, and yet would be ashamed of being thought "religious," and would not dare to avow that they desired to please Christ rather than people. The power of ridicule is truly wonderful! The bondage in which people live to the opinion of the world is astonishing!

Let us all pray daily for faith and courage to acknowledge Christ before the world. Of sin, worldliness or unbelief we may well be ashamed. We ought never to be ashamed of the Lord who died for us on the cross. In spite of laughter, mockery and hard words, let us boldly avow that we serve Christ. Let us often look forward to the day of second coming, and remember what he says in this place. Better a thousand times acknowledge Christ now, and be despised by people, than be disowned by Christ before his Father on the day of judgment.

Mark
Chapter 9

Christ's transfiguration *(9:1–13)*

The connection of this passage with the end of the last chapter ought never to be overlooked. Our Lord had been speaking of his own coming death and passion – of the necessity of self-denial if we would be his disciples – of the need of losing our lives if we want to have them saved. But in the same breath he goes on to speak of his future kingdom and glory. He takes off the edge of his "hard sayings" by promising a sight of that glory to some of those who heard him. And in the story of the transfiguration which is here recorded we see that promise fulfilled.

1. A vision of the glory of Christ's second coming
The first thing which demands our notice in these verses is the marvelous vision they contain of the glory which Christ and his people will have at his second coming.

There can be no doubt that this was one of the principal purposes of the transfiguration. It was meant to teach the disciples that though their Lord was lowly and poor in appearance now, he would one day appear in such royal majesty as fitted the Son of God. It was meant to teach them that when their Master came the second time, his saints, like Moses and Elijah, would appear with him. It was meant to remind them that though reviled and persecuted now, because they belonged to Christ, they would one day be clothed with honor and share in their Master's glory.

[The analogy between the glory assumed by our Lord at his transfiguration and the glory which the saints will receive at his resurrection, is well pointed out by Victor Antiochenus in a passage quoted by Du Veil. He says:

We must not suppose that there is to be any change of the natural form of man in the kingdom of heaven. For as the appearance of Christ was not in itself changed, but only illumined (or glorified) – so also the just who will be conformed to his glorious body will not be changed as to their outward form. Their bodies will only receive a certain accession of splendor and light, which St. Paul calls a change (1 Corinthians 15:52) but the Evangelists call a transfiguration.]

We have reason to thank God for this vision. We are often tempted to give up Christ's service, because of the cross and affliction which it entails. We see few with us, and many against us. We find our names cast out as evil, and all manner of evil said of us, because we believe and love the Gospel. Year after year we see our companions in Christ's service removed by death, and we feel as if we knew little about them except that they have gone to an unknown world and that we are left alone. All these things are trying to flesh and blood. No wonder that the faith of believers sometimes languishes, and their eyes fail while they look for their hope.

Let us see in the story of the transfiguration a remedy for such doubting thoughts as these. The vision of the holy mountain is a gracious pledge that glorious things are in store for the people of God. Their crucified Saviour will come again in power and great glory. His saints will all come with him, and are in safe keeping until that happy day. We may wait patiently. "When Christ, who is your life, appears, then you also will appear with him in glory" (Colossians 3:4).

2. Peter's strong expression

The second thing which demands our notice in this passage is the strong expression of the apostle Peter when he saw his Lord transfigured. "Rabbi," he said, "it is good for us to be here" (verse 5).

No doubt there was much in this saying which cannot be commended. It showed an ignorance of the purpose for which Jesus came into the world, to suffer and to die. It showed a forgetfulness of his brothers who were not with him, and of the dark world which so much needed his Master's presence. Above all, the proposal which he made at the same time to "put up three shelters" for Moses, Elijah and Christ, showed a low view of his Master's dignity, and implied that he did not know that someone greater than Moses and Elijah was there. In all these respects the apostle's exclamation is not to be praised, but to be blamed.

But having said this, let us not fail to remark what joy and happiness this glorious vision conferred on this warm-hearted disciple. Let us see in his fervent cry, "It is good for us to be here," what comfort and consolation the sight of glory can give to a true believer.

[The remark of Brentius on the glorious nature of the whole vision of the transfiguration is well worth quoting. Like most of that admirable commentator's expositions, it contains much in few words.

No synod on earth was ever more gloriously attended than this. No assembly was ever more illustrious. Here is God the Father, God the Son and God the Holy Spirit. Here are Moses and Elijah, the chief of the prophets. Here are Peter, James and John, the chief of the apostles.]

Let us look forward, and try to form some idea of the pleasure which the saints will experience when they at last meet the Lord Jesus at his second coming and meet to part no more. A vision of a few minutes was sufficient to warm and stir Peter's heart. The sight of two saints in glory was so cheering and life-giving that he wanted to enjoy more of it. What then shall we say when we see our Lord appear at the last day with all his saints? What shall we say when we ourselves are allowed to share in his glory and join the happy company, and feel that we shall go out no more from the joy of our Lord? These are questions that no man can answer. The happiness of that great day of gathering together is one that we cannot now conceive. The feelings of which Peter had a little foretaste will then be ours in full experience. We shall all say with one heart and one voice, when we see Christ and all his saints, "It is good for us to be here."

3. Testimony to Christ as the Messiah

The third thing which demands our notice in this passage is the distinct testimony it bears to Christ's office and dignity as the promised Messiah. We see this testimony first in the appearance of Moses and

Elijah, the representatives of the law and the prophets. They appear as witnesses that Jesus is the one of whom they spoke in old times, and of whom they wrote that he would come. They disappear after a few minutes, and leave Jesus alone, as though to show that they were only witnesses, and that our Master having come, the servants resign to him the chief place. We see this testimony, secondly, in the miraculous voice from heaven, saying, "This is my Son, whom I love. Listen to him!" (verse 7). The voice of God the Father which was heard at our Lord's baptism was heard once more at his transfiguration. On both occasions there was the same solemn declaration, "this is my Son, whom I love." On this last occasion, there was an addition of the most important words, "Listen to him!"

The whole conclusion of the vision was calculated to leave a lasting impression on the minds of the three disciples. It taught them in the most striking manner that their Lord was as far above them and the prophets as the master of a house is above the servants, and that they must in all things believe, follow, obey, trust and listen to him.

Finally, the last words of the voice from heaven are words that should always be in the minds of all true Christians. They should "listen to Christ." He is the great Teacher; those who want to be wise must learn from him. He is the light of the world: those who do not want to stray must follow him. He is the head of the church: those who want to be living members of his mystical body must always look to him. The grand question that concerns us all is not so much what people say, or ministers say, or what the church says, or councils say, but what Christ says. Let us listen to him. Let us remain in him. Let us lean on him. Let us look to him. He and only he will never fail us, never disappoint us and never lead us astray. Happy are those who know by experience the meaning of the text, "my sheep listen to my voice; I know them, and they follow me. I give them eternal life, and they shall never perish; no one can snatch them out of my hand" (John 10:27–28).

[The coming of Elijah, which forms the topic of conversation between our Lord and his disciples in the latter part of the passage now expounded, is a deep and mysterious subject.

1. According to one class of interpreters, the ministry of John the Baptist was the coming of Elijah. They consider that the prophecy of

Malachi 4:5–6, that Elijah the prophet would be sent before the great and dreadful day of the Lord, was completely fulfilled in John the Baptist, and that no other coming of Elijah is to be expected. This is the view maintained by the great majority of Protestant commentators, both English and foreign, from the Reformation to the present day.

2. According to another group of interpreters, a literal coming of Elijah has yet to take place. They consider that John the Baptist only went before our Lord in the "spirit and power of Elijah" (Luke 1:17) and that the words of Malachi are yet to be fulfilled. This is the view maintained by nearly all the Fathers, by the great majority of the Roman Catholic commentators, and by not a few modern Protestant theologians both English and continental.

If I must express an opinion, when great and learned theologians differ so widely, I must honestly confess that I decidedly incline to the second of the two interpretations above. I believe that a literal appearing of Elijah the prophet before the second coming of Christ may be expected. Dark and incomprehensible as the subject is, the scriptural arguments in favor of this view appear to me unanswerable. Any other view seems to do violence to the plain meaning of the words of Malachi 4:5–6, Matthew 17:11 and John 1:21. There seems no reason why there should not be a double "coming of Elijah" – the first "in spirit and power," when John the Baptist preached, and the second "literal and in person," when he comes at the end of the world, immediately before the great and dreadful day of the Lord.

The whole question is undoubtedly surrounded with difficulties, whatever view we adopt. I can only say that after patient and calm investigation I see much fewer difficulties in the way of the interpretation to which I lean than in the way of the other. I hold with Augustine, Jerome, Chrysostom, Hilary, Jansen, Brentius, Greswell, Alford and Stier that Malachi 4:5–6 is not yet completely fulfilled, and that Elijah the prophet will yet come. Those who can read Greek will find an interesting note on this subject in Cramer's Catena on St. Mark.]

The boy with an evil spirit healed (9:14–29)

The contrast between these verses and those which precede them in the chapter is very striking. We pass from the mount of transfiguration to a sad story of the work of the devil. We come down from the vision of glory, to a conflict with demonic possession. We exchange the blessed company of Moses and Elijah for the crude behavior of unbelieving teachers of the law. We leave the foretaste of millennial glory, and the solemn voice of God the Father testifying to God the Son, and return once more to a scene of pain, weakness and misery – a boy in agony of body, a father in deep distress and a little band of feeble disciples baffled by Satan's power and unable to give relief. The contrast, we must all feel, is very great. Yet it is but a faint picture of the change of scene that Jesus voluntarily undertook to witness when he first laid aside his glory and came into the world. And it is after all a vivid picture of the life of all true Christians. With them, as with their Master, work, conflict and scenes of weakness and sorrow will always be the rule. With them, too, visions of glory, foretastes of heaven and times on the mount will always be the exception.

1. The disciples' dependence on their Master

First, let us learn from these verses how dependent Christ's disciples are on the company and help of their Master.

We see this truth brought out in striking manner in the scene which meets our Lord's eyes when he came down from the mountain. Like Moses when he came down from Mount Sinai, he finds his little flock in confusion. He sees his nine apostles beset by a party of malicious teachers of the law, and baffled in an attempt to heal one who had been brought to them possessed with a devil. The very same disciples who a short time before had done many miracles and driven out many demons (Mark 6:13) had now met with a case too hard for them. They were learning by humbling experience the great lesson that "apart from me you can do nothing" (John 15:5). It was a useful lesson, no doubt, and worked out for their spiritual good. It would probably be remembered all the days of their lives. The things that we learn by smarting experience remain in our memories, while truths heard with the ear are often forgotten. But we may be sure it was a bitter lesson at the time. We do not love to learn that we can do nothing without Christ.

We need not look far to see many illustrations of this truth in the history of Christ's people in every age. The very people who at one time have done great exploits in the cause of the Gospel, at another time have failed entirely, and proved weak and unstable as water. The temporary recantations of Cranmer and Jewell are striking examples. The holiest and best of Christians have nothing to glory of. Their strength is not their own. They have nothing but what they have received. They have only to provoke the Lord to leave them for a while, and they will soon discover that their power has gone. Like Samson when his hair was cut, they are as weak as any other people.

Let us learn a lesson of humility from the failure of the disciples. Let us strive to realize every day our need of the grace and presence of Christ. With him we may do all things. Without him we can do nothing at all. With him we may overcome the greatest temptations. Without him the least may overcome us. Let our cry be every morning, "Do not leave us to ourselves; we do not know what a day may bring; if your Presence does not go with us, we cannot go up from here" (see Exodus 33:15).

2. Satan can injure us early in life

Second, let us learn from these verses how early in life we are liable to be injured by Satan. We read a fearful description of the miseries inflicted by Satan on the young man whose case is here recorded. And we are told that he had been in this awful state "from childhood" (verse 21).

There is a lesson of deep importnce here which we must not overlook. We must labor to do good to our children even from their earliest years. If Satan begins to harm them so early, we must not be behind him in diligence to lead them to God. How soon in life a child becomes responsible and accountable is a difficult question to solve. Perhaps far sooner than many of us suppose. One thing at all events is very clear: it is never too soon to strive and pray for the salvation of the souls of children – never too soon to speak to them as moral beings and tell them of God and Christ and right and wrong. The devil, we may be quite sure, loses no time in endeavoring to influence the minds of young people. He begins with them "from childhood." Let us work hard to counteract him. If young hearts can be filled by Satan, they can also be filled with the Spirit of God.

3. Faith and unbelief mixed in the heart

Third, let us learn from these verses how faith and unbelief can be mixed together in the same heart. The words of the child's father set this truth before us in a touching way. "I do believe," he cried to Jesus; "help me overcome my unbelief!"

We see in these words a vivid picture of the heart of many a true Christian. Among believers we find few indeed in whom trust and doubt, hope and fear, do not exist side by side. Nothing is perfect in the children of God so long as they live in the body. Their knowledge, love and humility are all more or less defective, and mingled with corruption. And as it is with their other graces, so it is with their faith. They believe, and yet have about them a remainder of unbelief.

What shall we do with our faith? We must *use it*. Weak, trembling, doubting, feeble as it may be, we must use it. We must not wait till it is great, perfect and powerful, but like the man in this passage turn it to account and hope that one day it will be more strong. "I do believe," he said.

What shall we do with our unbelief? We must *resist it*, and pray against it. We must not allow it to keep us back from Christ. We must take it to Christ, as we take all other sins and weaknesses, and cry to him for deliverance. Like the man in this passage, we must cry, "help me overcome my unbelief!"

These are the truths of experience. Happy are those who know something of them. The world is ignorant of them. Faith and unbelief, doubts and fears are all foolishness to the natural person. But let the true Christian study these things well, and thoroughly understand them. It is of the utmost importance to our comfort to know that a true believer may be known by inner warfare as well as by inner peace.

4. Christ's dominion over Satan and his agents

Fourth, let us note the complete dominion which our Lord exercises over Satan and all his agents. The spirit who was too strong for the disciples is at once driven out by the Master. He speaks with powerful authority, and Satan at once is obliged to obey. "I command you, come out of him and never enter him again" (verse 25).

We may leave the passage with comfortable feelings. He who is for us is greater than all those who are against us. Satan is strong, busy, active, malicious. But Jesus is able to save completely all those who come to God through him – from the devil as well as from sin – from the devil as well as the world. "By standing firm you will gain life" (Luke 21:19). Jesus still lives, and will not let Satan snatch us out of his hand. Jesus still lives, and will soon come again to deliver us entirely from the fiery darts of the wicked one. The great chain is prepared (Revelation 20:1). Satan will one day be bound. The God of peace will soon crush Satan under our feet (Romans 16:20).

[The expression "overwhelmed with wonder" (verse 15) deserves some notice. The Greek word is extremely strong. It certainly seems as if some traces of visible glory, or at any rate some expression of extraordinary majesty, appeared in our Lord's face after the transfiguration. It reminds us of the face of Moses shining when he came down from the mountain.]

The crucifixion predicted; humility commanded (9:30–37)

1. Christ repeats his prediction of his death and resurrection
Let us note in these verses our Lord's renewed announcement of his own coming death and resurrection. "He was teaching his disciples. He said to them, 'The Son of Man is going to be betrayed into the hands of men. They will kill him, and after three days he will rise'" (verse 31).

The dullness of the disciples in spiritual things appears once more, as soon as this announcement was made. There was good in the news as well as seeming evil – sweet as well as bitter – life as well as death – the resurrection as well as the cross. But it was all darkness to the bewildered twelve. "They did not understand what he meant and were afraid to ask him about it" (verse 32). Their minds were still full of their mistaken ideas of their Master's reign on earth. They thought that his earthly kingdom was going to appear immediately. Never are we so slow to understand as when prejudice and preconceived opinions darken our eyes.

The immense importance of our Lord's death and resurrection comes out strongly in this fresh announcement which he makes. It is not for nothing that he reminds us again that he must die. He would have us know that his death was the great end for which he came into the world. He would remind us that by that death the great problem was to be solved of how God could be just, and yet declare sinners to be righteous. He did not come to earth merely to teach, preach and work miracles. He came to pay the ransom for sin by his own blood and suffering on the cross. Let us never forget this. The incarnation, example and words of Christ are all of deep importance. But the grand object which demands our notice in the story of his earthly ministry is his death on Calvary.

2. The apostles' ambition and love of preeminence

Second, let us notice in these verses the ambition and love of preeminence which the apostles exhibited. "On the road . . . they had argued about who was the greatest" (verses 33–34).

How strange this sounds! Who would have thought that a few fishermen and tax collectors could have been overcome by rivalry and the desire of supremacy? Who would have expected that poor men who had given up everything for Christ's sake would have been troubled by strife and dissension as to the place and precedence which each one deserved? Yet so it is. The fact is recorded for our learning. The Holy Spirit has caused it to be written down for the perpetual use of Christ's church. Let us take care that it is not written in vain.

It is an awful fact, whether we like to admit it or not, that pride is one of the commonest sins which beset human nature. We are all born Pharisees. We all naturally think far better of ourselves than we ought. We all naturally imagine that we deserve something better than we have. It is an old sin. It began in the Garden of Eden, when Adam and Eve thought they had not got everything that their merits deserved. It is a subtle sin. It rules and reigns in many a heart without being detected, and can even wear the clothing of humility. It is a most soul-ruining sin. It prevents repentance, keeps people back from Christ, checks brotherly love and nips spiritual concern in the bud. Let us watch against it and be on our guard. Of all clothing, none is so graceful, none wears so well and none is so rare as true humility.

3. The standard of true greatness

Third, let us notice the unique standard of true greatness which our Lord sets before his disciples. He says to them, "If anyone wants to be first, he must be the very last, and the servant of all" (verse 35).

These words are deeply instructive. They show us that the maxims of the world are directly contrary to the mind of Christ. The world's idea of greatness is to rule, but Christian greatness consists in serving. The world's ambition is to receive honor and attention, but the desire of the Christian should be to give rather than receive, and to attend on others rather than be attended on. In short, the person who puts most effort into serving other people, and in being useful in the present time, is the greatest in the eyes of Christ.

[The words of Augustine on this point are worth reading. He says: "A bishop's office is a name of labor rather than of honor, so he who covets preeminence rather than usefulness may understand that he is not a bishop" (*The City of God*).]

Let us strive to make practical use of this heart-searching maxim. Let us seek to do good to other people and to mortify that self-pleasing and self-indulgence to which we are all so prone. Is there any service that we can render to our fellow Christians? Is there any kindness that we can do them, to help them and promote their happiness? If there is, let us do it without delay. It would be good for Christendom if empty boasts of churchmanship and orthodoxy were less frequent, and practical attention to our Lord's words in this passage more common. Those who are willing to be last of all, and servants of all, for Christ's sake are always few. Yet these are the people who do good, break down prejudices, convince unbelievers that Christianity is a reality, and shake the world.

4. Christ's encouragement to show kindness to the least of believers
Fourth, let us note what encouragement our Lord gives us to show kindness to the least and lowest who believe in his name. He teaches this lesson in a very touching way. He took a child in his arms, and said to his disciples, "Whoever welcomes one of these little children in my name welcomes me; and whoever welcomes me does not welcome me but the one who sent me" (verse 37).

The principle here laid down is a continuation of that which we have just considered. It is one which is foolishness to people without the Spirit. Flesh and blood can see no other way to greatness than crowns, rank, wealth and high position in the world. The Son of God declares that the way lies in devoting ourselves to the care of the weakest and lowest of his flock. He reinforces his declaration by marvelous words which are often read and heard without thought. He tells us that to receive one child in his name is to receive Christ, and to receive Christ is to receive God.

There is rich encouragement here for all who devote themselves to the charitable work of doing good to neglected souls. There is encouragement for everyone who labors to restore the outcasts to a place in society, to raise the fallen, to gather together the ragged children whom nobody cares for, to snatch the worst of characters from a life of sin like burning sticks from the fire, and to bring the wanderers home. Let all such people take comfort when they read these words. Their work may often be hard and discouraging. They may be mocked, ridiculed and held up to scorn by the world. But let them know that the Son of God notes all that they do, and is well pleased. Whatever the world may think, these are the people Jesus will delight to honor on the last day.

A tolerant spirit; self-sacrifice; the necessity of hell *(9:38–50)*

1. Religious toleration

First, we see in these verses the mind of Christ on the great subject of toleration in religion. The apostle John said to him, "Teacher, we saw a man driving out demons in your name and we told him to stop, because he was not one of us" (verse 38). The man was doing a good work without doubt. He was warring on the same side as the apostles, beyond question. But this did not satisfy John. He did not work in the company of the apostles. He did not fight in line with them. And therefore John had forbidden him. But let us hear now what the great head of the church decides! "'Do not stop him,' Jesus said. 'No one who does a miracle in my name can in the next moment say anything bad about me, for whoever is not against us is for us'" (verses 39–40).

Here is a golden rule indeed, and one that human nature sorely needs and has too often forgotten. Members of all branches of Christ's church are apt to think that no good can be done in the world unless it is done by their own party and denomination. They are so narrow-minded that they cannot conceive the possibility of working on any other pattern but that which they follow. They make an idol of their own particular ecclesiastical structure, and can see no merit in any other. They are like him who cried when Eldad and Medad prophesied in the camp, "Moses, my lord, stop them!" (Numbers 11:28).

To this intolerant spirit we owe some of the blackest pages of church history. Christians have repeatedly persecuted Christians for no better reason than that which is here given by John. They have practically proclaimed to their brothers and sisters, "you must either follow us or not work for Christ at all."

Let us be on our guard against this feeling. It is only too near the surface of all our hearts. Let us learn to realize that liberal, tolerant spirit which Jesus here recommends, and be thankful for good works wherever and by whomever they are done. Let us beware of the slightest inclination to stop and check others, merely because they do not choose to adopt our plans or work by our side. We may think our fellow Christians mistaken in some points. We may imagine that more would be done for Christ if they would join us, and if everyone worked in the same way. We may see many evils arising from religious dissension and divisions. But all this must not prevent us rejoicing if the works of the devil are destroyed and souls are saved. Is our neighbor warring against Satan? Is he really trying to labor for Christ? This is the grand question. Better a thousand times that the work should be done by other hands than not done at all. Happy is the person who knows something of the spirit of Moses when he said, "I wish that all the LORD's people were prophets" (Numbers 11:29), and of Paul when he says, "Christ is preached. And because of this I rejoice. Yes, and I will continue to rejoice" (Philippians 1:18).

[The remarks of Quesnel on this passage are interesting, and doubly so when we remember that the writer was a Roman Catholic. He says:

What John does here is an example of an indiscreet zeal for the interests of Christ. The most holy people sometimes have occasion to stop themselves engaging in covert rivalry. We very easily mingle our own interests with those of God, and our vanity uses the glory of his name only as a veil. A preacher sometimes imagines that his only desire is that people should follow Christ and adhere to his Word, when it is himself whom he desires they should follow, and to whom he is very glad to find them adhere. . . .

Christ permits many things in his church which are done without him commissioning them; but he makes them contribute to the establishment of his kingdom. Whatever reason we may have to fear that some people will not persevere in goodness, we must nonetheless allow them to continue in their endeavors when they appear to be at all useful. God himself authorizes such people, since it is he who performs the good in them.]

2. The need to give up anything that stands between us and our salvation

Second, we see in these verses the need to give up anything that stands between us and the salvation of our souls. The "hand" and the "foot" are to be cut off and the "eye" to be plucked out if they are a cause of sin. The things that are as dear to us as eye, foot or hand are to be thrown away and given up if they injure our souls, whatever pain the sacrifice may cost us.

This is a rule which seems stern and harsh at first sight. But our loving Master did not give the rule without cause. Compliance with it is absolutely necessary, since neglect of it is the sure way to hell. Our bodily senses are the channels through which many of our most formidable temptations approach us. Our bodily members are ready instruments of evil, but slow to do what is good. The eye, the hand and the foot are good servants when under right direction. But they need daily watching lest they lead us into sin.

Let us resolve by God's grace to make a practical use of our Lord's solemn injunction in this place. Let us regard it as the advice of a wise physician, the counsel of a tender father, the warning of a faithful friend. However people may ridicule us for our strictness, let us habitually "crucify our flesh with its affections and lusts." Let us deny ourselves any enjoyment rather than incur the peril of sinning against God. Let us walk in Job's steps: he says, "I made a covenant with my eyes" (Job 31:1). Let us remember Paul: he says, "I beat my body and make it my slave so that after I have preached to others, I myself will not be disqualified for the prize" (1 Corinthians 9:27).

3. The reality of future punishment

Third, we see in these verses the reality, awfulness and eternity of future punishment. Three times the Lord Jesus speaks of "hell." Three times (in the footnotes of the NIV, ed. note) he says, "their worm does not die, and the fire is not quenched." These are awful expressions. They call for reflection rather than exposition. They should be pondered, considered and remembered by all who claim to be Christians. It matters little whether we regard them as figurative and symbolic. If they are, one thing at least is very clear. The worm and the fire are symbols of real things. There is a real hell, and that hell is eternal.

There is no mercy in keeping back from people the subject of hell. Fearful and tremendous as it is, it ought to be pressed on everyone as one of the great truths of Christianity. Our loving Saviour speaks frequently of it. The apostle John in the book of Revelation often describes it. The servants of God in these days must not be ashamed of confessing their belief in it. Were there no boundless mercy in Christ for all who believe in him, we might well shrink from the awful topic. Were there no precious blood of Christ able to cleanse all sin, we might well keep silence about the wrath to come. But there is mercy for all who ask in Christ's name. There is a fountain open for all sin. Let us then boldly and unhesitatingly maintain that there is a hell, and beseech people to flee from it before it is too late. "Knowing what it is to fear the Lord," let us "try to persuade men" (2 Corinthians 5:11). It is not possible to say too much about Christ. But it is quite possible to say too little about hell.

Let the concluding words of our Lord ring in our ears as we leave the passage: "Have salt in yourselves, and be at peace with each other" (verse 50). Let us make sure that we have in our hearts the saving grace of the Holy Spirit, sanctifying, purifying, preserving from corruption our whole inner being. Let us watch the grace given to us with daily watchfulness, and pray to be kept from indifference and sin, lest we be overtaken in faults, bring misery on our consciences, and discredit on our religion. Above all let us live in peace with each other, not seeking great things, or striving for the preeminence, but clothed with humility, and loving all who love Christ in sincerity. These seem simple things. But great reward comes from attending to them.

[Verse 49 appears to baffle all the commentators: "Everyone will be salted with fire." The true meaning of these words and their connection with the context are problems which seem not yet solved. At all events, not one of the many interpretations which have been proposed so far is entirely satisfactory. We must confess that it is one of those knots which are not yet untied in the exposition of Scripture.

1. Some people think that our Lord is speaking only of the wicked and their future punishment, and that he means, "Every lost soul will be salted with the fire of hell." This appears to be the view held by Whitby.

2. Some people think that our Lord is speaking only of the righteous and their fiery trials in this life, by which they are purified and preserved from corruption, and that he means, "Every true disciple of mine will be as it were salted and passed through the fire of tribulation." Of those who think that our Lord speaks only of the righteous, some think that the "fire" means tribulation, and some the work of the Holy Spirit. Cartwright holds the last of these opinions, and Junius the first.

3. Some people think that our Lord is speaking of all members of his church, both good and bad, and that his meaning is the same as that of St. Paul where he says, "The fire will test the quality of each man's work" (1 Corinthians 3:13). According to this view, the meaning of the verse would be, "Everyone will finally be salted, tried, and tested by the fire of the last day."

I offer no opinion and make no comment on any of the above views. The objections which might be made against every one of them are neither few nor small. Whether these objections are insuperable or not is a point on which learned theologians differ widely, and a conclusion will perhaps never be attained until the Lord appears. My own conviction is that we must wait for more light, and regard the text at present as one of the "deep things" of God .]

Mark
Chapter 10

The right view of marriage expounded *(10:1–12)*

1. Christ's patient perseverance as a teacher
The opening verses of this passage show us the patient perseverance of our Lord Jesus Christ as a teacher. We are told that he came "into the region of Judea and across the Jordan. Again crowds of people came to him, and as was his custom, he taught them" (verse 1).

Wherever our Lord went, he was always about his Father's business, preaching, teaching and laboring to do good to souls. He threw away no opportunity. In the whole history of his earthly ministry we never read of an idle day. Of him it may be truly said that he sowed his seed by every stream (Isaiah 32:20) and that he sowed his seed in the morning and in the evening did not let his hand be idle (Ecclesiastes 11:6).

And yet our Lord knew every human heart. He knew perfectly well that the great proportion of his hearers were hardened and unbelieving. He knew, as he spoke, that most of his words fell to the ground uncared for and unheeded, and that so far as concerned the salvation of souls, most of his labor was in vain. He knew all this, and yet he labored on.

Let us see in this fact a standing pattern to all who try to do good to others, whatever their job may be. Let it be remembered by every minister and every missionary, by every schoolmaster and every Sunday-school teacher, by every district visitor and every lay worker, by every head of a house who has family prayers, and by every nurse who has the charge of children. Let all such people remember Christ's example and resolve to do likewise. We are not to give up teaching because we see no good done. We are not to relax our efforts because we see no fruit of our toil. We are to work on steadily, keeping before us the great principle that duty is ours and results are God's. There must be plowmen and sowers, as well as reapers and binders of sheaves. The honest master pays his laborers according to the work they do, and not according to the crops that grow on his land. Our Master in heaven will deal with all his servants in this way on the last day. He knows that success is not under their control. He knows that they cannot change hearts. He will reward them according to their labor, and not according to the fruits which have resulted from their labor. It is not "the good and *successful* servant" but the "good and *faithful* servant" to whom he will say, "Come and share your master's happiness!" (Matthew 25:21).

[Some remarks of Bishop Latimer on this point are well worth reading. They occur in a passage in one of his sermons on the parable of the wedding garment (*Works*, Parker Society, Vol. I, p. 286):

The man who had not the wedding garment was blamed because he professed one thing, and was indeed another. Why did not the king blame the preachers? There was no fault in them, they did their duties: they had no further commandment but to call men to the marriage. The garment he should have provided himself. Therefore he quarreleth not with the preachers, "What doth this fellow here? why suffered ye him to enter?" For their commission extended no further but only to call him. Many are grieved that there is so little fruit of their preaching. And when they are asked, "Why do you not preach, having so great gifts given you of God?" "I would preach," say they, "but I see so little fruit, so little amendment of life, that it maketh me weary:" a naughty answer: a very naughty answer. Thou art troubled with that which God gave thee no charge of: and leavest undone that which thou art charged with.

2. The dignity and importance of marriage

The greater portion of this passage is meant to show us the dignity and importance of the relationship of marriage. It is plain that the prevailing opinions of the Jews on this subject when our Lord was on earth were lax and low in the extreme. The binding character of the marriage tie was not recognized. Divorce for slight and trivial causes was allowable and common.

[The extent to which the Jews allowed divorce for absurd and frivolous causes would be almost incredible if we had not the evidence of their own Rabbinical writings on the subject. A full account of the matter will be found in Lightfoot's *Horae Hebraicae* on St. Matthew 5:31. One passage quoted by him will be sufficient to give the reader an idea of Jewish customs about divorce: "The school of Hillel says, If the wife cooks her husband's food ill by over-salting it, or over-roasting it, she is to be put away."]

The duties of husbands towards wives, and of wives towards husbands as a natural consequence, were little understood. To correct this state of things, our Lord sets up a high and holy standard of principles. He refers to the original institution of marriage at the creation, as the union of one man and one woman. He quotes and endorses the solemn words used at the marriage of Adam and Eve as words of perpetual significance: "a man will leave his father and mother and be united to his wife, and the two will become one flesh" (verse 7–8). He adds a solemn comment: "What God has joned together, let man not separate" (verse 9). And finally, in reply to the inquiry of his disciples, he declares that divorce followed by remarriage, except for the cause of unfaithfulness, is a breach of the seventh commandment.

[I am aware that the opinions I have expressed at the close of this paragraph are contrary to that of some learned theologians. I can only say that I have arrived at them deliberately, after calm investigation of the parallel passage in Matthew 19:9, and of the words of our Lord in Matthew 5:32. I decidedly believe that the remarriage forbidden by Christ is remarriage after a divorce for trivial and frivolous causes, and that his words do not apply to remarriage after divorce on account of unfaithfulness. Remarriage after divorce for frivolous causes is clearly adultery, for one simple reason: the divorce ought never to have taken place, and the divorced party is still a married person in the sight of God. Remarriage after divorce for unfaithfulness, by the same process of reasoning, is not adultery. Unfaithfulness dissolves the marriage tie altogether, and places the husband and wife once more in the position of unmarried people, or of a widower or widow.]

The importance of the whole subject on which our Lord here pronounces judgment can hardly be overrated. We ought to be very thankful that we have so clear and full an exposition of his mind upon it. The marriage relation lies at the very root of the social system of nations. The public morality of a people, and the private happiness of the families which compose a people, are deeply involved in the whole question of the law of marriage. The experience of all nations confirms the wisdom of our Lord's decision in this passage in the most stiking manner. It is a fact clearly ascertained, that polygamy and permission to obtain divorce on slight grounds have a direct tendency to promote immorality. In short, the nearer a nation's laws about marriage approach to the law of Christ, the higher has the moral tone of that nation always proved to be.

It is a good idea for all those who are married, or intend to marry, to ponder well the teaching of our Lord Jesus Christ in this passage. Of all relations of life, none ought to be regarded with such reverence and none taken in hand so cautiously as the relation of husband and wife. In no relation is so much earthly happiness to be found if it is entered upon discreetly, advisedly and in the fear of God. In none is so much misery seen to follow if it is taken in hand unadvisedly, lightly, wantonly and without thought. From no step in life does so much benefit come to the soul, if people marry "in the Lord." From none does the soul take so much harm if fancy, passion or any mere worldly motive is the only cause which produces the union. Solomon was the wisest of men, but "even he was led into sin by foreign women" (Nehemiah 13:26).

There is, unhappily, only too much necessity for impressing these truths upon people. It is a sad fact that few steps in life are generally taken with so much levity, self-will and forgetfulness of God as marriage. Few are the young couples who think of inviting Christ to their wedding! It is a sad fact that unhappy marriages are one great cause of the misery and sorrow of which there is so much in the world. People find out too late that they have made a mistake, and go in bitterness all their days. Happy are those who in the matter of marriage observe three rules. The *first* is to marry only in the Lord, and after prayer for God's approval and blessing. The *second* is not to expect too much from their partners, and to remember that marriage is, after all, the union of two sinners, and not of two angels. The *third* rule is to strive first and foremost for one another's sanctification. The more holy married people are, the happier they are. "Christ loved the church, and gave himself up for her, to make her *holy*" (Ephesians 5:25–26).

[There is an expression in this passage which claims special observation. The Pharisees told our Lord that "Moses permitted a man to write a certificate of divorce and send her away" (verse 4). The answer of our Lord is very remarkable. He says, "It was because your hearts were hard that Moses wrote you this law" (verse 5). And he then goes on to show that this permission to divorce was a proof that their forefathers had fallen below the original standard of marriage, and were dealt with as being in a weak and diseased state of soul. For he says, "But at the beginning of creation God 'made them male and female'" (verse 6).

The expression throws much light on some portions of the civil law of Moses. It shows us that it was an institution which in some of its requirements were specially adapted to the state of mind in which the Israelites were, on first leaving the land of Egypt. It was not intended in all its minute particulars to be a code of perpetual obligation. It was meant to lead on to something better and higher when the people were able to bear it. The possession of it was undoubtedly a great privilege, and one of which the Jews might justly glory. Yet in glorying they were to remember also that their law contained some grounds for humiliation. Its very permission to obtain divorce on light grounds was a standing witness of the hardness and cruelty of the people. It was thought better to tolerate such divorces than to have the nation filled with murder, adultery, cruelty and desertion. In short, the very law of which the Jew boasted was shown by our Lord to contain permissive statutes which were in reality written to his shame.

The expression throws light on the position of God's people in this world of sin. It shows us that there may be things *tolerated* and permitted by God, both in churches and states, not because they are the best things but because they are the things best suited to the church or state in which they are found. It is vain to expect perfection in any government, or in any church. If we have the essentials of justice in the one, and of truth in the other, we may be content. God tolerated many things in the government of Israel, until the time of reformation. Surely we may tolerate many things too. To spend our lives in searching after an imaginary state of perfection, either civil or ecclesiastical, is at best a waste of time. If God was pleased to allow some things in Israel "because their hearts were hard," we may well endure some things in churches and states which we do not entirely like. There is a balance of evil in every position in the world. There are imperfections everywhere. The state of perfection is yet to come.]

Young children brought to Christ; infant baptism *(10:13–16)*

The scene brought before us in these four verses is deeply interesting. We see young children brought to Christ "to have him touch them" (verse 13), and the disciples rebuking those who brought them. We are told that when Jesus saw this he was "indignant" (verse 14), and rebuked his disciples in words of a very remarkable tenor. And finally we are told that "he took the children in his arms, put his hands on them and blessed them" (verse 16).

1. The attention children should receive from the church
First, we learn from this passage how much attention the souls of children should receive from the church of Christ. The great head of the church found time to take special notice of children. Although his time on earth was precious, and grown men and women were perishing on every side for lack of knowledge, he did not think little boys and girls of small importance. He had room in his mighty heart even for them. He declared his goodwill for them by his outward gesture and deed. And not least, he has left on record words concerning them which his church should never forget: "the kingdom of God belongs to such as these" (verse 14).

We must never allow ourselves to suppose that little children's souls may be safely let alone. Their characters for life depend exceedingly on what they see and hear during their first seven years. They are never too young to learn evil and sin. They are never too young to receive religious impressions. They think in their childish way about God, and their souls, and a world to come, far sooner and far more deeply than most people are aware. They are far more ready to respond to appeals to their feeling of right and wrong than many suppose. They each have a conscience. God has mercifully not left himself without a witness in their hearts, fallen and corrupt as their natures are. They each have a soul which will live forever in heaven or hell. We cannot begin too soon to endeavor to bring them to Christ.

These truths ought to be diligently considered by every branch of the church of Christ. It is the bounden duty of every Christian congregation to make provision for the spiritual training of its chidren. The boys and girls of every family should be taught as soon as they can learn – should be brought to public worship as soon as they can behave with propriety – should be regarded with affectionate interest as the future congregation, which will fill our places when we are dead. We may incidentally expect Christ's blessing on all attempts to do good to children. No church can be regarded as being in a healthy state which neglects its younger members, and lazily excuses itself on the plea that "young people will be young" and that it is useless to try to do them good. Such a church shows plainly that it does not have the mind of Christ. A congregation which consists of none but grown-up people, whose children are idling at home or running wild in the streets or fields, is a most deplorable and unsatisfactory sight. The members of such a congregation may pride themselves on their numbers, and on the soundness of their own views. They may content themselves with loud assertions that they cannot change their children's hearts, and that God will convert them someday if he thinks fit. But they have yet to learn that Christ regards them as neglecting a solemn duty, and that Christians who do not use every means to bring children to Christ are committing a great sin.

2. Encouragement to bring young children to baptism

Second, let us learn from this passage how much encouragement there is to bring young children to be baptized. Of course it is not claimed that there is any mention of baptism, or even any reference to it, in the verses before us. All we mean to say is that the expressions and gestures of our Lord in this passage are a strong indirect argument in favor of infant baptism. It is on this account that the passage occupies a prominent place in the baptismal service of the Church of England.

The subject of infant baptism is undoubtedly a delicate and difficult one. Holy and praying people are unable to see alike on it. Although they read the same Bible, and claim to be led by the same Spirit, they arrive at different conclusions about this sacrament. The great majority of Christians hold that infant baptism is scriptural and right. A comparatively small section of the Protestant church, but one containing many eminent saints among its members, regards infant baptism as unscriptural and wrong. The difference is a sad proof of the blindness and weakness which remain even in the saints of God.

But the difference now referred to must not make members of the Church of England shrink from holding decided opinions on the subject. That church has declared plainly in its Articles that "the baptism of young children is in any wise to be retained, as most agreeable with the institution of Christ." To this opinion we need not be afraid to adhere.

It is agreed on all sides that infants may be elect and chosen by God for salvation – may be washed in Christ's blood, born again of the Spirit, have grace, be justified, sanctified and enter heaven. If these things are so, it is hard to see why they may not receive the outward sign of baptism.

It is agreed furthermore than infants are members of Christ's visible church by virtue of their parents' Christianity. What else can we make of St. Paul's words, "as it is, they are holy" (1 Corinthians 7:14)? If this is so, it is difficult to understand why an infant may not receive the outward sign of admission into the church, just as the Jewish child received the outward sign of circumcision.

The objection that baptism ought only to be given to those who are old enough to repent and believe does not appear a convincing one. We read in the New Testament that the "families" of Lydia and Stephanas were baptized (Acts 16:15 and 1 Corinthians 1:16), and that the jailer of Philippi and "all his family" were baptized (Acts 16:33). It is very difficult to suppose that in no one of these three cases were there any children.

The objection that our Lord Jesus Christ himself never directly commanded infants to be baptized is not a weighty one. The church of the Jews, to which he came, had always been accustomed to admit children into the church by the sign of circumcision. The very fact that Jesus says nothing about the age for baptizing goes far to prove that he intended no change to be made.

[In considering the arguments in favor of infant baptism, there are two facts which ought to be duly pondered. They are extra-scriptural facts, and I have therefore purposely omitted them from the thoughts above, but they are weighty facts and may help some minds in coming to a conclusion.

1. One fact is the testimony of history to the almost universal practice of infant baptism in the early church. The proof of this is to be found in Wall's *History of Infant Baptism*. If infant baptism is so entirely opposed to the mind of Christ, as some say that it is, it is at least a curious circumstance that the early church should have been so ignorant on the subject.

2. The other fact is the well-known practice of baptizing the infant children of proselytes in the Jewish church. The proof of this is to be found in Lightfoot's *Horae Hebraicae* on St. Matthew 3:6. He says, for instance (*Works*, Pitman ed., Vol. xi, p. 59):

The Anabaptists object, "It is not commanded to baptize infants, therefore they are not to be baptized." To whom I answer, "It is not forbidden to baptize infants, therefore they are to be baptized." And the reason is plain. For when paedobaptism in the Jewish church was so known, usual and frequent in the admission of proselytes, there was no need to strengthen it with any precept, when baptism passed into an evangelical sacrament. For Christ took baptism into his own hands, and into evangelical use as he found it; this only added that he might promote it to a worthier end, and larger use. The whole nation knew well enough that little children used to be baptized: there was no need of a precept for that which had ever, by common use, prevailed.

On the other hand, there was need of a plain and open prohibition, that infants and little children should not be baptized, if our Saviour would not have had them baptized. For since it was most common, in all ages foregoing, that little children should be baptized, if Christ had minded to abolish the custom he would have openly forbidden it. Therefore his silence and the silence of Scripture confirms paedobaptism, and continues it unto all ages.]

The subject may be safely left here. Few controversies have done so much harm, and led to so little spiritual fruit as the controversy about baptism. On none has so much been said and written without producing conviction. On none does experience seem to show that Christians had better leave each other alone and agree to differ.

The baptism that it concerns us all to know is not so much the baptism of water as the baptism of the Holy Spirit. Thousands are washed in baptismal waters who are never renewed by the Spirit. Have we been born again? Have we received the Holy Spirit, and been made new creatures in Christ? If not, it matters little when, where and how we have been baptized; we are still in our sins. Without a new birth there can be no salvation. May we never rest till we know and feel that we have passed from death to life, and are indeed born of God!

The rich young man; Christ's love to sinners; the peril of being rich *(10:17–27)*

This story is recorded no less than three times in the New Testament. Matthew, Mark and Luke were all inspired by one Spirit to write it for our learning. There is no doubt a wise purpose in this threefold repetition of the same simple facts. It is intended to show us that the lessons of the passage deserve particular notice from the church of Christ.

1. Human self-ignorance
First, let us learn from this passage the self-ignorance of mankind.

We are told of someone who "ran up to" our Lord and fell on his knees before him and asked the solemn question, "what must I do to inherit eternal life?" (verse 17). At first sight there was much that was promising in this man's case. He showed anxiety about spiritual things, while most around him were careless and indifferent. He showed a disposition to reverence our Lord, by kneeling to him, while teachers of the law and Pharisees despised him. Yet all this time this man was profoundly ignorant of his own heart. He hears our Lord recite those commandments which make up our duty to our neighbor, and at once declares, "all these I have kept since I was a boy" (verse 20). The searching nature of the moral law, its application to our thoughts and words as well as actions, are matters with which he is utterly unacquainted.

The spiritual blindness here exhibited is unhappily very common.

Myriads of people who claim to be Christians today have not an idea of their own sinfulness and guilt in the sight of God. They flatter themselves that they have never done anything very wicked. They have never murdered, or stolen, or committed adultery, or given false testimony. They cannot surely be in much danger of missing heaven, they believe. But they forget the holy nature of the God they are dealing with. They forget how often they break his law in temper, or imagination, even when their outward conduct is correct. They never study such parts of Scripture as Matthew 5, or at any rate they study it with a thick veil over their hearts and do not apply it to themselves. The result is that they are wrapped up in self-righteousness. Like the church of Laodicea, they are rich and have acquired wealth and do not need anything (Revelation 3:17). Self-satisfied they live, and self-satisfied too often they die.

Let us beware of this state of mind. So long as we think that we can keep the law of God, Christ does us no good. Let us pray for self-knowledge. Let us ask the Holy Spirit to convince us of sin, to show us our own hearts, to show us God's holiness, and so to show us our need of Christ. Happy is the person who has learned by experience the meaning of St. Paul's words, "Once I was alive apart from the law; but when the commandment came, sin sprang to life and I died" (Romans 7:9). Ignorance of the law and ignorance of the Gospel will generally be found together. If our eyes have really been opened to the spirituality of the commandments, we will never rest till we have found Christ.

2. Christ's love towards sinners

Second, let us learn from this passage the love of Christ towards sinners.

This is a truth which is brought out in the expression used by St. Mark, when in his account of this man's story he says that "Jesus looked at him and loved him" (verse 21). That love, beyond doubt, was a love of pity and compassion. Our Lord looked with pity on the strange mixture of earnestness and ignorance which the case before him presented. He saw with compassion a soul struggling with all the weakness and infirmity entailed by the fall – the conscience ill at ease, and aware that it wanted relief – the understanding sunk in darkness and blinded as to the first principles of spiritual religion. Just as we look with sorrow at some noble ruin, roofless and shattered, and unfit for man's use, yet showing many a mark of the skill with which it was designed and reared at first, so may we suppose that Jesus looked with tender concern at this man's soul.

We must never forget that Jesus feels love and compassion for the souls of the ungodly. Without controversy he feels a particular love for those who hear his voice and follow him. They are his sheep, given to him by the Father, and watched with a special care. They are his bride, joined to him in an everlasting covenant, and dear to him as part of himself. But the heart of Jesus is a wide heart. He has abundance of pity, compassion and tender concern even for those who are following sin and the world. He who wept over unbelieving Jerusalem is still the same. He would still gather into his bosom the ignorant and self-righteous, the faithless and impenitent, if they were only willing to be gathered (Matthew 23:37). We may boldly tell the chief of sinners that Christ loves them. Salvation is ready for the worst of people, if they will only come to Christ. If they are lost, it is not because Jesus does not love them, and is not ready to save. His own solemn words unravel the mystery: "men loved darkness instead of light" (John 3:19); "you refuse to come to me that you might have life" (John 5:40).

3. The danger of the love of money

Third, let us learn from this passage the immense danger of the love of money. This is a lesson which is twice enforced on our notice. Once it comes out in the conduct of the man whose story is related here. With all his professed desire for eternal life, he loved his money better than his soul. "He went away sad" (verse 22). Once it comes out in the solemn words of our Lord to his disciples, "How hard it is for those who trust in riches to enter the kingdom of God" (verse 24, NIV footnote, ed. note). "It is easier for a camel to go through the eye of a needle than for a rich man to enter the kingdom of God" (verse 25). The last day alone will fully prove how true those words are.

Let us watch against the love of money. It is a snare to the poor as well as to the rich. It is not so much the having money as the trusting in it which ruins the soul. Let us pray for contentment with such things as we have. The highest wisdom is to be of one mind with St. Paul: "I have learned to be content whatever the circumstances" (Philippians 4:11).

Leaving all for Christ; Christ's foreknowledge of his sufferings (10:28–34)

1. A glorious promise

The first thing which demands our attention in these verses is the glorious promise which they contain. The Lord Jesus says to his apostles, "I tell you the truth, no one who has left home or brothers or sisters or mother or father or children or fields for me and the gospel will fail to receive a hundred times as much in this present age (homes, brothers, sisters, mothers, children and fields – and with them, persecutions) and in the age to come, eternal life" (verses 29–30).

There are few wider promises than this in the Word of God. There is none certainly in the New Testament which holds out such encouragement for the life that now is. Let everyone who is fearful and faint-hearted in Christ's service look at this promise. Let all who are enduring hardness and tribulation for Christ's sake study this promise well and drink out of it comfort.

To all who make sacrifices on account of the Gospel, Jesus promises "a hundred times as much in this present age." They will have not only pardon and glory in the world to come. They will have even here on earth hopes and joys and tangible comforts sufficient to make up for all that they lose. They will find in the communion of saints new friends, new relations, new companions, more loving, faithful and valuable than any they had before their conversion. Their introduction into the family of God will be an abundant recompense for exclusion from the society of this world. This may sound startling and incredible to many ears. But thousands have found by experience that it is true.

To all who make sacrifices on account of the Gospel, Jesus promises "eternal life in the age to come." As soon as they put aside their earthly tent, they will enter a glorious existence, and in the morning of the resurrection will receive such honor and joy as pass man's understanding. Their light affliction for a few years will end in an everlasting reward. Their fights and sorrows while in the body will be exchanged for perfect rest and a conqueror's crown. They will dwell in a world where there is no death, no sin, no devil, no cares, no weeping, no parting, for the former things will have passed away. God has said it, and it will all be found true.

Where is the saint who will dare to say in the face of these glorious promises that there is no encouragement to serve Christ? Where is the man or woman whose hands are beginning to hang down, and whose knees are beginning to faint in the Christian race? Let all such people ponder this passage and take fresh courage. The time is short. The end is sure. Heaviness may remain for a night, but rejoicing comes in the morning. Let us wait patiently on the Lord.

2. A solemn warning

The second thing which demands our attention in these verses is the solemn warning which they contain. The Lord Jesus saw the secret self-conceit of his apostles. He gives them a word in season to check their high thoughts. "Many who are first will be last, and the last first" (verse 31).

How true were these words when applied to the twelve apostles! There stood among those who heard our Lord speak, a man who at one time seemed likely to be one of the foremost of the twelve. He was one who appeared more careful and trustworthy than any. He had the charge of the bag, and kept what was put in it. And yet that man fell away and came to a disgraceful end. His name was Judas Iscariot. Again, there did not stand among our Lord's hearers that day one who at a later period did more for Christ than any of the twelve. At the time when our Lord spoke he was a young Pharisee, brought up at the feet of Gamaliel and zealous for nothing so much as the law. And yet that young man in the end was converted to the faith of Christ, was not behind the chiefest apostles, and labored more abundantly than all. His name was Saul. Well might our Lord say, "the first will be last, and the last first."

How true were these words, when we apply them to the history of Christian churches! There was a time when Asia Minor, Greece and North Africa were full of practicing Christians, while England and America were heathen lands. Sixteen hundred years have made a mighty change. The churches of Africa and Asia have fallen into complete decay. The English and American churches are laboring to spread the Gospel over the world. Well might our Lord say, "the first shall be last, and the last first."

How true these words appear to believers, when they look back over their own lives and remember all they have seen from the time of their own conversion! How many began to serve Christ at the same time with themselves, and seemed to run well for a while. But where are they now? The world has got hold of one. False doctrine has beguiled another. A mistake in marriage has spoiled a third. Few indeed are the believers who cannot call to mind many such cases. Few have failed to discover by sorrowful experience that "the last are often first, and the first last."

Let us learn to pray for humility, when we read texts like this. It is not enough to begin well. We must persevere, and go on and continue in well-doing. We must not be content with the fair blossoms of a few religious convictions, joys, sorrows, hopes and fears. We must bear the good fruit of settled habits of repentance, faith and holiness. Happy the one who counts the cost, and resolves, having once begun to walk in the narrow way, by God's grace never to turn aside.

3. Christ's foreknowledge of his sufferings and death

The last thing that demands our attention in this passage is our Lord's clear foreknowledge of his own sufferings and death. Calmly and deliberately he tells his disciples of his coming passion at Jerusalem. One after another he describes all the leading details of his death. Nothing is kept back.

Let us note this well. There was nothing involuntary and unforeseen in our Lord's death. It was the result of his own free decision and deliberate choice. From the beginining of his earthly ministry he saw the cross before him, and went to it a willing sufferer. He knew that his death was the necessary payment that must be made to reconcile God and man. That payment he had covenanted and engaged to make at the price of his own blood. And so, when the appointed time came, like a faithful surety, he kept his word and died for our sins on Calvary.

Let us always bless God that the Gospel sets before us such a Saviour, so faithful to the terms of the covenant – so ready to suffer – so willing to be reckoned sin and a curse in our place. Let us not doubt that he who fulfilled his engagement to suffer will also fulfill his engagement to save all who come to him. Let us not only accept him gladly as our Redeemer and Advocate, but gladly give ourselves, and all we have, to his service. Surely if Jesus cheerfully died for us, it is a small thing to require Christians to live for him.

The ignorance of Zebedee's sons; Christ's example of humble devotion *(10:35–45)*

1. The ignorance of our Lord's disciples

First, let us note from this passage the ignorance of our Lord's disciples. We find James and John petitioning for the first places in the kingdom of glory. We find them confidently declaring their ability to drink of their Master's cup, and be baptized with their Master's baptism. In spite of all the plain warnings of our Lord, they clung obstinately to the belief that Christ's kingdom on earth was immediately going to appear. Despite their many shortcomings in Christ's service, they had no misgivings as to their power to endure anything which might come upon them. For all their faith, grace and love to Jesus, they neither knew their own hearts, nor the nature of the path before them. They still dreamed of temporal crowns and earthly rewards. They still did not know what sort of men they were.

There are few true Christians who do not resemble James and John when they first begin the service of Christ. We are apt to expect far more present enjoyment from our religion than the Gospel warrants us to expect. We are apt to forget the cross and the tribulation, and to think only of the crown. We form an incorrect estimate of our own patience and power of endurance. We misjudge our own ability to stand temptation and trial. And the result of all is that we often buy wisdom dearly, by bitter experience, after many disappointments and not a few falls.

Let the case before us teach us the importance of a solid and calm judgment in our religion. Like James and John, we are right to covet the best gifts, and tell all our desires to Christ. Like them we are right in believing that Jesus is King of kings and will one day reign on earth. But let us not, like them, forget that there is a cross to be borne by every Christian, and that "we must go through many hardships to enter the kingdom of God" (Acts 14:22). Let us not, like them, be over-confident in our own strength, and forward in professing that we can do anything that Christ requires. Let us, in short, beware of a boastful spirit when we first begin to run the Christian course. If we remember this, it may save us many a humbling fall.

2. Christ's praise of lowliness and devotion to others

Second, let us note from this passage what praise our Lord bestows on lowliness and devotion to the good of others. It seems that the ten were much displeased with James and John because of the request they made to their Master. Their ambition and love of preeminence were once more excited at the idea of anyone being placed above themselves. Our Lord saw their feelings, and like a wise physician proceeded at once to supply a corrective medicine. He tells them that their ideas of greatness were built on a mistaken foundation. He repeats with renewed emphasis the lesson already laid down in the preceding chapter, "whoever wants to become great among you must be your servant" (verse 9:43). And he backs everything up by the overwhelming argument of his own example: "Even the Son of Man did not come to be served, but to serve" (verse 45).

[The remarks of Quesnel on this passage are worth reading. He says:

The ambition of clergymen is a great scandal in the church, and frequently causes rivalries, enmities, divisions, schisms and wars. The displeasure of the apostles gives us an imperfect shadow of all this. If apostles, trained up in the school of humility and love, are not free from this vice, what will ambition not do in souls wholly immersed in flesh and blood, having no motive other than what comes from their passions, no law other than their own desires?

Those who are appointed solely for heaven's work strangely forget themselves when they vie with the great ones of the earth in haughtiness and grandeur. It is very difficult to be both a spiritual pastor and a temporal prince; and to combine humility with grandeur, meekness with dominion, and the constant care of a pastor with the care of secular affairs.

The greatest prelate in the church is the one who is most like Christ in humility, love and continual attendance on his flock, and who looks on himself as a servant of the children of God.]

Let all who desire to please Christ watch and pray against self-esteem. It is a feeling which is deeply rooted in our hearts. Thousands have come out from the world, taken up the cross, professed to desert their own righteousness and believe in Christ, who have felt irritated and annoyed when a brother has been more honored than themselves. These things ought not to be so. We ought often to ponder the words of St. Paul, "Do nothing out of selfish ambition or vain conceit, but in humility consider others better than yourselves" (Philippians 2:3). We are blessed if we can sincerely rejoice when others are exalted, though we ourselves are overlooked and passed by!

Above all, let those who desire to walk in Christ's steps labor to be useful to others. Let them lay themselves out to do good in their day and generation. There is always a vast field for doing it, if people have the will and inclination. Let them never forget that true greatness does not consist in being an admiral or a general, a statesman or an artist. It consists in devoting ourselves body, soul and spirit to the blessed work of making other people more holy and more happy. It is those who exert themselves by the use of scriptural means to lessen the sorrow and increase the joy of all around them – the Howards, the Wilberforces, the Martyns, the Judsons of a country – who are truly great in the sight of God. While they live they are laughed at, mocked, ridiculed and often persecuted. But their memorial is on high. Their names are written in heaven. Their praise endures forever. Let us remember these things, and while we have time do good to everyone, and be servants of all for Christ's sake. Let us strive to leave the world better, holier, happier than it was when we were born. A life spent in this way is truly Christlike, and brings its own reward.

3. The language Christ uses of his death

Third, let us notice in this passage the language which our Lord uses in speaking of his own death. He says that the Son of Man came "to give his life as a ransom for many" (verse 45).

This is one of those expressions which ought to be carefully treasured up in the minds of all true Christians. It is one of the texts which prove incontrovertibly the atoning character of Christ's death. That death was no common death, like the death of a martyr, or of other holy men. It was the public payment by an almighty representative of the debts of sinful people to a holy God. It was the ransom which a divine surety undertook to provide in order to procure liberty for sinners, tied and bound by the chain of their sins. By that death Jesus made a full and complete satisfaction for our countless transgressions. He bore our sins in his own body on the tree. The Lord laid on him the iniquity of us all. When he died, he died for us. When he suffered, he suffered in our place. When he hung on the cross, he hung there as our substitute. When his blood flowed, it was the price of our souls.

Let all who trust in Christ take comfort in the thought that they build on a sure foundation. It is true that we are sinners, but Christ has borne our sins. It is true that we are poor helpless debtors, but Christ has paid our debts. It is true that we deserve to be shut up forever in the prison of hell. But, thanks be to God, Christ has paid a full and complete ransom for us. The door is wide open. The prisoners may go free. May we all know this privilege by heartfelt experience, and walk in the blessed liberty of the children of God.

[The way in which our Lord uses the word baptism in the passage now expounded deserves careful notice. He says to two disciples who were already baptized with water, "Can you . . . be baptized with the baptism I am baptized with?" (verse 38). The expression is very remarkable. It is a clear proof that in the New Testament a sacramental dipping or sprinkling with water is not always necessarily implied by the word baptism. It establishes the fact that there is such a thing as being baptized, in a certain sense, without the use of any outward ordinance at all.

This is a point that ought to be remembered in interpreting some of the passages in the epistles where the words "baptism" and "baptized" are used. In such texts, for instance, as "baptism that now saves you" (1 Peter 3:21) or "all of you who were baptized into Christ have put on Christ" (Galatians 3:27) it is clear that something more is contained than any mere outward ordinance. In both cases, the baptism of water is undoubtedly meant, but it is no less evident that something is implied also of deeper moment than any ordinance humanly administered. It both cases it is a baptism which is accompanied by true faith, and a heart-reception of Christ, such as was the baptism of the Philippian jailer. To quote such texts in support of what is commonly called the baptismal regeneration of infants is to wrest and pervert them from their proper meaning. The conclusion of the text in St. Peter, for example, seems to place this beyond question. He emphatically warns us not to suppose that he means nothing more than the washing of water, or bodily reception of a sacrament, by the word baptism.

It has been a wise act on the part of translators of the New Testament to adhere to the Greek words "baptize" and "baptism" in rendering the Bible into the vernacular tongue of each nation. No other words could possibly imply all that the two Greek words convey. All other expressions would either weaken the sense of the inspired writers, or convey a false impression to the mind of the reader. To take one solitary instance, what could be more meager or unsatisfactory than to render the passage now before us in the following way: "Can you be sprinkled with the sprinkling, or dipped with the dipping, that I am sprinkled or dipped with?" The firmness of the British and Foreign Bible Society on this point ought to be a cause of thankfulness to all the Protestant churches. In resolving to use the Greek words "baptize" and "baptism," in all their versions, they have exercised a wise discretion.]

Blind Bartimaeus healed *(10:46–52)*

We read in these verses an account of one of our Lord's miracles. Let us see in it, as we read, a vivid picture of spiritual things. It is not as though we were studying a story which concerns us personally no more than the exploits of Caesar or Alexander; we have before us a picture which ought to be deeply interesting to the soul of every Christian.

1. An example of strong faith
First, we have here an example of strong faith. We are told that as Jesus went out of Jericho, a blind man named Bartimaeus "was sitting by the roadside begging. When he heard that it was Jesus of Nazareth, he began to shout, 'Jesus, Son of David, have mercy on me!'" (verses 46–47).

Bartimaeus was blind in body, but not in soul. The eyes of his understanding were open. He saw things which Annas and Caiaphas, and hosts of formally educated teachers of the law and Pharisees, never saw at all. He saw that Jesus of Nazareth, as our Lord was contemptuously called – Jesus who had lived for thirty years in an obscure Galilean village – this very Jesus was the Son of David, the Messiah of whom prophets had prohesied long ago. He had witnessed none of our Lord's mighty miracles. He had not had the opportunity of seeing dead people raised with a word, and lepers healed by a touch. Of all these privileges his blindness totally deprived him. But he had heard the report of our Lord's mighty works and, hearing, had believed. He was satisfied from mere hearsay, that he of whom such wonderful things were reported must be the promised Saviour and must be able to heal him. And so when our Lord drew near, he cried, "Jesus, Son of David, have mercy on me!"

Let us strive and pray that we may have the same precious faith. We too are not allowed to see Jesus with our bodily eyes. But we have the report of his power, and grace, and willingness to save, in the Gospel. We have exceeding great promises from his own lips, written down for our encouragement. Let us trust those promises implicitly, and commit our souls to Christ unhesitatingly. Let us not be afraid to repose all our confidence in his own gracious words, and to believe that what he has undertaken to do for sinners, he will surely perform. What is the beginning of all saving faith but a soul's venture on Christ? What is the life of saving faith when once begun, but a continual leaning on an unseen Saviour's word? What is the first step of a Christian but a crying, like Bartimaeus, "Jesus have mercy on me"? What is the daily course of a Christian but keeping up the same spirit of faith? "Even though you do not see him now, you believe in him and are filled with an inexpressible and glorious joy" (1 Peter 1:8).

2. An example of determined perseverance

Second, we have in these verses an example of determined perseverance in the face of difficulties. We are told that when Bartimaeus began to cry out, "Jesus, Son of David, have mercy on me," he met with little encouragement from those who were near him. On the contrary, "many rebuked him and told him to be quiet" (verse 48). But he was not to be stopped. If others did not know the misery of blindness, he did. If others did not think it worthwhile to take such trouble in order to obtain relief, he at any rate knew better. He did not care about the rebukes of unfeeling bystanders. He did not mind the ridicule which his persistence probably brought on him. "He shouted all the more," and his shouting obtained his heart's desire, and he received his sight.

Let all who wish to be saved take good note of this conduct of

Bartimaeus, and walk diligently in his steps. Like him, we must not care what others think and say of us when we seek the healing of our souls. There will never be any lack of people telling us that it is "too soon" or "too late," that we are going "too fast" or "too far," that we need not pray so much or read our Bibles so much, or be so anxious about salvation. We must pay no attention to such people. Like Bartimaeus, we must cry all the more, "Jesus, have mercy on me."

What is the reason that people are so half-hearted in seeking Christ? Why are they so soon deterred, and checked, and discouraged in drawing near to God? The answer is short and simple. They do not feel their own sins sufficiently. They are not thoroughly convinced of the plague of their own hearts, and the disease of their own souls. Once let people see their own guilt as it really is, and they will never rest till they have found pardon and peace in Christ. It is those who, like Bartimaeus, really know their own deplorable state, who persevere like Bartimaeus and are finally healed.

3. An example of how gratitude to Christ should constrain us

Third, we have in these verses an example of the constraining influence which gratitude to Christ ought to have on our souls. Bartimaeus did not return home as soon as he was restored to sight. He would not leave the healer from whom he had received such mercy. At once he devoted the new powers which his cure gave him, to the Son of David who had worked the cure. His story concludes with the touching expression, he "followed Jesus along the road" (verse 52).

Let us see in these simple words a living picture of the effect that the grace of Christ ought to have on everyone who tastes it. It ought to make him a follower of Jesus in his life, and to draw him with mighty power into the way of holiness. Freely pardoned, he ought to give himself freely and willingly to Christ's service. Bought at so mighty a price as the blood of Christ, he ought to devote himself heartily and thoroughly to him who redeemed him. Grace really experienced will make us feel daily, "What shall I give to the Lord for all his benefits?" It did so for the apostle Paul: he says, "Christ's love compels us" (2 Corinthians 5:14). It will do so for all true Christians at the present day. The person who boasts of having an interest in Christ, while not following Christ in his life, is a miserable self-deceiver and is ruining his own soul. "Those who are led by the Spirit of God are sons of God" (Romans 8:14).

Have we had our eyes opened by the Spirit of God? Have we yet been taught to see sin, Christ, holiness and heaven in their true light? Can we say, "One thing I do know. I was blind but now I see!" (John 9:25)? If so, we shall know in our own experience the things we have been reading about. If not, we are still on the broad road that leads to destruction, and have everything to learn.

Mark
Chapter 11

Christ's entry into Jerusalem, and his poverty *(11:1–11)*

The event described in these verses is exceptional in the history of our Lord's earthly ministry. Generally speaking, we see Jesus withdrawing himself from public notice – often passing his time in the remote parts of Galilee – not infrequently remaining in the desert – and so fulfilling the prophecy that he would "not shout or cry out, or raise his voice in the streets" (Isaiah 42:2). Here, and here only, our Lord appears to drop his private character and of his own choice to call public attention to himself. He deliberately makes a public entry into Jerusalem, at the head of his disciples. He voluntarily rides into the holy city, surrounded by a vast multitude crying "Hosanna," like King David returning to his palace in triumph. All this too was done at a time when myriads of Jews had gathered in Jerusalem from every land to keep the Passover. We may well believe that the holy city rang with the news of our Lord's arrival. It is probable that there was not a house in Jerusalem in which the entry of the prophet of Nazareth was not known and talked of that night.

These things should always be remembered in reading this portion of our Lord's history. It is not for nothing that this entry into Jerusalem is four times related in the New Testament. It is evident that it is a scene in the earthly life of Jesus which Christians are intended to study with special attention. Let us study it in that spirit, and see what practical lessons we may learn from the passage for our own souls.

1. A public act
First, let us observe how public an act our Lord purposely made the last

act of his life. He came to Jerusalem to die, and he desired that all Jerusalem should know it. When he taught the deep things of the Spirit, he often spoke to no one but his apostles. When he delivered his parables, he often addressed no one but a crowd of poor and ignorant Galileans. When he worked his miracles, he was generally at Capernaum, or in the land of Zebulun and Naphtali. But when the time came for him to die, he made a public entry into Jerusalem. He drew the attention of rulers, priests, elders, teachers of the law, Greeks and Romans to himself. He knew that the most wonderful event that ever happened in this world was about to take place. The eternal Son of God was about to suffer in the place of sinful mankind. The great sacrifice for sin was about to be offered up. The great Passover Lamb was about to be slain. The great atonement for a world's sin was about to be made. He therefore ordered it so that his death was eminently a public death. He overruled things in such a way that the eyes of all Jerusalem were fixed on him, and when he died, he died in front of many witnesses.

Let us see here one more proof of the unspeakable importance of the death of Christ. Let us treasure up his gracious sayings. Let us strive to walk in the steps of his holy life. Let us prize his intercession. Let us long for his second coming. But never let us forget that the crowning fact in all we know of Jesus Christ is his death on the cross. From that death flow all our hopes. Without that death we would have nothing solid beneath our feet. May we prize that death more and more every year we live; and in all our thoughts about Christ, may we rejoice in nothing so much as the great fact that he died for us!

2. Voluntary poverty

Second, let us observe in this passage the voluntary poverty which our Lord underwent when he was on earth. How did he enter Jerusalem when he came to it on this remarkable occasion? Did he come in a royal chariot, with horses, soldiers and a retinue around him, like the kings of this world? We are told nothing of the kind. We read that he borrowed the colt of a donkey for the occasion, and sat on his disciples' clothing for lack of a saddle. This was in perfect keeping with all the tenor of his ministry. He never had any of the riches of this world. When he crossed the Sea of Galilee, it was in a borrowed boat. When he rode into the holy city, it was on a borrowed beast. When he was buried, it was in a borrowed tomb.

We have in this simple fact an instance of that marvelous union of weakness and power, riches and poverty, the Godhead and the humanity, which may be so often traced in the history of our blessed Lord.

[I use the word "weakness" in this passage advisedly. There is scriptural warrant for it in the text "He was crucified in weakness" (2 Corinthians 13:4). Nevertheless I wish it to be clearly understood that I utterly disclaim the idea of there being any *moral* weakness in the human nature of Christ. The only weakness I mean is that sinless infirmity which is inseparably connected with flesh and blood, and from which Adam, before the fall, was not exempt. I believe that our Lord shared all such weakness to the fullest extent.

Whether or not our Lord's riding on a donkey instead of a horse was a mark of humiliation is a point on which opinions differ widely. Some dwell on the fact that the donkey in oriental countries was an animal that even kings rode, and refer to Judges 5:10 ("You who ride on white donkeys . . ."). Others think that the choice of a donkey was purposely made as emblematic of our Lord's lowly nature. Gerhard in his commentary refers to a saying of Tertullian that the Gentiles called Christians "asinarii" in ridicule because they believed in Christ who rode on a donkey, and even accused them of worshiping a donkey's head!]

When we read the Gospels, how can we fail to observe that Jesus, who could feed thousands with a few loaves, was himself sometimes hungry – that he who could heal the sick and infirm was himself sometimes weary – that he who could drive out demons with a word was himself tempted – and that he who could raise the dead could himself submit to die? We see the very same thing in the passage before us. We see the power of our Lord in his bending the wills of a vast crowd to conduct him into Jerusalem in triumph. We see the poverty of our Lord in his borrowing a donkey to carry him when he made his triumphal entry. It is all wonderful, but there is a fitness in it all. It is meet and right that we should never forget the union of the divine and human natures in our Lord's person. If we saw his divine acts only, we might forget that he was human. If we saw his times of poverty and weakness only, we might forget that he was God. But we are intended to see in Jesus divine strength and human weakness united in one person. We cannot explain the mystery; but we may take comfort in the thought that this is our Saviour, our Christ – one able to sympathize because he is human, but almighty to save because he is God.

Finally, let us see in the simple fact that our Lord rode on a borrowed donkey one more proof that poverty is in itself no sin. The causes which occasion much of the poverty there is around us, are undoubtedly very sinful. Drunkenness, extravagance, profligacy, dishonesty, idleness, which produce so much of the destitution in the world, are unquestionably wrong in the sight of God. But to be born poor, and to inherit nothing from our parents – to work with our own hands for our bread, and to have no land of our own – all this is not sinful at all. The honest poor person is as honorable in the sight of God as the richest king. The Lord Jesus Christ himself was poor. Silver and gold he did not have. He often had nowhere to lay his head. Though he was rich, yet for our sakes he became poor. To be like him in circumstances cannot in itself be wrong. Let us do our duty in that state of life to which God has called us, and if he thinks fit to keep us poor let us not be ashamed. The Saviour of sinners cares for us as well as for others. The Saviour of sinners knows what it is to be poor.

Christ's humanity; the fig-tree cursed; the temple cleansed (11:12–21)

1. Christ's humanity

We see in the beginning of this passage one of the many proofs that our Lord Jesus Christ was really man. We read that "Jesus was hungry" (verse 12). He had a nature and bodily constitution like our own in everything, sin only excepted. He could weep, rejoice and suffer pain. He could be weary and need rest. He could be thirsty and need drink. He could be hungry and need food.

Expressions like this should teach us *the humility of Christ.* How wonderful they are when we reflect on them! He who is the eternal God – he who made the world and all that it contains – he from whose hand the fruits of the earth, the fish of the sea, the fowls of the air, the beasts of the field all had their beginning – he, even he chose to suffer hunger when he came into the world to save sinners. This is a great mystery. Kindness and love like this pass our understanding. No wonder St. Paul speaks of the "unsearchable riches of Christ" (Ephesians 3:8).

Expressions like this should teach us *Christ's power to sympathize* with his believing people on earth. He knows their sorrows by experience. He can sympathize with our weaknesses. He has had experience of a body and its daily needs. He has himself suffered the severe sufferings that the human body is liable to. He has tasted pain, weakness, weariness, hunger and thirst. When we tell him of these things in our prayers, he knows what we mean and is no stranger to our troubles. Surely this is just the Saviour and Friend that poor aching, groaning human nature requires!

2. The danger of unfruitfulness in religion

Second, we learn from these verses the great danger of unfruitfulness and formality in religion. This is a lesson which our Lord teaches in a remarkable typical action. We are told that, coming to a fig-tree in search of fruit and finding on it "nothing but leaves" (verse 13), he pronounced on it the solemn sentence, "May no one ever eat fruit from you again" (verse 14). And we are told that the next day the fig-tree was found "withered from the roots" (verse 20). We cannot doubt for a moment that this whole transaction was a picture of spiritual things. It was a parable in deeds, as full of meaning as any of our Lord's parables in words.

[There are two difficulties connected with the story of the withered fig-tree, which weigh considerably on some minds and therefore deserve notice.

1. It is a difficulty for some people that our Lord should have pronounced any curse at all on the fig-tree. They say that it looks like a needless destruction of an innocent and unoffending creature, and out of keeping with the spirit of Deuteronomy 20:19.

Such objectors appear to forget that the withering of the fig-tree was not a mere empty exhibition of power, like the miracles claimed for Muhammad and other false prophets. It was a powerful symbolic act, teaching deep spiritual lessons, lessons of such importance as might well justify the destruction of one of God's unintelligent creatures, in order to convey them. Remembering this, we have no more right to object to it than to object to the daily offering of a lamb under Mosaic law. In that offering the life of an innocent and unoffending creature was daily taken away. But taking the life of the lamb each day was justified by the great purpose of setting before human eyes the one sacrifice for sin. Just in the same way we may justify our Lord's taking the life of the tree.

2. It is a difficulty for some people that the account of St. Mark contains the words, "it was not the season for figs" (verse 13). They ask to be told why our Lord should have gone to the tree seeking fruit, when the fig season had not yet arrived.

The answers to this difficulty are various. The simplest of them appears to be as follows: the season for figs, as a general rule, had not yet come, but our Lord seeing a fig-tree covered with leaves, unlike other fig-trees, had a right to suppose that figs were to be found on it, and therefore came to it. In favor of this view it may be said that it supplies an exact illustration of the state of the Jewish church when our Lord was on earth. It was not the season for figs, that is, the nations of the earth were all in darkness, and bore no fruit to the glory of God. But among the nations there was one covered with leaves, that is the Jewish church, full of light, knowledge, privileges and high profession. Seeing this fig-tree full of leaves, our Lord came to it to find out if it had any fruit; that is, he came to the Jews justly expecting them to have fruit according to their outward profession. But when our Lord came to this leafy Jewish fig-tre, he found it utterly destitute of fruit, faithless and unbelieving. And the end was that he pronounced sentence on it, gave it over to be destroyed by the Romans, and scattered the Jews over the earth.]

But who were the people to whom this withered fig-tree was intended to speak? It was a sermon of three-fold application, a sermon that ought to speak loudly to the conscience of all who claim to be Christians. Though withered and dried up, the fig-tree still speaks.

There was a voice in it for *the Jewish church*. Rich in the leaves of a formal religion, but barren of all fruits of the Spirit, that church was in fearful danger at the very time when this withering took place. It would have been good for the Jewish church if it had had eyes to see its peril!

There was a voice in the fig-tree for *all the branches of Christ's visible church* in every age, and every part of the world. There was a warning against an empty profession of Christianity, unaccompanied by sound doctrine and holy living, which some of those branches would have done well to lay to heart.

But above all there was a voice in that withered fig-tree for *all worldly, hypocritical and false-hearted Christians*. It would be good if everyone who is content with a reputation for being alive, when in reality they are dead, would only see their own faces in the mirror of this passage.

Let us take care that we each individually learn the lesson that this fig-tree conveys. Let us always remember that baptism, church membership, receiving the Lord's Supper and a diligent use of the outward forms of Christianity are not sufficient to save our souls. They are leaves, nothing but leaves, and without fruit will not hide the nakedness of our souls from the eye of an all-seeing God, or give us boldness when we stand before him on the last day. No! We must bear fruit, or be lost forever. There must be fruit in our hearts and fruit in our lives, the fruit of repentance toward God and faith toward our Lord Jesus Christ, and true holiness in our behavior. Without such fruits as these a profession of Christianity will only sink us lower into hell.

3. Reverence for places of worship

Third, we learn from this passage how reverently we ought to use places which are set apart for public worship. This is a truth which is taught us in a striking manner by our Lord Jesus Christ's conduct when he went into the temple. We are told that he "began driving out those who were buying and selling there. He overturned the tables of the money changers and the benches of those selling doves" (verse 15). And we are told that he enforced this action by warrant of Scripture, saying, "Is it not written: 'My house will be called a house of prayer for all nations'? But you have made it 'a den of robbers'" (verse 17).

We need not doubt that there was a deep meaning in this action of our Lord on this occasion. Like the cursing of the fig-tree, the whole transaction was eminently typical. But in saying this, we must not allow ourselves to lose sight of one simple and obvious lesson which lies on the surface of the passage. That lesson is the sinfulness of careless and irreverent behavior in the use of buildings set apart for the public service of God. It was not so much as the house of sacrifice, but as

171

the "house of prayer," that our Lord purified the temple. His action clearly indicates the feeling with which every "house of prayer" should be regarded. A Christian place of worship no doubt is in no sense so sacred as the Jewish temple. It is not built after a divine model, and intended to serve as an example of heavenly things. But because these things are so, it does not follow that a Christian place of worship is to be used with no more reverence than a private dwelling, or a shop, or an inn. There is surely a decent reverence which is due to a place where Christ and his people regularly meet together and public prayer is offered up – a reverence which it is foolish and unwise to brand as superstitious, and confuse with Popery. There is a certain feeling of sanctity and solemnity which ought to belong to all places where Christ is preached, and souls are born again, a feeling which does not depend on any human consecration, and ought to be encouraged rather than checked. At all events the mind of the Lord Jesus in this passage seems very plain. He takes notice of people's behavior in places of worship, and all irreverence or profanity is an offense in his sight.

Let us remember these verses whenever we go to the house of God, and take care that we go in a serious frame, and do not offer the sacrifice of idols. Let us recall where we are, what we are doing, what business we are about and in whose presence we are engaged. Let us beware of giving God a mere formal service, while our hearts are full of the world. Let us leave our business and money at home, and not carry them with us to church. Let us beware of allowing any buying and selling in our hearts, in the midst of our religious assemblies. The Lord who drove out buyers and sellers from the temple is still alive, and when he sees such conduct he is very displeased.

The importance of faith; the need to forgive *(11:22–26)*

1. The importance of faith
First, let us learn from these words of our Lord Jesus Christ the immense importance of faith.

This is a lesson which our Lord teaches first by a proverbial saying. Faith will enable us to accomplish great works, and overcome difficulties as great and formidable as throwing a mountain into the sea.

[It is clear that a promise like this of removing mountains must be taken ion a figurative sense. It appears to be a proverbial expression, and to be used as such by St. Paul in 2 Corinthians 13:2. Moreover it is a promise that must be interpreted with sober and reasonable limitations. We have no right to expect that whatever we take it into our heads to ask of God will at once be done for us, whether it is for his glory and our sanctification or not. We have no warrant for presuming that in every difficulty and trouble God will at once work a miracle and deliver us from our anxety, as soon as we make it a subject of prayer. The things about which we must pray must be things having special reference to our own vocation and providential position. Moses at the head of the twelve tribes of Israel, Elijah on Mount Carmel and Paul in the Philippian prison might confidently expect miraculous intervention in answer to prayer, in a way that private individuals may not expect in our days. Above all, we must not think to tell God the time and way in which he must remove mountains for us.]

Afterwards the lesson is impressed on us still further by a general exhortation to exercise faith when we pray. "Whatever you ask for in prayer, believe that you have received it, and it will be yours" (verse 24). This promise must of course be taken with a reasonable qualification. It assumes that a believer will ask things which are not sinful, and which are in accordance with the will of God. When he asks such things, he may confidently believe that his prayer will be answered. To use the words of St. James, "when he asks, he must believe and not doubt" (James 1:6).

The faith here commended must be distinguished from that faith which is essential to justification. In principle undoubtedly all true faith is one and the same. It is always trust or belief. But in the object and operations of faith there are diversities, which it is useful to understand. Justifying faith is that act of the soul by which a person lays hold on Christ, and has peace with God. Its special object is the atonement for sin which Jesus made on the cross. The faith spoken of in the passage now before us is a more general grace, the fruit and companion of justifying faith, but still not to be confused with it. It is rather a general confidence in God's power, wisdom and goodwill towards believers. And its special objects are the promises, the Word and the character of God in Christ.

Confidence in God's power and will to help every believer in Christ, and in the truth of every word that God has spoken, is the grand secret of success and prosperity in our religion. In fact, it is the very root of saving Christianity. "This is what the ancients were commended for" (Hebrews 11:2). "Anyone who comes to him must believe that he exists and that he rewards those who earnestly seek him" (Hebrews 11:6). To know the full worth of it in the sight of God, we should often study Hebrews 11.

Do we desire to grow in grace, and in the knowledge of our Lord Jesus Christ? Do we wish to make progress in our religion, and become strong Christians, and not mere babes in spiritual things? Then let us pray daily for more faith, and watch our faith with most jealous watchfulness. Here is the cornerstone of our religion. A flaw or weakness here will affect the whole condition of our inner man. According to our faith will be the degree of our peace, our hope, our joy, our decision in Christ's service, our boldness in confession, our strength in work, our patience in trial, our resignation in trouble, our tangible comfort in prayer. All, all will hinge on the proportion of our faith. Happy are those who know how to rest their whole weight continually on a covenant God, and to walk by faith, not by sight. "The one who trusts will never be dismayed" (Isaiah 28:16).

2. The necessity of forgiving others

Second, let us learn from these verses the absolute necessity of a forgiving spirit towards others. This lesson is here taught us in a striking way. There is no immediate connection between the importance of faith, of which our Lord had just been speaking, and the subject of forgiving injuries. But the connecting link is prayer. First we are told that faith is essential to the success of our prayers. But then it is added, no prayers can be heard which do not come from a forgiving heart. "When you stand praying, if you hold anything against anyone, forgive him, so that your Father in heaven may forgive you your sins" (verse 26).

The value of our prayers, we can all understand, depends exceedingly on the state of mind in which we offer them. But the point before us is one which receives far less attention than it deserves. Our prayers must not only be earnest, fervent and sincere, and in the name of Christ. They must come from a forgiving heart. We have no right to look for mercy if we are not ready to extend mercy to our brothers and sisters. We cannot really feel the sinfulness of the sins we ask to have pardoned if we cherish malice towards other people. We must have the heart of a brother or sister towards our neighbor on earth, if we wish God to be our Father in heaven. We must not flatter ourselves that we have the Spirit of adoption if we cannot bear and forbear.

This is a heart-searching subject. The quantity of malice, bitterness and party-spirit among Christians is fearfully great. No wonder so many prayers seem to be thrown away and unheard. It is a subject which ought to come home to all classes of Christians. All have not equal gifts of knowledge and speech in their approaches to God. But all can forgive other people. It is a subject which our Lord Jesus Christ has taken special pains to impress on our minds. He has given it a prominent place in that pattern of prayers, the Lord's prayer. We are all familiar from our infancy with the words, "Forgive us our trespasses, as we forgive those who trespass against us." It would be good for many people if they would consider what those words mean!

Let us leave the passage with serious self-examination. Do we know what it is to be of a forgiving spirit? Can we overlook the injuries that we receive from time to time in this evil world? Can we pass over a transgression and pardon an offense? If not, where is our Christianity? If not, why should we wonder that our souls do not prosper? Let us resolve to amend our ways in this matter. Let us determine by God's grace to forgive, even as we hope to be forgiven. This is the nearest approach we can make to the mind of Christ Jesus. This is the character which is most suitable to a poor sinful child of Adam. God's free forgiveness of sins is our highest privilege in this world. God's free forgiveness will be our only title to eternal life in the world to come. Then let us be forgiving during the few years that we are here upon earth.

[The expression "when you stand praying" (verse 25) ought not to be overlooked. It is one of those forms of speech in the Bible which ought to teach all Christians not to be dogmatic in laying down minute rules about the externals of religion, and especially about the precise manner, gesture, or posture in which a believer ought to pray. If you are fully persuaded that you can hold closer communion with God, and pour out your heart more freely and without distraction, while standing rather than kneeling, I dare not tell you that you are wrong.

The great spirit to insist on is the absolute necessity of praying with the heart. The last words of Sir Walter Raleigh to his executioner on the scaffold are a beautiful illustration of the right view of the question: "Friend, it matters little how a man's head lies, if his heart be right in the sight of God."]

The spiritual blindness of the chief priests and teachers of the law; mental dishonesty in prejudiced believers (11:27–33)

1. Spiritual blindness in high church officials
First, let us observe in these verses how much spiritual blindness may be in the hearts of those who hold high ecclesiastical office. We see "the chief priests, the teachers of the law and the elders" coming to Jesus, and raising difficulties and objections in the way of his work (verse 27).

These men, we know, were the accredited teachers and rulers of the Jewish church. They were regarded by the Jews as the fountain and spring-head of religious knowledge. They were, most of them, regularly ordained to the position they held, and could trace their orders by direct descent from Aaron. And yet we find these very men, at the time when they ought to have been instructors of others, full of prejudice against the truth, and bitter enemies of the Messiah!

[The following remarks from Gerhard's commentary are worth reading:

The church is not tied to those teachers who are in the regular succession, for they frequently err from the path of truth. In such cases the church ought not to follow their errors, but to embrace the truth as set forth in the word. Thus, Aaron setting up the golden calf – Uriah the high priest in the time of Ahaz, building a new altar – Pashur and the other priests in Jeremiah's time, all erred most grievously. And in this very passage, the priests sitting in Moses' seat reject the Messiah himself, and impugn his authority. But if those who succeeded Aaron in the divinely appointed priesthood of the Old Testament could err, and in fact did occasionally err, how much more likely to err are the Popes of Rome, who cannot prove from God's Word that the Pope's office has been instituted by Christ in the New Testament.]

These things are written to show Christians that they must beware of depending too much on ordained ministers. They must not look up to ministers as Popes, or regard them as infallible. The orders of no church confer infallibility, whether they be episcopal, presbyterian or independent. Bishops, priests and deacons at their best are only flesh and blood, and may err both in doctrine and practice, as well as the chief priests and elders of the Jews. Their acts and teaching must always be tested by the Word of God. They must be followed so far as they follow Scripture, and no further. There is only one Priest and Bishop of souls who makes no mistakes. That one is the Lord Jesus Christ. In him alone is no weakness, no failure, no shadow of infirmity. Let us learn to lean more entirely on him. Let us "not call anyone on earth 'Father'" (Matthew 23:9). So doing, we shall never be disappointed.

2. Envy and unbelief make people discredit God's ministers
Second, let us observe how envy and unbelief make men throw discredit on the commission of those who work for God. These chief priests and elders could not deny the reality of our Lord's miracles of mercy. They could not say that his teaching was sinful. What then did they do? They attacked his claim to attention, and demanded his authority: "'By what authority are you doing these things?' they asked. 'And who gave you this authority?'" (verse 28).
[Brentius has some sensible remarks on the unreasonableness of the chief priests and Pharisees, who would neither keep the temple from the encroachment of the buyers and sellers, nor let others do it for them. They would neither exercise the lawful authority which was in their hands, nor allow our Lord to exercise it for them. He shows the similarity of their conduct to that of the Greek and Roman churches, and to that of a foolish head of a family who neither corrects his children himself, nor likes anyone to correct them for him. And he concludes by saying, "Let us learn that everyone should do his own duty, or else yield up his place to another. Let us not be like the dog in the manger, who would neither eat the hay himself, nor yet allow the ox to eat it." The history of the church of Christ contains only too much of

the dog in the manger! Ministers and teachers have often neglected the souls of their people shamefully, and yet found fault with anyone who has tried to do good, and haughtily demanded his authority!

The reflections of the Roman Catholic writer, Quesnel, on this subject are remarkable:

> Those who find themselves vanquished by truth, generally endeavor to reject authority. There are no persons more forward to demand of others a reason for their actions, than those who think they may do everything themselves without control.]

There can be no doubt whatever that, as a general principle, all who undertake to teach others should be properly appointed to the work. The writer to the Hebrews declares that this was the case with our Lord, in the matter of the priestly office: "No one takes this honor upon himself; he must be called by God, just as Aaron was" (Hebrews 5:4). And even now, when the office of the sacrificing priest no longer exists, the words of the twenty-third Article of the Church of England are wise and scriptural: "It is not lawful for any man to take upon him the office of public preaching, or ministering the sacraments in the congregation, before he be lawfully called and sent to execute the same." But it is one thing to maintain the lawfulness of an outward call to minister in sacred things, and quite another to assert that it is the one thing needed, without which no work for God can be done. This is the point on which the Jews evidently erred in the time of our Lord's earthly ministry, and on which they have unhappily followed them down to the present day.

Let us beware of this narrow spirit, and specially in these last ages of the world. Unquestionably we must not undervalue order and discipline in the church. It is just as valuable there as it is in an army. But we must not suppose that God is absolutely tied to the use of ordained people. We must not forget that there may be an inward call of the Holy Spirit without any outward, human call – just as there may be an outward, human call without any inward call of the Holy Spirit. The first question, after all, is this: "Is this person for Christ, or against him? What does he teach? How does he live? Is he doing good?" If questions like these can be answered satisfactorily, let us thank God and be content. We must remember that a physician is useless, however high his degree and diploma, if he cannot cure diseases, and a soldier useless, however well dressed and drilled, if he will not face the enemy on the day of battle. The best doctor is the one who can cure, and the best soldier the one who can fight.

3. Prejudice against the truth

Third, let us observe what dishonesty and equivocation unbelievers may be led into by prejudice against the truth. The chief priests and elders dared not answer our Lord's question about John's baptism. They dared not say it was from men, because they feared the people. They dared not admit that it was from heaven, because they saw our Lord would say, "Why did you not believe him? He witnessed plainly about me." What then did they do? They told a direct lie. They said, "We don't know" (verse 33).

It is a melancholy fact that dishonesty like this is far from being uncommon among unconverted people. There are thousands who evade appeals to their conscience by answers which are not true. When pressed to attend to their souls, they say things which they know are not correct. They love the world and their own way, and like our Lord's enemies are determined not to give them up, but like them also are ashamed to say the truth. And so they answer exhortations to repentance and decision by false excuses. One pretends to be unable to understand the doctrines of the Gospel. Another assures us that they really "try" to serve God, but make no progress. A third claims to have every wish to serve Christ but "has no time." All these are often nothing better than miserable equivocations. As a general rule, they are worthless as the chief priests' answer, "We don't know."

The plain truth is that we ought to be very slow to give credit to the unconverted person's professed reasons for not serving Christ. We may be reasonably sure that when they say, "I cannot," the real meaning of their heart is "I will not." A really honest spirit in religious matters is a mighty blessing. Once someone is willing to live up to their light, and act up to their knowledge, they will soon know the doctrine of Christ, and come out from the world (John 7:17). The ruin of thousands is simply this, that they deal dishonestly with their own souls. They allege pretended difficulties as the cause of their not serving Christ, while in reality they "love darkness instead of light," and have no honest desire to change (John 3:19).

Mark
Chapter 12

The parable of the tenants *(12:1–12)*

These verses contain a historical parable. The history of the Jewish nation from the day that Israel left Egypt down to the time of the destruction of Jerusalem is here set before us as in a mirror. In the metaphor of the vineyard and the tenants, the Lord Jesus tells the story of God's dealings with his people for fifteen hundred years. Let us study it attentively, and apply it to ourselves.

1. God's special kindness to the Jews

First, let us observe God's special kindness to the Jewish church and nation. He gave them special privileges. He dealt with them as someone might deal with a piece of land which he separates and hedges in for "a vineyard" (verse 1). He gave them good laws and ordinances. He set them in a good land, and drove out seven nations before them. He passed over greater and more powerful nations to show them favor. He left Egypt alone, and Assyria, and Greece and Rome, and showered down mercies on a few million people in Palestine. The vienyard of the Lord was the house of Israel. No family under heaven ever received so many notable and distinguishing privileges as the family of Abraham.

And we too, can we say that we have received no special mercies from God? We cannot say so. Why are we not a heathen country, like China? Why are we not a land of idolaters, like India? We owe it all to the distinguishing favor of God. It is not for our goodness and worthiness, but of God's free grace, that our country is what it is among the nations of the earth. Let us be thankful for our mercies, and know the hand from which they come. Let us not be high-minded, but humble, lest we provoke God to take our mercies away. If Israel had special national privileges, so also have we. Let us mark this well, and take care, lest what happened to Israel should happen also to us.

2. God's patience towards the Jewish nation

Second, let us observe God's patience and long-suffering towards the Jewish nation. What is their whole history as recorded in the Old Testament, but a long record of repeated provocations and repated pardons? Over and over we read of prophets being sent to them, and warnings being delivered, but too often entirely in vain. One servant after another came to the vineyard of Israel and asked for fruit. One servant after another was "sent away empty-handed" by the Jewish farmers (verse 3), and no fruit borne by the nation to the glory of God. "They mocked God's messengers, despised his words and scoffed at his prophets" (2 Chronicles 36:16). Yet hundreds of years passed by before "the wrath of the LORD was aroused against his people and there was no remedy." Never was there a people so patiently dealt with as Israel.

And we too, have we no long-suffering of God to be thankful for? Beyond doubt, we have abundant cause to say that our Lord is patient. He does not deal with us according to our sins, or reward us according to our iniquities. We have often provoked him to take our light away, and to deal with us as he has dealt with Tyre, Babylon and Rome. Yet his long-suffering and loving-kindness still continue. Let us beware that we do not presume on his goodness too far. Let us hear in his mercies a loud call to us to bear fruit, and let us strive to abound in that righteousness which alone exalts a nation (Proverbs 14:34). Let every family in the land feel its responsibility to God, and then the whole nation will be seen showing his praise.

3. Human hardness seen in the history of the Jews

Third, let us observe the hardness and wickedness of human nature, as exemplified in the history of the Jewish people.

It is difficult to imagine a more striking proof of this truth than the summary of Israel's dealing with God's messengers, which our Lord sketches in this parable. Prophet after prophet was sent to them in vain. Miracle after miracle was worked among them, without any lasting effect. The Son of God himself, loved by God, at last came down to them, and was not believed. God himself was seen in the flesh, living among them, and "they took him and killed him" (verse 8).

There is no truth so little realized and believed as the desperate wickedness of the human heart. Let this parable always be reckoned among the standings proofs of it. Let us see in it what men and women can do in the full blaze of religious privlieges – in the midst of prophecies and miracles – in the presence of the Son of God himself. "The sinful mind is hostile to God" (Romans 8:7). Only once, when Jesus became a man and lived on earth, did people see God face to face. They saw him holy, harmless, undefiled, going about doing good. Yet they would not have him, rebelled against him and at last killed him. Let us dismiss from our minds the idea that there is any innate goodness or natural rectitude in our hearts. Let us put away the common idea that seeing and knowing what is good is enough to make someone a Christian. The great experiment has been made in the case of the Jewish nation. We too, like Israel, might have among us miracles, prophets and the company of Christ himself in the flesh, and yet, like Israel, have them in vain. Nothing but the Spirit of God can change the heart. We must be "born again" (John 3:7).

4. The pricked conscience may remain impenitent

Fourth, let us observe that people's consciences may be pricked, and yet they may continue impenitent. The Jews, to whom our Lord addressed the solemn historical parable which we have been reading, saw clearly that it applied to themselves. They felt that they and their ancestors were the farmers to whom the vineyard was rented, and who ought to have given fruit to God. They felt that they and their ancestors were the wicked laborers who had refused to give the owner of the vineyard his dues, and had shamefully treated his servants, beating some and killing some (verse 5). Above all, they felt that they themselves were planning the last crowning act of wickedness, which the parable described. They were about to kill the well-beloved Son, and throw him out of the vineyard (verse 8). All this they knew perfectly well. "They knew he had spoken the parable against them" (verse 12). Yet though they knew it, they would not repent. Though convicted by their own consciences, they were hardened in sin.

Let us learn from this awful fact that knowledge and conviction alone save no one's soul. It is quite possible to know that we are wrong, and be unable to deny it, and yet to cling to our sins obstinately, and perish miserably in hell. The thing that we all need is a change of heart and will. For this let us pray earnestly. Till we have this, let us never rest. Without this, we shall never be real Christians, and reach heaven. Without it we may live all our lives, like the Jews, knowing inwardly that we are wrong and yet, like the Jews, persevere in our own way, and die in our sins.

The tax, and the claims of Caesar and of God *(12:13–17)*

1. Different opinions united against Christ

First, let us observe in the beginning of this passage how people of different religious opinions can unite in opposing Christ. We read of "Pharisees and Herodians" coming together to catch our Lord in his words (verse 13), and perplex him with a hard question. The Pharisee was a superstitious person who cared for nothing but the outward forms and ceremonies of religion. The Herodian was a mere man of the world who despised all religion and cared more for pleasing other people than God. Yet when a mighty teacher came among them assailing the ruling passions of both alike, and sparing neither formalist nor worldling, we see them making common cause and uniting in a common effort to stop his teaching.

It has always been like this from the beginning of the world. We may see the same thing going on today. People of the world and people of empty formal religion have little real sympathy with one another. They dislike one another's principles and despise one another's ways. But there is one thing which they both dislike even more, and that is the pure Gospel of Jesus Christ. And so, whenever there is a chance of opposing the Gospel, we always see them act together. We must expect no mercy from them: they will show none. We must never reckon on their divisions: they will always patch up an alliance to resist Christ.

2. A subtle question

Second, let us observe the exceeding subtlety of the question they asked our Lord: "Is it right to pay taxes to Caesar or not? Should we pay or shouldn't we?" (verses 14–15). Here was a question which it seemed at first sight impossible to answer without peril. If our Lord had replied, "Give," the Pharisees would have accused him before the priests as one who regarded the Jewish nation as subject to Rome. If our Lord had replied, "Do not give," the Herodians would have accused him before Pilate as a seditious person who taught rebellion against the Roman government. The trap was indeed well planned. Surely we may see in it the cunning hand of someone more than human. That old serpent the devil was there.

We shall do well to remember that of all questions which have perplexed Christians, none have ever proved so intricate and puzzling as the sort of questions which the Pharisees and Herodians here put. ["Nothing is more likely to ensnare ministers," wrote Matthew Henry, "than bringing them to meddle with controversies about civil rights, and to settle landmarks between the prince and the subjects, which it is fit should be done, while it is not at all fit that they should have the doing of it."] What is due to Caesar, and what is due to God – where the rights of the church end, and where the rights of the state begin – what are lawful civil claims and what are lawful spiritual claims – all these are hard knots and deep problems which Christians have often found it difficult to untie, and almost impossible to solve. Let us pray to be delivered from them. Never does the cause of Christ suffer so much as when the devil succeeds in bringing churches into collisions and law-suits with the civil power. In such collisions precious time is wasted, energies are misapplied, ministers are diverted from their proper work, the souls of people suffer and a church's victory often proves only one degree better than a defeat. "Give peace in our time, O Lord," is a prayer of wide meaning, and one that should often be on a Christian's lips.

3. Christ's wise answer

Third, let us observe the marvelous wisdom which our Lord showed in his answer to his enemies.

Their flattering words did not deceive him. He "knew their hypocrisy" (verse 15). His all-seeing eye detected the "silver dross" over the earthenware (Proverbs 26:23, NIV footnote, ed. note) which stood before him. He was not deceived, as too many of his people are, by glowing language and fine speeches.

He made the daily practice of his own enemies supply him with an answer to their cunning question. He tells them to bring him a denarius, a common coin which they themselves were in the habit of using. He asks them (verse 16) whose portrait and inscription are stamped on that denarius. They are obliged to reply, "Caesar's." They were themselves using a Roman coin, issued and circulated by the Roman government. By their own confession they were in some way under the power of the Romans, or this Roman money would not have been current among them. At once our Lord silences them by the memorable words, "Give to Caesar what is Caesar's and to God what is God's" (verse 17). He tells them to pay tribute to the Roman government in temporal things, for by using its money they admitted that they were bound to do so. Yet he tells them to give obedience to God in spiritual things, and not to suppose that duty to an earthly sovereign and a heavenly sovereign are incapable of being reconciled with each other. In short, he tells the proud Pharisee not to refuse his dues to Caesar, and the worldly Herodian not to refuse his dues to God.

Let us learn from this masterly decision the great principle that true Christianity was never meant to interfere with a person's obedience to the civil power. So far from this being the case it ought to make him a quiet, loyal and faithful subject. He ought to regard the authorities that exist as "established by God" (Romans 13:1), and to submit to their rules and regulations, so long as the law is enforced, though he may not thoroughly approve of them. If the law of the land and the law of God come in collision, no doubt his course is clear – he must obey God rather than man. Like the three children, though he serves a heathen king, he must not bow down to an idol. Like Daniel, though he submits to a tyrannical government, he must not give over praying in order to please the ruling powers.

[Sibelius quotes a passage from Augustine on the Psalms which is worth reading as an illustration of the subject now before us:

Julian was an unbelieving emperor. He was an apostate, a wicked man, and an idolater. And yet Christian men served as soldiers under this unbelieving emperor. When the cause of

Christ was concerned, they acknowledged no commander but the one in heaven. When the emperor wished them to worship idols or burn incense to them, they preferred honoring God before him. But when he said, "Draw out in order of battle, march against that nation," they obeyed him. They drew a distinction between their eternal master and their temporal master; and yet were submissive to their temporal master for their eternal master's sake.]

Let us often pray for a larger measure of that spirit of wisdom which dwelt so abundantly in our blessed Lord. Many are the evils which have arisen in the church of Christ from a morbid and distorted view of the relative positions of the civil government and of God. Many are the rents and divisions which have been occasioned by lack of sound judgment as to their comparative claims. Happy is the person who remembers our Lord's decision in this passage, understands it rightly and makes a practical application to the present time.

The Sadducees, and the doctrine of the resurrection (12:18–27)

These verses relate a conversation between our Lord Jesus Christ and the Sadducees. The religion of these men, we know, was little better than unbelief. They said there was "no resurrection" (verse 18). They too, like the Pharisees, thought to entangle and perplex our Lord with hard questions. The church of Christ must not expect to fare better than its Master. Empty formal religion on one side, and unbelief on the other, are two enemies for whose attacks we must always be prepared.

1. Unfair arguments
First, we learn from this passage how much unfairness may often be detected in the arguments of unbelievers.

The question put by the Sadducees is a striking illustration of this. They tell him of a woman who married seven brothers in succession, had no children, and outlived her seven husbands. They ask "whose wife" of all the seven the women would be "at the resurrection" (verse

23). It may well be surmised that the case was a supposed and not a real one. On the face of it, there is the strongest evidence of improbability. The chances against such a case occurring in reality, any actuary would tell us, are almost infinite. But that was nothing to the old Sadducees. All they cared for was to raise a difficulty, and if possible to put our Lord to silence. They had not the face openly to deny the doctrine of the resurrection. The possible consequences of the doctrine were the ground which they chose to take up.

There are three things which we shall do well to remember, if unhappily we have at any time to argue with unbelievers.

For one thing, let us remember that an unbeliever will always try to press us with the *difficulties and abstruse things of religion,* and especially with those which are connected with the world to come. We must avoid this mode of argument as far as possible. It is leaving the open field to fight in a jungle. We must endeavor, as far as we can, to make our discussion turn on the great plain facts and evidences of Christianity.

For another thing, let us remember to be on our guard against *unfairness and dishonesty in argument.* It may seem hard and uncharitable to say this. But experience proves that it is necessary. Thousands of people who claim to be unbelievers have confessed later on in life that they had never studied the Bible which they claimed to deny, and though well-read in the works of skeptics and unbelievers, had never calmly examined the foundations of Christianity.

Above all, let us remember that every unbeliever has a *conscience.* We may always appeal confidently to this. The very people who talk most loudly and disdainfully against religion are often feeling conscious, even while they talk, that they are wrong. The very argument which they have sneered at and ridiculed will often prove at last not to have been thrown away.

2. Religious error due to ignorance of the Bible

Second, we learn from this passage how much of religious error may be traced to ignorance of the Bible. Our Lord's first words in reply to the Sadducees declare this plainly. He says, "Are you not in error because you do not know the Scriptures . . . ?" (verse 24).

The truth of the principle here laid down is proved by facts in almost every age of church history. The reformation in Josiah's day was closely connected with the discovery of the book of the law. The false doctrines of the Jews in our Lord's time were the result of neglecting the Scriptures. The dark ages of Christendom were times when the Bible was kept back from the people. The Protestant Reformation was mainly effected by translating and circulating the Bible. The churches which are most flourishing at the present are churches which honor the Bible. The nations which enjoy most moral light are nations in which the Bible is most known. The parishes in our land where there is most true religion are those in which the Bible is most studied. The godliest families are Bible-reading families. The holiest men and women are Bible-reading people. These are simple facts which cannot be denied.

Let these things sink deeply into our hearts, and bear fruit in our lives. Let us not be ignorant of the Bible, lest we fall into some deadly error. Let us rather read it diligently and make it our rule of faith and practice. Let us labor to spread the Bible over the world. The more the book is known, the better the world will be. Not least, let us teach our children to value the Bible. The very best inheritance we can give them is a knowledge of the Scriptures.

3. The resurrection state

Third, we learn from this passage how different will be the state of things after the resurrection, from the state in which we live now. Our Lord tells us that "when the dead rise, they will neither marry nor be given in marriage; they will be like the angels in heaven" (verse 25).

It would be foolish to deny that there are many difficulties connected with the doctrine of the life to come. It must be so. The world beyond the grave is a world unseen by mortal eye, and therefore unknown. The conditions of existence there are necessarily hidden from us, and if more were told, we should probably not understand it. Let it suffice us to know that the bodies of the saints will be raised, and, though glorified, will be like their bodies on earth – so like, that those who knew them once will know them again. But though raised with a real body, the risen saint will be completely freed from everything which is now an evidence of weakness and infirmity. There will be nothing like Muhammad's gross and sensual paradise in the Christian's future existence. Hunger and thirst being no more, there will be no need of food. Weariness and fatigue being no more, there will be no need of sleep. Death being no more, there will be no need of births to supply the place of those who are removed. Enjoying the full presence of God and his Christ, men and women will no more need the marriage union in order to help one another. Able to serve God without weariness and attend on him without distraction, doing his will perfectly and seeing his face continually, clothed in a glorious body, they will be "like the angels in heaven."

There is comfort in all this for the true Christian. In the body that we now have we often "groan and are burdened" from a daily sense of weakness and imperfection (2 Corinthians 5:4). We are now tried by many cares about this world – what to eat, what to drink and what to put on, how to manage our affairs, where to live and what company to choose. In the world to come, everything will be changed. Nothing will be lacking to make our happiness complete.

One thing only we must carefully bear in mind. Let us take care that we "rise to live" and not "rise to be condemned" (John 5:29). To the believer in the Lord Jesus, the resurrection will be the greatest of blessings. To the worldly, the godless and the profane, the resurrection will be a misery and a curse. Let us never rest till we are one with Christ and Christ in us, and then we may look forward with joy to a life to come.

[The text by which our Lord silenced the Sadducees, and proved the resurrection to be a scriptural doctrine, has been a cause of surprise to many Bible readers. Some have wondered that our Lord should have chosen this text, when others far more plain might have been adduced. Some have been unable to see the force and cogency of the text as any proof at all of the resurrection of the body.

As to the particular fitness of the text as a proof, compared with others we are perhaps very poor judges. It may well be suspected that there is a fullness of meaning in some texts of Scripture which in our hasty and superficial reading we have not yet fathomed. At any rate it is clear that to a Jewish hearer of the Lord the argument was so forcible as to be unanswerable. The quotation and the famous one in John 10:34 go far to show that the Jewish mind saw a depth of meaning in scriptural expressions, which many of us in modern times have not at all seen yet. It is a matter on which we have much to learn.

As to the text "I am the God of Abraham, the God of Isaac, and the

God of Jacob" being a convincing proof of the resurrection of the body, there is a passage in Bishop Pearson which is worth reading. He says of this text as quoted by our Lord:

> With the force of this argument the multitude was astonished, and the Sadducees silenced. For under the name of God was understood a great benefactor, a God of promise, and to be "*their* God" was to bless them and reward them; as in them to be "his servants" and "his people" was to believe in him and obey him. Now Abraham, Isaac and Jacob had not received the promise which they expected, and therefore God after their death desiring still to be called "their God," he thereby acknowledgeth that he had a blessing and a reward for them still, and consequently that he will raise them to another life, in which they may receive it. So that the argument of our Saviour is the same which the Jews have drawn from another place of Moses (Exodus 6:3–4), "I appeared to Abraham, to Isaac and to Jacob as God Almighty, but by my name the LORD I did not make myself known to them. I also established my covenant with them to give them the land of Canaan." It is not said, "to give their sons," but "to give *them* the land," and therefore because while they lived here they enjoyed it not, they must rise again that they may receive the promise.]

The teachers of the law, and the greatest commandment (12:28–34)

These verses contain a conversation between our Lord Jesus Christ and "one of the teachers of the law" (verse 28). For the third time in one day we see our Lord tried by a hard question. Having put to silence the Pharisees and Sadducees, he is asked to decide a point on which much difference of opinion prevailed among the Jews: "Of all the commandments, which is the most important?" (verse 28). We have reason to bless God that so many hard questions were put to our Lord. Without them the marvelous words of wisdom which his three answers contain might never have been spoken at all. Here, as in many other cases, we see how God can bring good out of evil. He can make the most malicious assaults of his enemies work round to the good of his church, and redound to his own praise. He can make the enmity of Pharisees and Sadducees and teachers of the law minister instruction to his people. Little did the three questioners in this chapter think what benefit their crafty questions would confer on all Christendom. "Out of the eater, something to eat" (Judges 14:14).

1. Christ's high standard of duty

First, let us observe in these verses how high is our Lord Jesus Christ's standard of duty to God and man.

The question that the teacher of the law put was a very wide one: "Of all the commandments, which is the most important?" (verse 28). The answer he received was probably very unlike what he expected. At any rate, if he thought that our Lord would comment to him the observance of some outward form or ceremony, he was mistaken. He hears these solemn words: "'Love the Lord your God with all your heart and with all your soul and with all your mind and with all your strength.' The second is this: 'Love your neighbor as yourself'" (verses 30–31).

How striking is our Lord's description of the *feeling* with which we ought to regard both God and our neighbor! We are not merely to obey the one, or to abstain from injuring the other. In both cases we are to give far more than this. We are to give love, the strongest of all affections, and the most comprehensive. A rule like this includes everything. It makes all petty details unnecessary. Nothing will be intentionally lacking where there is love.

How striking again is our Lord's description of the *measure* in which we should love God and our neighbor! We are to love God better than ourselves, with all the powers of our inner being. We cannot love him too well. We are to love our neighbors as ourselves, and to deal with them in all respects as we would like them to deal with us. The marvelous wisdom of this distinction is clear and plain. We may easily go wrong in our affections towards others, either by thinking too little or too much of them. We therefore need the rule to love them as ourselves, neither more nor less. We cannot go wrong in our affections towards God in the matter of excess. He is worthy of all we can give him. We are therefore to love him with all our heart.

Let us keep these two grand rules continually before our minds, and use them daily in our journey through life. Let us see in them a summary of all that we ought to aim at in our practice, both as regards God and our neighbor. By them let us test every difficulty of conscience that may happen to beset us, as to right and wrong. Happy are those who try to frame their lives according to these rules.

Let us learn from this brief exposition of the true standard of duty, how great is the need in which we all naturally stand of the atonement and mediation of our Lord Jesus Christ. Where are the men or women who can say with truth that they have perfectly loved God and perfectly loved their neighbor? Where is the person on earth who must not plead "guilty" when tried by such a law as this? No wonder the Scripture says, "There is no one righteous, not even one," and, "Therefore no one will be declared righteous in his sight by observing the law" (Romans 3:10, 20). It is only gross ignorance of the requirements of God's law which makes people undervalue the Gospel. The person who has the clearest view of the moral law will always be the person with the highest sense of the value of Christ's atoning blood.

2. How far one may go in religion without being a true Christian

Second, let us observe in these verses how far a person may go in religion, and still not be a true disciple of Christ.

The teacher of the law, in the passage now before us, was evidently a man of more knowledge than most of his equals. He saw things which many teachers of the law and Pharisees never saw at all. His own words are a strong proof of this. "God is one and there is no other but him. To love him with all your heart, with all your understanding and with all your strength, and to love your neighbor as yourself is more important than all burnt offerings and sacrifices" (verses 32–33). These words are remarkable in themselves, and doubly remarkable when we remember who the speaker was, and the generation among whom he lived. No wonder we read next that our Lord said, "You are not far from the kingdom of God" (verse 34).

But we must not shut our eyes to the fact that we are nowhere told that this man became one of our Lord's disciples. On this point there is a lamentable silence. The parallel passage in St. Matthew throws not a gleam of light on his case. The other parts of the New Testament tell us nothing about him. We are left to draw the painful conclusion that, like the rich young man, he could not make up his mind to give everything up and follow Christ; or that, like the chief rulers mentioned elsewhere, he "loved praise from men more than praise from God" (John 12:43). In short, though "not far from the kingdom of God," he probably never entered into it, and died outside.

Cases like that of this teacher of the law are unhappily far from being uncommon. There are thousands on every side who, like him, see much and know much of religious truth, and yet live and die uncommitted. There are few things which are so much overlooked as the length to which people may go in religious attainments and yet never be converted, and never saved. May we all mark well this man's case, and take care!

Let us beware of resting our hopes of salvation on mere intellectual knowledge. We live in days when there is great danger of doing so. Education makes children acquainted with many things in religion, of which their parents were once utterly ignorant. But education alone will never make a Christian in the sight of God. We must not only know the leading doctrines of the Gospel with our heads, but receive them into our hearts, and be guided by them in our lives. May we never rest till we have truly repented, really believed, and have been made new creatures in Christ Jesus. If we rest satisfied with being "not far from the kingdom," we shall find at last that we are shut out forevermore.

Christ in the Psalms; a warning against hypocrisy; the widow's offering (12:35–44)

We have seen in the earlier part of this chapter how the enemies of our Lord endeavored to catch him in his words. We have seen how the Pharisees, the Sadducees and the teachers of the law in turn put hard question to him – questions, we can hardly fail to observe, more likely to bring strife than edification. The passage before us begins with a question of a very different sort. Our Lord himself asks it. He asks his enemies about Christ and about the meaning of Holy Scripture. Such questions are always truly profitable. It would be good for the church if theological discussions were less about trifles and more about weighty matters and things necessary to salvation.

1. Christ in the Old Testament

First, we learn from these verses how much there is about Christ in the Old Testament Scriptures. Our Lord wants to expose the ignorance of the Jewish teachers about the true nature of the Messiah. He does it by referring to a passage in the book of Psalms, and showing that the teachers of the law did not rightly understand it. And in so doing he shows us that one subject, about which David was inspired by the Holy Spirit to write, was Christ.

We know from our Lord's own words in another place that the Old Testament Scriptures "testify about" Christ (John 5:39). They were intended to teach people about Christ by symbols, imagery and prophecy, till he himself appeared on earth. We should always keep this in mind in reading the Old Testament, but never so much as in reading the Psalms. Christ is undoubtedly to be found in every part of the Law and the Prophets, but nowhere is he so much to be found as in the book of Psalms. His experience and sufferings at his first coming into the world, his future glory and his final triumph at his second coming are the chief subjects of many a passage in that wonderful part of God's Word. It is a true saying that we should look for Christ quite as much as David in reading the Psalms.

Let us beware of undervaluing or despising the Old Testament. In its place and proportion, the Old Testament is just as valuable as the New. There are probably many rich passages in that part of the Bible, which have never yet been fully explorerd. There are deep things about Jesus in it which many people walk over as if over hidden gold mines, and do not know the treasures beneath their feet. Let us reverence *all* the Bible. All of it is given by inspiration, and all of it is profitable. One part throws light on another, and no part can ever be neglected without loss and damage to our souls. A boastful contempt for the Old Testament Scriptures has often proved the first step towards infidelity.

2. The sin of hypocrisy

Second, let us learn from these verses how odious is the sin of hypocrisy in the sight of Christ. This is a lesson which is taught us by our Lord's warning against the teachers of the law. He exposes some of their notorious practices – their ostentatious manner of dressing, their love of the honor and praise of other people rather than of God, their love of money disguised under a concern for widows, their long-protracted public devotions intended to make people think them eminently godly. And he winds up everything by the solemn declaration, "Such men will be punished most severely" (verse 40).

Of all the sins into which people can fall, none seems to be as exceedingly sinful as false profession of belief, and hypocrisy. At all events, none have drawn from our Lord's mouth such strong language, and such heavy denunciations. It is bad enough to be led away captive by open sin, and to serve various different lusts and pleasures. But it is even worse to pretend to have a religion, while in reality we serve the world. Let us beware of falling into this abominable sin. Whatever we do in religion, let us never wear a cloak. Let us be real, honest, thorough and sincere in our Christianity. We cannot deceive an all-seeing God. We may take poor short-sighted humans by a little talk and religious claims, a few clichés and a show of devoutness. But God is not mocked. He discerns the thoughts and intentions of the heart. His all-seeing eye pierces through the paint and varnish and tinsel which cover the unsound heart. The day of judgment will soon be here. The "joy of the godless lasts but a moment" (Job 20:5). His end will be shame and everlasting contempt.

One thing, however, must never be forgotten in connection with the subject of hypocrisy. Let us not flatter ourselves, because some people make a false profession of religion, that others need not make any profession at all. This is a common delusion, and one against which we must carefully guard. It does not follow, because some people bring Christianity into contempt by professing what they do not really believe and feel, that we should run to the other extreme, and bring it into contempt by a cowardly silence and by keeping our religion out of sight. Let us rather be doubly careful to adorn our doctrine by our lives. Let us prove our sincerity by the consistency of our conversation. Let us show the world that there is true coin, as well as counterfeit coin, and that the visible church contains Christians who can witness a good confession, as well as Pharisees and teachers of the law. Let us confess our Master modestly and humbly, but firmly and decidedly, and show the world that although some people may be hypocrites, there are other who are honest and true.

3. Self-denying liberality

Third, let us learn from these verses how pleasing to Christ is self-denying liberality in giving. This is a lesson which is taught us in a striking manner, by our Lord's commendation of a certain poor widow. We are told that he "watched the crowd" putting their voluntary contributions for God's service into the public collecting box or "treasury" (verse 41). He saw that "many rich people threw in large amounts." At last he saw this poor widow put in all she had for her daily maintenance. And then we hear him pronounce the solemn words, "This poor widow has put more into the treasury than all the others" (verse 43) – more in the sight of him who looks not merely at the amount given, but at the ability of the giver – not merely at the quantity contributed, but at the motive and heart of the contributor.

There are few of our Lord's sayings so much overlooked as this. There are thousands who remember all his doctrinal speeches, and yet contrive to forget this little incident in his earthly ministry. The proof of this is to be seen in the meager and sparing contributions which are made every year by Christ's church to do good in the world. The proof is to be seen in the miserably small incomes of all the missionary societies, in proportion to the wealth of the churches. The proof is to be seen in the long annual lists of self-complacent modest subscribers, of whom many could easily give hundreds of pounds. The stinginess of professing Christians in all matters which concern God and religion is one of the crying sins of the day, and one of the worst signs of the times. The givers to Christ's cause are but a small section of the visible church. Not one baptized person in twenty, probably, knows anything of being "rich towards God" (Luke 12:21). The vast majority spend pounds on themselves, and give not even pence to Christ.

Let us mourn over this state of things, and pray God to amend it. Let us pray him to open our eyes and awaken our hearts and stir up a spirit of liberality. Above all, let us each do our own duty, and give liberally and gladly to every Christian object, while we can. There will be no giving when we are dead. Let us give as those who remember that the eyes of Christ are upon us. He still sees exactly what each person gives, and knows exactly how much is left behind. Above all, let us give as the disciples of a crucified Saviour, who gave himself for us, body and soul, on the cross. Freely we have received. Let us freely give.

[It is probable, according to Arius Montanus and Brentius, that the words "all she had to live on" mean "all her daily income," and not all her property.

It may be well to remark in this connection that nothing can be more absurd than to say, as some do, that they contribute "their mite" to a cause when they probably contribute some trifling sum which they do not miss, and which bears not the most remote proportion to the widow's scale of liberality. People contribute "their mite" when they contribute half their daily income, and not till then.]

Mark
Chapter 13

The beginning of the prophecy on the Mount of Olives
(13:1–8)

This chapter is full of prophecy – prophecy of which part has been fulfilled, and part remains to be fulfilled. Two great events form the subject of this prophecy. One is the destruction of Jerusalem, and the consequent end of the Jewish dispensation. The other is the second coming of our Lord Jesus Christ, and the winding up of the state of things under which we now live. The destruction of Jerusalem was an event which happened only forty years after our Lord was crucified. The second coming of Christ is an event which is yet to come, and we may yet live to see it with our own eyes.

[I think it right to repeat here what I said in commenting on the report of our Lord's prophecy given by St. Matthew, respecting the destruction of Jerusalem. I believe that in the prophecy now under consideration, our Lord had in view a *second* siege of Jerusalem and a *second* period of distress accompanying that siege, as well as the first siege and distress when the city was taken by Titus. Zechariah 14 appears to me to be unanswerable proof that such a siege is to be expected.

I see no other way of explaining the close connection which appears in the prophecy between the "distress" here foretold (verse 19) and the "Son of Man coming in the clouds with great power and glory" (verse 26). To interpret the coming of the Son of Man as the coming of the Roman army in judgment on the Jews appears to me positive trifling with Scripture.

The view that our Lord is prophesying about *two* sieges of Jerusalem and *two* tremendous periods of distress which would fall especially on the Jews, and of his own second coming as an event which would immediately follow the second siege, makes the whole chapter plain and intelligible.

All these events ought to be deeply interesting to believers, and would be especially so to Jewish believers, like the apostles, in whose time the temple was still standing, the Jewish dispensation not yet put aside and Jerusalem not yet destroyed.]

Chapters like this ought to be deeply interesting to every true Christian. No history ought to receive so much of our attention as the past and future history of the church of Christ. The rise and fall of worldly empires are events of comparatively small importance in the sight of God. Babylon, Greece, Rome, France and England are as nothing in God's eyes beside the mystical body of Christ. The march of armies and the victories of conquerors are mere trifles in comparison with the progress of the Gospel and the final triumph of the Prince of Peace. May we remember this in reading prophetic Scripture! "Blessed is the one who reads" (Revelation 1:3).

1. The prediction concerning the temple

The first thing that demands our attention in the verses before us is the prediction of our Lord concerning the temple at Jerusalem.

The disciples, with the natural pride of Jews, had called their Master's attention to the architectural splendor of the temple. "Look!" they said. "What massive stones! What magnificent buildings!" (verse 1).

[It may be as well to remark that the temple here spoken of was in a certain sense the third temple in order which had been built at Jerusalem. The first was built by Solomon and destroyed by Nebuchadnezzar. The second was built by Ezra and Nehemiah. The third, if it may be so called, was enlarged and almost rebuilt, about the time of our Lord Jesus Christ's birth, by Herod. The enormous size of the stones used in building it, and the general magnificence of the whole fabric, are attested not only by Josephus but by heathen writers.]

They received an answer from the Lord very different from what they expected, a heart-saddening answer, and one well calculated to stir up inquisitive thoughts in their minds. No word of admiration falls from his lips. He does not commend the design or workmanship of the gorgeous structure before him. He appears to lose sight of the form and comeliness of the material building in his concern for the wickedness of the nation to which it belonged. "Do you see all these great buildings?" he replies. "Not one stone here will be left on another; every one will be thrown down" (verse 2).

Let us learn from this solemn saying that the true glory of a church does not consist in its buildings for public worship, but in the faith and godliness of its members. The eyes of our Lord Jesus Christ could find no pleasure in looking at the very temple which contained the holy of holies and the golden candlestick and the altar of burnt offering. Much less, we may suppose, can he find pleasure in the most splendid place of worship among professing Christians, if his Word and his Spirit are not honored in it.

We shall all do well to remember this. We are naturally inclined to judge things by the outward appearance, like children who value poppies more than corn. We are too apt to suppose that where there is a stately ecclesiastical building and a magnificent ceremonial – carved stone and stained glass – fine music and gorgeously dressed ministers, there must be some real religion. And yet there may be no religion at all. It may be all form and show and appeal to the senses. There may be nothing to satisfy the conscience, nothing to cure the heart. It may prove on enquiry that Christ is not preached in that stately building, and the Word of God not expounded. The ministers may perhaps be utterly ignorant of the Gospel, and the worshipers may be dead in transgressions and sins. We need not doubt that God sees no beauty in such a building as this. We need not doubt the Parthenon had no glory in God's sight compared to the dens and caves where the early Christians worshiped, or that the meanest room where Christ is preached today is more honorable in his eyes than the cathedral of St. Peter's at Rome.

Let us however not run to the absurd extreme of supposing that it does not matter what kind of building we set apart for God's service. There is no Popery in making a church handsome. There is no true religion in having a dirty, mean, shabby and disorderly place of worship. "Everything should be done in a fitting and orderly way" (1 Corinthians 14:40). But let it be a settled principle in our religion, however beautiful we make our churches, to regard pure doctrine and holy practice as their principal ornaments. *Without* these two things, the noblest ecclesiastical edifice is radically defective. It has no glory if God is not there. *With* these two things, the humblest brick cottage where the Gospel is preached is lovely and beautiful. It is consecrated by Christ's own presence and the Holy Spirit's own blessing.

2. How the prophecy commences

The second thing that demands our attention in these verses is the remarkable manner in which our Lord commences the great prophecy of this chapter.

We are told that four of his disciples, aroused no doubt by his warning prediction about the temple, asked him for further information. "Tell us," they said, "when will these things happen? And what will be the sign that they are all about to be fulfilled?" (verse 4).

The answer which our Lord gives to these questions begins at once with a prediction of coming false doctrine and coming wars. If his disciples thought he would promise them immediate success and temporal prosperity in this world, they were soon undeceived. So far from telling them to expect a speedy victory of truth, he tells them to look out for the rise of error. "Watch out that no one deceives you. Many will come in my name, claiming, 'I am he'" (verses 5–6). So far from telling them to expect a general reign of peace and quietness, he tells them to prepare for wars and troubles. "Nation will rise against nation, and kingdom against kingdom. There will be earthquakes in various places, and famines. These are the beginning of birth-pains" (verse 8).

There is something deeply instructive in this opening of our Lord's prophetic discourse. It seems like the keynote of what his church is to expect between his first and second advents. It looks as if it were specially intended to correct the mistaken views not only of his apostles but of the vast body of professing Christians in every age. It looks as if our Lord knew well that we are always catching at the idea of a "good time coming," and as if he would give us plain notice that there will be no "good time" till he returns. It may not be pleasant to us to hear such tidings. But it is in strict accordance with what we read in the prophet Jeremiah: "From early times the prophets who preceded you and me have prophesied war, disaster and plague against many countries and great kingdoms. But the prophet who prophesies peace will be recognized as one truly sent by the LORD only if his prediction comes true" (Jeremiah 28:8–9).

Let us learn from our Lord's opening prediction to be moderate in our expectations. Nothing has created so much disappointment in the church of Christ as the extravagant expectations in which many of its members have indulged. Let us not be carried away by the common idea that the world will be converted before the Lord Jesus returns, and the earth filled with the knowledge of the Lord. It will not be so. There is nothing in Scripture to justify such expectations. Let us cease to expect a reign of peace. Let us rather look for wars. Let us cease to expect everyone to be made holy by any existing means – schools, missions, preaching or anything of the kind. Let us rather look for the rise of Antichrist himself. Let us understand that we live in a day of election, and not of universal conversion. There will be no universal peace till the Prince of Peace appears. There will be no universal holiness till Satan is bound. It may cost us much to hold such opinions as these. But there is not a church or congregation on earth whose state does not show that these opinions are true, and that "many are invited, but few are chosen" (Matthew 22:14). It may bring on us the unkind remarks and the unfavorable judgment of many. But the end will prove who is right and who is wrong. For that end let us wait patiently. Let us labor, teach, work and pray. But let it not surprise us if we find our Lord's word strictly true: narrow is the road that leads to life, and only a few find it (Matthew 7:14).

What Christ's people must expect between his first and second advents *(13:9–13)*

In reading the prophecies of the Bible concerning Christ's church, we shall generally find judgment and mercy blended together. They are seldom all bitter without any sweet, seldom all darkness without any light. The Lord knows our weakness and readiness to faint, and has taken care to mingle consolations with threatenings, kind words with hard words, like warp and woof in a garment. We may notice this throughout the book of Revelation. We may see it all through the prophecy we are now considering. We may note it in these few verses.

1. Troubles

First, let us observe what troubles our Lord tells his people to expect between the time of his first and second comings. Trouble, no doubt, is everyone's lot since the day Adam fell. It came in with the thorns and thistles. "Man is born to trouble as surely as sparks fly upward" (Job 5:7). But there are special troubles to which believers in Jesus Christ are liable, and of these our Lord gives them plain warning.

They must expect trouble *from the world*. They must not look for the help of "governors and kings" (verse 9). They will find their ways and their doctrines bring them no favor in high places. On the contrary, they will often be imprisoned, beaten and brought before judgment seats as criminals for no other reason than their adherence to the Gospel of Christ.

They must expect trouble from *their own relations*. "Brother will betray brother to death, and a father his child" (verse 12). Their own flesh and blood will often forget to love them, out of hatred of their religion. They will find sometimes that the enmity of the worldly mind against God is stronger than even the ties of family and blood.

We shall do well to lay these things to heart and to count the cost of being a Christian. We must think it no strange thing if our religion brings with it some bitter things. Our lot, no doubt, is cast in favorable times. The boundary lines have fallen for Christians in our country in pleasant places (Psalm 16:6). We have no reason to be afraid of death or imprisonment, if we serve Christ. But, for all that, we must make up our minds to endure a certain proportion of hardship, if we are real, thorough and committed Christians. We must be content to put up with laughter, ridicule, mockery, slander and petty persecution. We must even bear hard words and unkindness from our nearest and dearest relations. The "offense of the cross" is not over. "The man without the Spirit does not accept the things that come from the Spirit of God" (1 Corinthians 2:14). Those who are "born in the ordinary way" will persecute those who are "born by the power of the Spirit" (Galatians 4:29). The utmost consistency of life will not prevent it. If we are converted, we must never be surprised to find that we are hated for Christ's sake.

2. Encouragement

Second, let us observe what rich encouragement the Lord Jesus holds out to his persecuted people. He sets before them three rich cordials to cheer their souls.

For one thing, he tells us that *"the Gospel must first be preached to all nations"* (verse 10). It must be, and it will be. In spite of men and devils, the story of the cross of Christ will be told in every part of the world. The gates of Hades will not overcome it. Despite persecution, imprisonment and death there will never lack a succession of faithful people who will proclaim the glad news of salvation by grace. Few may believe them. Many of their hearers may continue hardened in sin. But nothing will prevent the Gospel being preached. The word will never be chained, though those who preach it may be imprisoned and slain (2 Timothy 2:9).

For another thing, our Lord tells us that *those who are placed in special trial for the Gospel's sake will have special help* in their time of need. The Holy Spirit will assist them in making their defense. They will have speech and wisdom which their adversaries will not be able to gainsay or resist. As it was with Peter and John and Paul, when brought before Jewish and Roman councils, so it will be with all true-hearted disciples. How thoroughly this promise has been fulfilled the stories of Hus, Luther, Latimer, Ridley and Baxter abundantly prove. Christ has been faithful to his word.

For another thing, our Lord tells us that *patient perseverance will result in final salvation.* "He who stands firm to the end will be saved" (verse 13). Not one of those who endure tribulation will miss his reward. All will at last reap a rich harvest. Though they sow in tears, they will reap with songs of joy (Psalm 126:5). Their light and momentary troubles will achieve an eternal weight of glory (2 Corinthians 4:17).

Let us gather comfort from these comforting promises for all true-hearted servants of Christ. Persecuted, vexed and mocked as they are now, they will find at length they are on the victorious side. Beset, perplexed, tried as they sometimes are, they will never find themselves entirely forsaken. Though cast down, they will not be destroyed. Let them possess their souls in patience. The end of all that they see going on around them is certain, fixed and sure. The kingdom of this world shall yet become the kingdom of their God and of his Christ (Revelation 11:15). And when the scoffers and ungodly, who so often insulted them, are put to shame, believers will receive a crown of glory that will never fade away (1 Peter 5:4).

[There is a promise in this passage which is often much perverted. I allude to the implied promise contained in the words, "Do not worry beforehand about what to say. Just say whatever is given you at the time" (verse 11).

The perversion I mean consists in supposing that this passage warrants ministers in getting up to preach unprepared every Sunday, and in expecting special help from the Holy Spirit in addressing regular congregations, when they have neither meditated, read nor taken pains about their subject.

A moment's reflection must show any reader that such an application of this passage is utterly unjustifiable. The passage has no reference whatever to the regular sabbath sermon of a minister, and only holds out the promise of special help in special times of need.

It would be good for the church if this were more remembered than it is. At present it may be feared this promise is not infrequently made an excuse for ministerial idleness and undigested sermons. People seem to forget when they enter the pulpit that what costs nothing is worth nothing, and that the "foolishness" of preaching and foolish preaching are widely different things.]

Providing for our own safety; privileges of the elect (13:14–23)

1. Providing for our own safety

First, we are taught in these verses that it is legitimate to take steps to provide for our own personal safety. The language of our Lord Jesus Christ on the subject is clear and unmistakable: "Let those who are in Judea flee to the mountains. Let no one on the roof of his house go down or enter the house to take anything out. Let no one in the field go back to get his cloak. . . . Pray that this will not take place in winter" (verses 14–18). Not a word is said to make us suppose that flight from danger, in certain circumstances, is unworthy of a Christian. As to the time prophesied of in this passage, people may differ widely. But as to the lawfulness of taking measures to avoid peril, the teaching of the passage is plain.

The lesson is one of wide application, and of much usefulness. Christians are not to neglect to take steps in the things of this life because they are Christians, any more than in the things of the life to come. Believers are not to suppose that God will take care of them and provide for their needs if they do not make use of the means and common sense which God has given them, as well as other people. Beyond doubt they may expect the special help of their Father in heaven in every time of need. But they must expect it in the diligent use of lawful means. To profess to trust God, while we idly sit still and do nothing, is nothing better than enthusiasm and fanaticism, and brings religion into contempt.

The Word of God contains several instructive examples on this subject, and we shall do well to take heed of them. The conduct of Jacob when he went to meet his brother Esau is a striking case in point. He first prays a most touching prayer and then sends his brother a carefully arranged present (Genesis 32:9–15). The conduct of Hezekiah when Sennacherib came against Jerusalem is another case. "With us," he tells the people, "is the LORD our God to help us and to fight our battles." And yet, at the same time, he built up the walls of the city and made weapons and shields (2 Chronicles 32:8, 5). The conduct of St. Paul is another case. Frequently we read of his fleeing from one place to another to preserve his life. Once we see him let down from the walls of Damascus by a basket. Once we hear him telling the soldiers on board the Alexandrian corn ship, "Unless these men stay with the ship, you cannot be saved" (Acts 27:31). We know the great apostle's faith and confidence. We know his courage and reliance on his Master. And yet we see that even he never despised the taking of steps to secure his own safety. Let us not be ashamed to do likewise.

One thing only let us bear in mind. Let us not rest upon means while we use them. Let us look far beyond them to the blessing of God. It is a great sin to be like Asa and not seek help from the Lord but only from the physicians (2 Chronicles 16:12). To use all means diligently, and then leave the whole event in the hands of God, is the mark at which a true believer ought to aim.

2. The privileges of the elect

Second, we are taught in these verses the great privileges of God's elect. Twice in the passage our Lord uses a remarkable expression about them. He says of the great time of distress, "If the Lord had not cut short those days, no one would survive. But for the sake of the elect, whom he has chosen, he has shortened them" (verse 20). He says again of the false Christs and false prophets, that they will "perform signs and miracles to deceive the elect – if that were possible" (verse 22).

It is plain from this and other passages in the Bible that God has an elect people in the world. They are those, according to the seventeenth Article of the Church of England, whom "he has constantly decreed by his counsel, secret to us, to deliver from curse and damnation; those whom he hath chosen in Christ out of mankind, and decreed to bring by Christ to an everlasting salvation, as vessels made to honor." To them, and them only, belong the great privileges of justification, sanctification and final glory. They, and they only, "are called by the Spirit in due season." They, and they only, "obey the calling. They are made sons of God by adoption. They are made like the image of God's only begotten Son, Jesus Christ. They walk religiously in good works, and at length, by God's mercy, attain to everlasting felicity." To them belong the precious promises of the Gospel. They are the bride, the Lamb's wife. They are the holy Catholic church, which is Christ's body. They are those whom God especially cares for in the world. Kings, princes, noblemen, rich men are all nothing in God's eyes compared to his elect. These things are plainly revealed in Scripture. Human pride may not like them. But they cannot be gainsaid.

The subject of election is, no doubt, deep and mysterious. Unquestionably it has been often sadly perverted and abused. But the misuse of truths must not prevent us from using them. Rightly used, and fenced with proper cautions, election is a doctrine "full of sweet, pleasant and unspeakable comfort." Before we leave the subject, let us see what these cautions are.

For one thing, we must never forget that God's election does not destroy our accountability for our own soul. The same Bible which speaks of election always addresses us as free agents, and calls on us to repent, to believe, to seek, to pray, to strive, to labor. "In our doings," as Article 17 most wisely says, "that will of God is to be followed, which we have expressly declared unto us in the Word of God."

For another thing, let us never forget that the great thing we have to do is to *repent and believe the Gospel*. We have no right to take any comfort from God's election unless we can show plain evidence of repentance and faith. We are not to stand still, troubling ourselves with anxious speculations about whether we are elect or not, when God commands us plainly to repent and believe (Acts 17:30 and 1 John 3:23). Let us cease to do evil. Let us learn to do good. Let us break off from sin. Let us lay hold on Christ. Let us draw near to God in prayer. So doing, we shall soon know and feel whether we are God's elect. To use the words of an old divine, we must begin at the "grammar school" of repentance and faith, before we go to the "university" of election. It was when Paul remembered the faith, hope and love of the Thessalonians that he said, "we know, brothers loved by God, that he has chosen you" (1 Thessalonians 1:4).

[The meaning of the "abomination that causes desolation" in this passage (verse 14) has always perplexed the commentators. The most common view undoubtedly is that it means the Roman armies, who executed God's judgment on the Jewish nation.

It may be questioned whether this interpretation completely fulfills the prophecy. I venture, though with much diffidence, to suggest that a more complete and literal accomplishment yet remains to come. The remarkable words of St. Paul to the Thessalonians appear to me scarcely to have received yet a complete fulfillment: "He will oppose and will exalt himself over everything that is called God or is worshiped, so that he sets himself up in God's temple, proclaiming himself to be God" (2 Thessalonians 2:4). I confess that it seems to me by no means improbable that a personal Antichrist, yet to be revealed at Jerusalem, may prove the final accomplishment of these words. I desire to avoid dogmatism on the subject. I only suggest it as a possible and probable thing.]

Christ's second coming described; the importance of observing the signs of the time *(13:24–31)*

This part of our Lord's prophecy on the Mount of Olives is entirely unfulfilled. The events described in it are all yet to take place. They may possibly take place in our own day. The passage therefore is one which we ought always to read with particular interest.

1. The majesty of Christ's second coming

First, let us observe what solemn majesty will attend our Lord Jesus Christ's second coming to this world. The language that is used about the sun, moon and stars conveys the idea of some universal convulsion of the universe at the close of the present dispensation. It reminds us of the apostle Peter's words, "The heavens will disappear with a roar; the elements will be destroyed by fire" (2 Peter 3:10). At such a time as this, amid terror and confusion, exceeding all that even earthquakes or hurricanes are known to produce, people "will see the Son of Man coming in clouds with great power and glory" (verse 26).

The second coming of Christ will be utterly unlike the first. He came the first time in weakness, a tender infant born of a poor woman in the manger at Bethlehem, unnoticed, unhonored and scarcely known. He will come the second time in royal dignity, with the armies of heaven around him, to be known, recognized and feared by all the tribes of the earth. He came the first time to suffer – to bear our sins – to be reckoned a curse – to be despised, rejected, unjustly condemned and slain. He will come the second time to reign – to put down every enemy beneath his feet – to take the kingdoms of this world for his inheritance – to rule them with righteousness – to judge everybody, and to live forevermore.

How vast the difference! How mighty the contrast! How startling the comparison between the second advent and the first! How solemn the thoughts that the subject ought to stir up in our minds!

Here are *comforting* thoughts for Christ's friends. Their own King will soon be here. They will reap according as they have sown. They will receive a rich reward for all that they have endured for Christ's sake. They will exchange their cross for a crown.

Here are *confounding* thoughts for Christ's foes. That same Jesus of Nazareth, whom they have so long despised and rejected, will at length have the preeminence. That very Christ whose Gospel they have refused to believe will appear as their judge; helpless, hopeless and speechless they will have to stand before his bar. May we all lay these things to heart, and learn wisdom!

2. The gathering of Christ's elect

Second, let us observe that the first event after the Lord's second coming will be the gathering of his elect. "He will send his angels and gather his elect from the four winds" (verse 27).

The safety of the Lord's people will be provided for, when judgment falls upon the earth. He will do nothing till he has placed them beyond the reach of harm. The flood did not begin till Noah was safe in the ark. The fire did not fall on Sodom till Lot was safe within the walls of Zoar. The wrath of God on unbelievers will not be let loose till believers are hidden and secure.

The true Christian may look forward to the advent of Christ without fear. However terrible the things that come on the earth, his Master will take care that no harm comes to him. He may well bear patiently the partings and separations of this present time. He will have a joyful meeting, by and by, with all his brothers and sisters in the faith, of every age, country, people and language. Those who meet on that day will meet to part no more. The great gathering is yet to come (2 Thessalonians 2:1–2).

3. The signs of our own times

Third, let us observe how important it is to note the signs of our own times. Our Lord tells his disciples to "learn this lesson from the fig-tree" (verse 28). Just as its budding leaves tell men that summer is near, so the fulfillment of events in the world around us should teach us that the Lord's coming "is near, right at the door" (verse 28).

All true Christians should observe carefully the public events of their own day. It is not only a duty to do this, but a sin to neglect it. Our Lord reproved the Jews for not interpreting the signs of the times (Matthew 16:3). They did not see that the scepter was passing away from Judah, and the weeks of Daniel running out. Let us beware of falling into their error. Let us rather open our eyes and look at the world around us. Let us mark the drying up of the Turkish power and the increase of missionary work in the world. Let us mark the revival of Popery and the rise of new and subtle forms of unbelief. Let us mark the rapid spread of lawlessness and contempt for authority. What are these things but the budding of the fig-tree? They show us that this world is wearing out, and needs a new and better dynasty. It needs its rightful king, namely Jesus. May we stay awake and keep our clothes with us (Revelation 16:15), and live ready to meet our Lord!

4. The certainty of fulfillment

Fourth, let us observe in these verses how carefully our Lord asserts the certainty of his predictions being fulfilled. He speaks as though he foresaw the incredulity and skepticism of these times. He warns us emphatically against it: "Heaven and earth will pass away, but my words will never pass away" (verse 31).

We ought never to allow ourselves to suppose that any prophecy is improbable or unlikely to be fulfilled, merely because it is contrary to past experience. Let us not say, "Where is the likelihood of Christ coming again? Where is the likelihood of the world being burned up?" We have nothing to do with "likely or unlikely" in such matters. The only question is, "what is written in God's word?" The words of St. Peter should never be forgotten: "in the last days scoffers will come, scoffing and following their own evil desires" (2 Peter 3:3–4).

We would do well to ask ourselves what we would have thought if we had lived on earth two thousand years ago. Would we have thought it more probable that the Son of God would come on earth as a poor man and die, or that he would come on earth as a King and reign? Would we not have said at once that if he came at all he would come to reign and not to die? Yet we know that he did come as "a man of sorrows" and died on the cross. Then let us not doubt that he will come the second time in glory, and reign as a King forevermore.

Let us leave the passage with a thorough conviction of the truth of every jot of its predictions. Let us believe that every word of it will prove in the end to have been fully accomplished. Above all, let us strive to live under an abiding sense of its truth, like good servants ready to meet their master. Then, whatever be the fulfillment of it, or however soon, we shall be safe.

[I am aware that some interpreters of this passage explain its language very differently from myself. Many regard the "sun, moon and stars" as emblems of kings and governors, the "coming of the Son of Man" as a general expression meaning any great display of divine power, and the "sending of his angels" as nothing more than the sending of ministers and messengers of the Gospel to gather together the people of God.

I will only say that I can see no ground or warrant for such interpretations. They appear to me to be a dangerous tampering with the plain literal meaning of Scripture, and to give great leverage to the Arian, the Socinian and the Jew in the arguments that they respectively bring forward in support of their own particular views.

I take this opportunity of expressing my decided opinion that the word "generation" in the verse "this generation will certainly not pass away" (verse 30) can only mean "this nation or people – the Jewish nation – will not pass away."

The view that it means "the generation of people who are alive now while I am speaking" would make our Lord say what was not true. His words were in no sense completely fulfilled when the generation to which he spoke had passed away.

The view that it means "the same generation which is alive when these things begin will also see them accomplished" appears to me untenable for one simple reason. It is not the natural meaning of the Greek words from which our translation is made.]

The uncertainty of the time of Christ's second coming; the duty to keep awake *(13:32–37)*

These verses conclude St. Mark's report of our Lord's prophecy on the Mount of Olives. They ought to form a personal application of the whole discourse to our consciences.

1. The time is purposely withheld
First, we learn from these verses that the exact time of our Lord Jesus Christ's second coming is purposely withheld from his church. The event is certain. The precise day and hour are not revealed. "No one knows about that day or hour, not even the angels in heaven" (verse 32).

[There is undoubtedly some difficulty in the words of our Lord, "No one knows about that day, not even the angels in heaven, nor the Son." The question has often been raised, "How can the Lord Jesus be ignorant of anything, since he is true God, and says himself, 'I and my Father are one'?" How can the expression be reconciled with the saying that in him are hidden "all the treasures of wisdom and knowledge" (Colossians 2:3)?

The answer to these questions is to be found in our deep ignorance of the great mystery of the union of two natures in one Person. That our Lord Jesus Christ was at the same time perfect God and perfect man we know. That these two distinct natures were both found together in his Person, we also know. But how, and in what way, and to what exent the divine nature did not always operate in him so as to overshadow the human nature, I believe it to be impossible for mortal humans to explain. Enough for us to know that we sometimes see in our Lord's words and actions the "man Christ Jesus" and sometimes see the "God over all blessed forever." But though we see clearly, and admire, we cannot explain. We can only say, in the present instance, that our Lord spoke as a man and not as God.

Bullinger, in an able note on the subject, gives an interesting quotation from Cyril, of which the following passage is a portion:

> Just as the Saviour was willing to endure hunger, and thirst, and other suffering of this kind, so also, as man, he is ignorant of "that great day." For he sometimes speaks as God, and sometimes as man, in order that he may show himself to be both true God and true man. As God he said to his disciples, "Our friend Lazarus is asleep," when no one had told him. As man he asked the sister of Lazarus, when he came to them at the end of his journey, "Where have you laid him?" He who, when far off, knew that Lazarus was dead, how could he be ignorant, when present, of the place where the body of Lazarus was? It is utterly improbable that he should have known the one thing and been ignorant of the other. But the truth is, that he knew both as God, while he was ignorant of both as man. Therefore, in the same way, he both did not know and yet knew "that day and that hour." As man he did not know. As God he knew.

It is a sensible remark of Gualter, that pressing an excessively literal interpretation of texts like this is the sure way to revive old heresies and

214

to bring into doubt sometimes the divine and sometimes the human nature of Christ.]

There is deep wisdom and mercy in this intentional silence. We have reason to thank God that the thing has been hidden from us. Uncertainty about the date of the Lord's return is calculated to keep believers in an attitude of constant expectation, and to preserve them from despondency. What a dreary prospect the early church would have had before it, if it had known for certain that Christ would not return to earth for at least fifteen hundred years! The hearts of men like Athanasius, Chrysostom and Augustine might well have sunk within them if they had been aware of the centuries of darkness through which the world would pass before their Master came back to take the kingdom. What a life-giving motive, on the other hand, true Christians have perpetually had for a close walk with God! They have never known, in any age, that their Master might not come suddenly to take account of his servants. This very uncertainty has supplied them with a reason for living always ready to meet him.

There is one caution connected with the subject, which must not be overlooked. We must not allow the uncertainty of the time of our Lord's second coming to prevent our giving attention to the unfulfilled prophecies of Scripture. This is a great delusion, but one into which, unhappily, many Christians fall. There is a wide distinction to be drawn between dogmatic and positive assertions about dates, and a humble, prayerful searching into the good things yet to come. Against dogmatism about times and seasons, our Lord's words in this place are a standing caution. But as to the general profitableness of studying prophecy, we can have no plainer authority than the apostle Peter's words: "you will do well to pay attention to it" (2 Peter 1:19); and the apostle John's words in Revelation: "Blessed is the one who reads the words of this prophecy" (Revelation 1:3).

2. Practical duties

Second, we learn from these verses what are the practical duties of all true believers in the prospect of the second coming of Jesus Christ. Our Lord mentions three things to which his people should attend. He tells them plainly that he is coming again one day, in great power and glory. He tells them at the same time that the precise hour and date of that coming are not known. What then are his people to do? They are to keep awake. They are to pray. They are to work.

We are to *keep awake*. We are to live always on our guard. We are to keep our souls in a wakeful, lively state, prepared at any time to meet our Master. We are to beware of anything like spiritual lethargy, dullness, deadness and torpor. The company, the employment of time, the society which induces us to forget Christ and his second coming should be marked, noted and avoided. "Let us not be like others, who are asleep," says the apostle, "but let us be alert and self-controlled" (1 Thessalonians 5:6).

We are to *pray*. We are to keep up habits of regular communion and relations with God. We are to allow no strangeness to come between us and our Father in heaven, but to speak with him daily, so that we may be ready at any moment to see him face to face. Moreover, we are to pray specially about the Lord's coming, that we may be "found spotless, blameless and at peace with him" (2 Peter 3:14), and that our hearts may at no time be "weighed down" with the cares of this life, and so the day come upon us unawares (Luke 21:34).

Finally, we are to *work*. We are to realize that we are all servants of a great Master, who has given work to everyone and expects that work to be done. We are to labor to glorify God, each in our particular sphere and relation. There is always something for everyone to do. We are to strive each of us to shine as a light – to be the salt of our own times – to be faithful witnesses for our Master, and to honor him by conscientiousness and consistency in our daily conversation. Our great desire must be to be found not idle and sleeping, but working and doing.

["Be doing something," says Jerome, "that the devil may always find you engaged." Towards the end of Calvin's life, when his friends wanted him to do less work for his health's sake, he would say: "Would you have my Master find me idle?"]

Such are the simple injunctions to which our Lord wants us to attend. They ought to stir up in the hearts of all who claim to be Christians great self-examination. Are we looking for our Saviour's return? Do we long for his appearing? Can we say with sincerity, "Come, Lord Jesus"? Do we live as if we expected Christ to come again? These are questions which demand serious consideration. May we give them the attention which they deserve!

Does our Lord require us to neglect any of the duties of life, in the expectation of his return? He requires nothing of the kind. He does not tell the farmer to neglect his land, or the laborer his work, the merchant his business or the lawyer his calling. All he asks is that baptized people should live up to the faith into which they were baptized – should live as penitent people – live as believing people – live as people who know that "without holiness no one can see the Lord." So living, we are ready to meet our Master. If we do not live in this way, we are neither fit for death, judgment nor eternity. To live in this way is to be truly happy, because it is to be tuly prepared for anything that may come upon the earth. Let us never be content with a lower standard of practical Christianity than this. The last words of the prophecy are particularly solemn: "What I say to you, I say to everyone: 'Watch!'" (verse 37).

Mark
Chapter 14

The chief priests' plots; the anointing at Bethany *(14:1-9)*

This chapter begins that part of St. Mark's Gospel which describes our Lord's sufferings and death. Hitherto we have chiefly seen our Saviour as our prophet and teacher. We have now to see him as our High Priest. Hitherto we have had to consider his miracles and sayings. We have now to consider his vicarious sacrifice on the cross.

1. God can overrule human wickedness
First, let us observe in these verses how God can disappoint the designs of wicked people and overrule them to his own glory.

It is plain from St. Mark's words, and the parallel passage in St. Matthew, that our Lord's enemies did not intend to make his death a public transaction. They were looking for some sly way to arrest Jesus and kill him. "But not during the Feast," they said, "or the people may riot" (verses 1-2). In short, it would appear that their original plan was to do nothing till the feast of the passover was over, and the passover worshipers had returned to their own homes.

The overruling providence of God completely defeated this political design. The betrayal of our Lord took place at an earlier time than the chief priests had expected. The death of our Lord took place on the very day when Jerusalem was most full of people, and the Passover feast was at its height. In every way the counsel of these wicked men was turned to foolishness. They thought they were going to put an end forever to Christ's spiritual kingdom; and in reality they were helping to establish it. They thought to have made him vile and contemptible by the crucifixion; and in reality they made him glorious. They thought to have put him to death quietly, and without being observed; and instead they were compelled to crucify him publicly, before the whole nation of the Jews. They thought to have silenced his disciples and stopped their teaching; and intead they supplied them with a text and a subject forevermore. So easy is it for God to cause human wrath to praise him (Psalm 76:10).

There is comfort in all this for true Christians. They live in a troubled world, and are often tossed to and fro by anxiety about public events. Let them rest themselves in the thought that everything is ordered for good by an all-wise God. Let them not doubt that everything in the world around them works together for their Father's glory. Let them recall the words of the second Psalm: "The kings of the earth take their stand and the rulers gather together against the LORD" (Psalm 2:2). And yet it goes on: "The One enthroned in heaven laughs; the LORD scoffs at them" (Psalm 2:4). It has been so in the past. It will be so in the future.

2. Good works undervalued
Second, let us observe in these verses how good works are sometimes undervalued and misunderstood. We are told of the good work of a certain woman, in pouring ointment on our Lord's head in a house at Bethany.

[The question has often been raised whether there were one, two or three women who anointed our Lord during his earthly ministry. Theophylact is of opinion that there were three. For this opinion much may be said:

1. The woman spoken of in Luke 7 appears first in order. The city in which this anointing took place does not appear to be Bethany. The woman is spoken of as having been "a sinner" (Luke 7:40). The house is described as that of a Pharisee. The anointing was of our Lord's "feet," and not of his "head." There is strong internal evidence that the whole transaction took place at a comparatively early period of our Lord's ministry. All these points should be noticed.

2. The anointing described by St. John appears next in order. This, we are clearly told, was "six days" before the passover. The person who anointed our Lord was Mary, the sister of Lazarus. The part of him anointed was again his "feet," and not his "head." These points ought also to be noticed.

3. The anointing described by St. Matthew and St. Mark comes third in order. This, we are told, was only "two days" before the feast of the passover. In this case we are not told the name of the woman who anointed our Lord. But we are told that the ointment was poured on his "head."

The question of course occurs to our minds: "Is it likely and probable that this event would take place no less than three times?" In reply to that it may be fairly said that to anoint a person as a mark of honor and respect was far more common in our Lord's time than we suppose; and that anointing was a far more frequent practice than we in our climate can imagine. And it seems perfectly possible that the same thing may have happened three times.

The main difficulty, of course, is the close similarity of the language used at the anointing described by John, and at that described by Matthew and Mark. This can only be explained by supposing that our Lord twice said the same things.]

She did it, no doubt, as a mark of honor and respect, and in token of her own gratitude and love towards him. Yet this act of hers was blamed by some. Their cold hearts could not understand such costly liberality. They called it "waste." They were indignant, and "rebuked her harshly" (verses 4–5).

The spirit of these narrow-minded fault-finders is unhappily all too common. Their followers and successors are to be found in every part of Christ's visible church. There is never any lack of people who decry what they call "extremes" in religion, and are incessantly recommending what they term "moderation" in the service of Christ. If someone devotes time, money and affection to the pursuit of worldly things, they do not blame him. If he gives himself up to the service of money, pleasure or politics, they find no fault. But if the same person devotes himself and all he has to Christ, they can scarcely find words to express their sense of his folly. "He is beside himself." "He is out of his mind." "He is a fanatic." "He is an enthusiast." "He is too righteous." "He is an extremist." In short, they regard it as "waste."

Let charges like these not disturb us if we hear them made against us because we strive to serve Christ. Let us bear them patiently, and remember that they are as old as Christianity itself. Let us pity those who make such charges against believers. They show plainly that they have no sense of obligation to Christ. A cold heart makes a slow hand. Once a person understands the sinfulness of sin and the mercy of Christ in dying for them, they will never think anything too good or too costly to give to Christ. They will rather feel, "How can I repay the LORD for all his goodness to me?" (Psalm 116:12). They will fear wasting their time, talents, money, affections on the things of this world. They will not be afraid of wasting them on the Saviour. They will fear going to extremes about business, money, politics or pleasure, but will not be afraid of doing too much for Christ.

3. Christ's estimation of service done to him

Third, let us observe how highly our Lord esteems any service done to himself. Nowhere, perhaps, in the Gospels do we find such strong praises bestowed on any person as this woman here receives. Three points in particular stand out prominently in our Lord's words, which many who now ridicule and blame others for their religion's sake would do well to consider.

For one thing, our Lord says, *"Why are you bothering her?"* (verse 6). A heart-searching question that, and one which all who persecute others because of their religion would find it hard to answer! What cause can they show? What reason can they give for their conduct? None! None at all. They trouble others out of envy, malice, ignorance and dislike of the true Gospel.

For another thing, our Lord says, *"She has done a beautiful thing to me"* (verse 6). How great and marvelous is that praise, from the lips of the King of kings! Money is often given to the church, or left to charities, from ostentation or other false motives. But it is the person who loves and honors Jesus himself who really "does good works."

For another thing, our Lord says, *"She did what she could"* (verse 8). No stronger word of commendation than that could possibly have been used. Thousands live and die without grace, and are lost eternally, who are always saying, "I try all I can. I do all I can." And yet in saying so, they tell as great a lie as Ananias and Sapphira. Few, it may be feared, are to be found like this woman, and really deserve to have it said of them that they "do what they can."

Let us leave the passage with practical self-application. Let us, like this holy woman whose conduct we have just heard described, devote ourselves and all we have to Christ's glory. Our position in the world may be lowly, and our means of usefulness few. But let us, like her, do what we can.

Finally, let us see in this passage a sweet foretaste of things yet to come on the day of judgment. Let us believe that the same Jesus who here pleaded the cause of his loving sevrant, when she was blamed, will one day plead for all who have been his servants in this world. Let us work on, remembering that his eye is on us and that all we do is noted in his book. Let us take no notice of what people say or think of us because of our religion. The praise of Christ at the last day will more than compensate for all we suffer in this world from unkind tongues.

Judas agrees to betray Christ; the time of the crucifixion (14:10–16)

In these verses, St. Mark tells us how our Lord was delivered into the hands of his enemies. It came about through the treachery of one of his own twelve disciples. The false apostle, Judas Iscariot, betrayed him.

1. The lengths to which false profession of religion may go
First, we ought to note in this passage the lengths a person may go to in a false profession of religion.

It is impossible to conceive a more striking proof of this painful truth than the story of Judas Iscariot. If ever there was a man who at one time looked like a true disciple of Christ, and seemed likely to reach heaven, that man was Judas. He was chosen by the Lord Jesus himself to be an apostle. He was privileged to be a companion of the Messiah, and an eyewitness of his mighty works, thoughout his earthly ministry. He was an associate of Peter, James and John. He was sent out to preach the kingdom of God, and to work miracles in Christ's name. He was regarded by all the eleven apostles as one of themselves. He was so like his fellow disciples that they did not suspect him of being a traitor. And yet this very man turns out at last a false-hearted chid of the devil – departs entirely from the faith – assists our Lord's deadliest enemies, and leaves the world with a worse reputation than anyone since the days of Cain. Never was there such a fall, such an apostasy, such a miserable end to a fair beginning – such a total eclipse of a soul!

And how can this amazing conduct of Judas be accounted for? There is only one answer to that question. "The love of money" was the cause of this unhappy man's ruin. That same groveling covetousness which enslaved the heart of Balaam and brought leprosy to Gehazi was the destruction of Iscariot's soul. No other explanation of his behavior will satisfy the plain statements of Scripture. His act was an act of mean covetousness, without a redeeming feature about it. The Holy Spirit declares plainly, "he was a thief" (John 12:6). And his case stands before the world as an eternal comment on the solemn words, "the love of money is a root of all kinds of evil" (1 Timothy 6:10).

Let us learn from the sad story of Judas to be "clothed with humility," and to be content with nothing short of the grace of the Holy Spirit in our hearts. Knowledge, gifts, professing Christ, privileges, church membership, power of preaching, praying and talking about religion are all useless things if our hearts are not converted. They are all no better than a resounding gong or a clanging cymbal if we have not put off the old man and put on the new. They will not deliver us from hell. Above all, let us remember our Lord's caution to "be on your guard aginst all kinds of greed" (Luke 12:15). It is a sin that spreads like gangrene, and once admitted into our hearts may lead us finally into every wickedness. Let us pray to be content with what we have (Hebrews 13:5). The possession of money is not the one thing needed. Riches entail great peril on the souls of those who have them. The true Christian ought to be far more afraid of being rich than of being poor.

2. The connection between the Passover and Christ's death

Second, we ought to note in this passage the intentional connection between the time of the Jewish Passover and the time of Christ's death. We cannot doubt for a moment that it was not by chance but by God's providential appointment that our Lord was crucified in the Passover week, and on the very day that the Passover lamb was slain. It was meant to draw the attention of the Jewish nation to him as the true Lamb of God. It was meant to bring to their minds the true object and purpose of his death. Every sacrifice, no doubt, was intended to point the Jew onward to the one great sacrifice for sin which Christ offered. But none, certainly, was so striking an image and symbol of our Lord's sacrifice as the slaying of the Passover lamb. It was preeminently an ordinance which was "to lead us to Christ" (Galatians 3:24). Never was there a symbol so full of meaning in the whole circle of Jewish ceremonies as the Passover was at its original institution.

Did the Passover remind the Jews of the marvelous deliverance of their ancestors out of the land of Egypt, when God killed the first-born? No doubt it did. But it was also meant to be a sign to them of the far greater redemption and deliverance from the bondage of sin which was to be brought in by our Lord Jesus Christ.

Did the Passover remind the Jews that by the death of an innocent lamb the families of their ancestors were once exempted from the death of their first-born? No doubt it did. But it was also meant to teach them the far higher truth that the death of Christ on the cross was to be the life of the world.

Did the Passover remind the Jews that the sprinkling of blood on the door-posts of their ancestors' houses preserved them from the sword of the destroying angel? No doubt it did. But it was also meant to show them the far more important doctrine that Christ's blood sprinkled on the human conscience cleanses it from all stain of guilt, and brings safety from the wrath to come.

Did the Passover remind the Jews that none of their ancestors were safe from the destroying angel unless they actually ate of the slain lamb? No doubt it did. But it was meant to guide their minds to the far higher lesson that all who want to receive benefit from Christ's atonement must actually feed on him by faith, and receive him into their hearts.

Let us recall these things, and weigh them well. We shall then see a special appropriateness and beauty in the time set by God for our Lord Jesus Christ's death on the cross. It happened at the very time when the mind of all Israel was being directed to the deliverance from Egypt, and to the events of that wonderful night when it took place. The lamb killed and eaten by every member of the family, the destroying angel, the safety within the blood-sprinkled door, would have been talked over and considered in every Jewish household, the very week that our blessed Lord was killed. It would be strange indeed if such a remarkable death as his, at such a time, did not set many minds thinking, and open many eyes. To what extent we shall never know till the last day.

Let it be a rule with us in the reading of our Bibles to study the types and ordinances of the Mosaic law with prayerful attention. They are all full of Christ. The altar, the scapegoat, the daily burnt offering, the day of atonement are all so many signposts pointing to the great sacrifice offered by our Lord on Calvary. Those who neglect to study the Jewish ordinances, as dark, dull and uninteresting parts of the Bible, only show their own ignorance and miss great advantages. Those who examine them with Christ as the key to their meaning will find them full of Gospel light and comforting truth.

[It may be well to observe in this connection that it is debatable whether the common view of the word "Passover" is the correct one. At any rate, the following passage from Bishop Lowth on Isaiah 31:5 deserves careful consideration. He says:

The common notion of God's passing over the houses of the Israelites is, that in going through the land of Egypt to smite the first-born, seeing the blood on the door of the houses of the Israelites, he passed over, or skipped those houses, and forbore to smite them. But that this is not the true notion of the thing, will be plain from considering the words of the sacred historian, where he describes very explicitly the action: "For Jehovah will pass through to smite the Egyptians; and when he seeth the blood on the lintels and on the two side posts, Jehovah *will spring forward over or before the door*, and will not suffer the destroyer to come into your houses to smite you" (Exodus 12:23). Here are manifestly two distinct agents, with which the notion of passing over is not consistent; for that supposes but one agent. The two agents are, the destroying angel passing through to smite every house, and Jehovah the protector, keeping pace with him, who seeing the door of the Israelites marked with blood, leaps forward, throws himself with a sudden motion in the way, opposes the destroying angel, and protects and saves that house against him, nor suffers him to smite it.

The words of Isaiah 31:5 ought to be studied attentively, in order to understand the fitness and propriety of this interpretation.]

The institution of the Lord's Supper *(14:17–25)*

These verses contain St. Mark's account of the institution of the Lord's Supper. The simplicity of the description deserves special observation. It would have been good for the church if people had not departed from the simple statements of Scripture about this blessed sacrament! It is a sad fact that it has been corrupted by false explanations and superstitious additions, until its real meaning, in many parts of Christendom, is utterly unknown. Let us, however, at present dismiss from our minds all matters of controversy and study the words of St. Mark with a view to our own personal edification.

1. Self-examination should precede reception

First, let us learn from the passage that self-examination should precede the reception of the Lord's Supper. We cannot doubt that this was one object of our Lord's solemn warning, "one of you will betray me – one who is eating with me" (verse 18). He meant to stir up in the minds of his disciples those very searchings of heart which are here so touchingly recorded: "They were saddened, and one by one they said to him, 'Surely not I'" (verse 19). He meant to teach his whole church throughout the world that the time of drawing near to the Lord's table should be a time for diligent self-inquiry.

The benefit of the Lord's Supper depends entirely on the spirit and frame of mind in which we receive it. The bread which we there eat, and the wine which we there drink, have no power to do good to our souls, as medicine does good to our bodies, without the cooperation of our hearts and wills. They will not convey any blessings to us by virtue of the minister's consecration, if we do not receive them rightly, worthily and with faith. To assert, as some do, that the Lord's Supper must do good to all communicants whatever be the state of mind in which they receive it, is a monstrous and unscriptural figment, and has given rise to gross and wicked superstitions.

The state of mind which we should look for in ourselves, before going to the Lord's table, is well described in the Church of England Catechism. We ought to "examine ourselves whether we repent truly of our former sins, whether we firmly resolve to lead a new life, whether we have a lively faith in God's mercy through Christ, and a thankful remembrance of his death, and whether we are in charity with all men." If our conscience can answer these questions satisfactorily, we may receive the Lord's Supper without fear. More than this God does not require of any communicant. Less than this ought never to content us.

Let us look at ourselves in the matter of the Lord's Supper. It is easy to err on either side. On the one hand, we are not to be content with staying away from the Lord's table under the vague plea of unfitness. This is disobeying a plain command of Christ, and thus we are living in sin. But on the other hand we are not to go to the Lord's table as a mere form, and without thought. As long as we receive the sacrament in that state of mind, we derive no good from it, and are guilty of a great transgression. It is an awful thing to be unfit for the sacrament, for this is to be unfit to die. It is a no less awful thing to receive it unworthily, for this is most provoking to God. The only safe course is to be a committed servant of Christ, and to live the life of faith in him. Then we may draw near with boldness and take the sacrament for our comfort.

2. The object is to remind us of Christ's sacrifice

Second, let us learn from these verses that the principal object of the Lord's Supper is to remind us of Christ's sacrifice for us on the cross. The bread is intended to remind us of the "body" of Christ, which was wounded for our transgressions. The wine is intended to remind us of the "blood" of Christ, which was shed to cleanse us from all sin. The atonement and propitiation which our Lord effected by his death as our surety and substitute stand out prominently in the whole ordinance. The false doctrine which some teach, that his death was nothing more than the death of a very holy man who left us an example of how to die, turns the Lord's Supper into an unmeaning ordinance, and cannot possibly be reconciled with our Lord's words at its institution.

A clear understanding of this point is of great importance. It will place us in the right position of mind, and teach us how we ought to feel in drawing near to the Lord's table.

It will produce in us true _humility_ of spirit. The bread and wine will remind us how sinful sin must be when nothing but Christ's death could atone for it.

It will produce in us _hopefulness_ about our souls. The bread and wine will remind us that though our sins are great, a great price has been paid for our redemption.

Not least, it will produce in us gratitude. The bread and wine will remind us how great is our debt to Christ, and how deeply bound we are to glorify him in our lives. May these be the feelings that we experience whenever we receive the Lord's Supper!

3. Its spiritual benefits and the people who may expect them

Third, we learn from these verses the nature of the spiritual benefits which the Lord's Supper is intended to convey, and the people who have a right to expect them. We may gather this lesson from the significant actions which are used in receiving this sacrament. Our Lord commands us to "eat" bread and to "drink" wine. Now eating and drinking are the acts of a living person. The object of eating and drinking is to be strengthened and refreshed. The conclusion we are meant to draw is clearly that the Lord's Supper is appointed for "the strengthening and refreshing of our souls," and that those who ought to partake of it are those who are real living Christians. All these will find this sacrament a means of grace. It will assist them to rest in Christ more simply, and to trust in him more entirely. The visible symbols of bread and wine will aid, confirm and bring life to their faith.

A right view of this point is of the utmost moment in these times. We must always beware of thinking that there is any way of eating Christ's body and drinking Christ's blood but by faith – or that receiving the Lord's Supper will give anyone a different interest in Christ's sacrifice on the cross from that which faith gives. Faith is the one grand means of communication between the soul and Christ. The Lord's Supper can aid, confirm and bring life to faith, but can never supersede it, or supply its absence. Let this never be forgotten. Error on this point is a most fatal delusion, and leads to many superstitions.

Let it be a settled principle in our Christianity that no unbeliever ought to go to the Lord's table, and that the sacrament will not do our souls the slightest good if we do not receive it with repentance and faith. The Lord's Supper is not a converting or justifying ordinance, and those who come to it unconverted and unjustified will go away no better than they came, but rather worse. It is an ordinance for believers, and not for unbelievers – for the living, and not for the dead. It is meant to sustain life, but not to impart it – to strengthen and increase grace, but not to give it – to help faith to grow, but not to sow or plant it. Let these things sink down into our hearts and never be forgotten.

Are we alive to God? This is the great question. If we are, let us go to the Lord's Supper and receive it thankfully, and never turn our backs on the Lord's table. If we do not go, we commit a great sin.

Are we still dead in sin and worldliness? If we are, we have no business at the communion. We are on the broad road that leads to destruction. We must repent. We must be born again. We must be joined to Christ by faith. Then, and not till them, we are fit to be communicants.

[There are two expressions in verse 25 which deserve a special notice. One is "the fruit of the vine." The other is "the kingdom of God."

1. The words "fruit of the vine," applied by our Lord to the cup of wine which he had just been giving to his disciples in the institution of the Lord's Supper, appear entirely to overthrow the doctrine of transubstantiation. The wine, it appears, did not really and literally become Christ's blood as the Roman Catholics say. Our Lord himself speaks of it as the juice of grapes, "the fruit of the vine." It is clear therefore that when he said of that cup of wine before, "this is my blood" (verse 24), he meant nothing more than "this represents – is a symbol of – my blood."

2. The words "kingdom of God," applied by our Lord to a time and state of things still in the future, appear to show plainly that he did not consider God's kingdom to have come when he spoke. Moreover the words have not yet received a fulfillment, as it is not known that our Lord administered the Lord's Supper to his disciples after his resurrection. The words therefore are meant to turn our minds towards the time of our Lord's second coming. Then, and not till then, "the kingdom of God" will be fully set up. Then, and not till then, we shall sit down at the marriage supper of the Lamb, and drink the new wine in the kingdom.]

Christ's foreknowledge of his disciples' weakness; the self-ignorance of believers (14:26–31)

1. Christ's foreknowledge of his disciples' weakness
First, we see in these verses how well our Lord knew how weak his disciples would be. He tells them plainly what they were going to do:

"You will all fall away" (verse 27). He tells Peter in particular of the astounding sin which he was about to commit: "Today – yes, tonight – before the cock crows twice you yourself will disown me three times" (verse 30).

Yet our Lord's foreknowledge did not prevent his choosing these twelve disciples to be his apostles. He allowed them to be his intimate friends and companions, knowing perfectly well what they would one day do. He granted them the mighty privilege of being continually with him and hearing his voice, with a clear foresight of the sad weakness and lack of faith which they would exhibit at the end of his ministry. This is remarkable, and deserves to be continually remembered.

Let us take comfort in the thought that the Lord Jesus does not throw off his believing people because of failures and imperfections. He knows what they are. He takes them, as the husband takes the wife, with all their blemishes and defects, and, once joined to him by faith, will never put them away. He is a merciful and compassionate High Priest. It is his glory to pass over the transgressions of his people and to cover their many sins. He knew what they were before conversion – wicked, guilty and defiled; yet he loved them. He knows what they will be after conversion – weak, erring and frail; yet he loves them. He has undertaken to save them, notwithstanding all their shortcomings, and what he has undertaken he will perform.

Let us learn to pass a charitable judgment on the conduct of those who claim to believe. Let us not set them down in a low place and say they have no grace, because we see in them much weakness and corruption. Let us remember that our Master in heaven bears with their infirmities, and let us try to bear with them too. The church of Christ is little better than a great hospital. We ourselves are all, more or less, weak, and all daily need the skillful treatment of the heavenly Physician. There will be no complete cures till the resurrection day.

2. Comfort missed by indifference

Second, we see in these verses how much comfort professing Christians may miss by indifference and inattention. Our Lord spoke plainly of his resurrection: "After I have risen, I will go ahead of you into Galilee" (verse 28). Yet his words appear to have been thrown away, and spoken in vain. Not one of his disciples seems to have noticed them, or treasured them up in his heart. When he was betrayed, they deserted him. When he was crucified, they were almost in despair. And when he rose again on the third day, they would not believe that it was true. They had heard of it frequently with the hearing of the ear, but it had never made any impression on their hearts.

What an exact picture we have here of human nature! How often we see the very same thing among professing Christians today! How many truths we read year by year in the Bible, and yet remember them no more than if we had never read them at all! How many words of wisdom we hear in sermons heedlessly and thoughtlessly, and live on as if we had never heard them! The days of darkness and affliction come upon us by and by, and then we prove unarmed and unprepared. On sick-beds and in mourning we see a meaning in texts and passages which we at one time heard listlessly and unconcernedly. Things flash across our minds at such times and make us feel ashamed that we had not noticed them before. We then remember that we read them and heard them and saw them, but they made no impression on us. Like Hagar's well in the wilderness, they were close at hand, but, like Hagar, we never saw them (Genesis 21:19).

Let us pray for a quick understanding in hearing and reading God's Word. Let us search into every part of it, and not lose any precious truth in it for lack of care. So doing, we shall lay up a good foundation against the time to come, and in sorrow and sickness be found armed.

Let us note how little reason ministers have to be surprised if the words that they preach in sermons are often unnoticed and unheeded. They only drink of the same cup with their Master. Even he said many things which were not noticed when first spoken. And yet we know that "no one ever spoke like this man." "A student is not above his teacher, nor a servant above his master" (Matthew 10:24). We need patience. Truths that seem neglected at first often bear fruit after many days.

3. Ignorant self-confidence

Third, we see in these verses how much ignorant self-confidence may sometimes be found in the hearts of professing Christians. The apostle Peter could not think it possible that he could ever disown his Lord. "Even if I have to die with you," he says, "I will never disown you" (verse 31). And he did not stand alone in his confidence. The other disciples were of the same opinion. "All the others said the same" (verse 31).

Yet what did all this confident boasting come to? Twelve hours did not pass before all the disciples deserted our Lord and fled. Their loud protestations were all forgotten. The present danger swept all their promises of fidelity clean away. So little do we know how we shall act in any particular position until we are placed in it! So much do present circumstances alter our feelings!

Let us learn to pray for humility. "Pride goes before destruction, a haughty spirit before a fall" (Proverbs 16:18). There is far more wickedness in all our hearts than we know. We never can tell how far we might fall if once placed in temptation. There is no degree of sin into which the greatest saint may not run if not upheld by the grace of God, and if they do not watch and pray. The seeds of every wickedness lie hidden in our hearts. They only need a convenient time to spring up into a mischievous vitality. "So, if you think you are standing firm, be careful that you don't fall!" (1 Corinthians 10:12). "He who trusts in himself is a fool" (Proverbs 28:26). Let our daily prayer be, "Uphold me, and I shall be delivered" (Psalm 119:117).

The agony in the garden; the apostles' weakness (14:32–42)

The story of our Lord's agony in the garden of Gethsemane is a deep and mysterious passage of Scripture. It contains things which the wisest divines cannot fully explain. Yet it has upon its surface plain truths of most momentous importance.

1. The burden of a world's sin

First, let us note how keenly our Lord felt the burden of a world's sin. It is written that he "began to be deeply distressed and troubled. 'My soul is overwhelmed with sorrow to the point of death,' he said to them" (verses 33–34) – and that "he fell to the ground and prayed that if possible the hour might pass from him" (verse 35).

There is only one reasonable explanation of these expressions. It was no mere fear of the physical suffering of death which drew them from our Lord's lips. It was a sense of the enormous load of human guilt, which began at that time to press upon him in a special way. It was a sense of the unutterable weight of our sins and transgressions which were then specially laid upon him. He was "becoming a curse for us" (Galatians 3:13). He was taking up our infirmities and carrying our sorrows, according to the covenant he came on earth to fulfill. He who had no sin was being made sin for us (2 Corinthians 5:21). His holy nature felt acutely the hideous burden laid on him. These were the reasons of his extraordinary sorrow.

We ought to see in our Lord's agony in Gethsemane the exceeding sinfulness of sin. It is a subject on which the thoughts of professing Christians are far below what they should be. The careless, light way in which such sins as swearing, Sabbath-breaking, lying and the like are often spoken of is a painful evidence of the low condition of our moral feelings. Let the recollection of Gethsemane have a sanctifying effect on us. Whatever others do, let us never "mock at making amends for sin" (Proverbs 14:9).

2. Prayer in time of trouble

Second, let us note what an exmaple our Lord gives us of the importance of prayer in time of trouble. In the hour of his distress we find him employing this great remedy. Twice we are told that when his soul was exceeding sorrowful, he "prayed" (verses 35 and 39).

We shall never find a better prescription than this for bearing affliction patiently. The first person to whom we should turn in our trouble is God. The first complaint we should make should be in the form of a prayer. The reply may not be given immediately. The relief we want may not be granted at once. The thing that tries us may never be removed and taken away. But the mere act of pouring out our hearts, and unbosoming ourselves at a throne of grace will do us good. The advice of St. James is wise and weighty: "Is any one of you in trouble? He should pray" (James 5:13).

3. Submission of will to the will of God

Third, let us note what a striking example our Lord gives of submission of will to the will of God. Deeply as his human nature felt the pressure of a world's guilt, he still prays that "if possible the hour might pass from him" (verse 35). "Take this cup from me. Yet not what I will, but what you will" (verse 36).

[People are so apt to run into error on the subject of the divine and human natures in Christ, that the following quotation from Petter on Mark may be worth reading.

There are two distinct wills in Christ. But although they be truly distinct and different one from the other, yet they are not contrary one to the other, but they are subordinate each to the other; the human will of Christ being always subject to his divine will, and most ready to be ordered and ruled by it. Therefore here we see that he doth submit his will, as he was man, to the divine will of the Father, which divine will of the Father was also Christ's own will. This truth we are to hold and maintain against those old heretics, which were called Monothelites, because they held there was but one kind of will in Christ, namely his divine will. This heresy sprung up in the Eastern church about 600 years after Christ; and it did very much molest and trouble the church for many years. It was a branch of the gross heresy of Eutyches which sprung up 200 years before. The Eutyches confounded the two natures in Christ, holding that as there was but one Person after the personal union, so there was but one nature in Christ, viz. the divine nature, the human nature being swallowed up. To maintain this the better, his followers maintained that Christ had but one kind of will. This heresy was condemned by the 6th general council at Constantinople, as well as by other ancient councils. And the fathers of the church in those times did confute it by these very words of our Saviour which we have now in hand.]

We can imagine no higher degree of perfection that that which is here set before us. To take patiently whatever God sends – to like nothing but what God likes – to wish nothing but what God approves – to prefer pain, if it please God to send it, rather than ease, if God does not think fit to bestow it – to lie passive under God's hand, and know no will but his – this is the highest standard at which we can aim, and of this our Lord's conduct in Gethsemane is a perfect pattern.

Let us strive and labor to have "the mind that was in Christ" in this matter. Let us daily pray and endeavor to be enabled to mortify our self-will. It is for our happiness to do so. Nothing brings us so much misery on earth as having our own way. It is the best proof of real grace to mortify self-will. Knowledge, gifts, convictions, feelings and wishes are all very uncertain evidences. They are often to be found in unconverted people. But a continually increasing disposition to submit our own wills to the will of God is a far more healthy symptom. It is a sign that we are really "growing in grace, and in the knowledge of Jesus Christ."

4. Weakness even in the best Christians

Fourth, let us note in these verses how much weakness may be found even in the best Christians. We have a painful illustration of this truth in the conduct of Peter, James and John. They slept when they ought to have kept watch and prayed. Though invited by our Lord to watch with him, they slept. Though warned a short time before that danger was at hand, and their faith likely to fail, they slept. Though fresh from the Lord's table, with all its touching solemnities, they slept. Never was there a more striking proof that the best of people are only human, and that so long as saints are in the body they are subject to weakness.

These things are written for our learning. Let us take care that they are not written in vain. Let us always be on our guard against the slothful, indolent, lazy spirit in religion, which is natural to us all, and specially in the matter of our private prayers. When we feel that spirit creeping over us, let us remember Peter, James and John in the garden, and take care.

The solemn advice which our Lord addresses to his disciples should often ring in our ears: "Watch and pray so that you will not fall into temptation. The spirit is willing, but the body is weak" (verse 38). It should be the Christian's daily motto from the time of his conversion to the hour of his death.

Are we true Christians? Do we want to keep our souls awake? Let us not forget that we have within us a double nature – a ready spirit and weak body – a bodily nature inclined to evil, and a spiritual nature inclined to good. These two are contrary one to the other (Galatians

5:17). Sin and the devil will always find helpers in our hearts. If we do not crucify and rule over the body, it will often rule over us and bring us to shame.

Are we true Christians, and do we want to keep our souls awake? Then let us never forget to "watch and pray." We must watch like soldiers – we are in enemy territory. We must always be on our guard. We must fight a daily fight and war a daily warfare. The Christian's rest is yet to come. We must pray without ceasing, regularly, habitually, carefully and at stated times. We must pray as well as watch, and watch as well as pray. Watching without praying is self-confidence and self-conceit. Praying without watching is enthusiasm and fanaticism. Those who know their own weakness, and knowing it both watch and pray, are those who will be upheld and not allowed to fall.

Christ taken prisoner by his enemies *(14:43–52)*

1. The nature of the kingdom little understood
First, let us notice in these verses how little our Lord's enemies understood the nature of his kingdom. We read that Judas came to take him "with a crowd armed with swords and clubs" (verse 43). It was evidently expected that our Lord would be vigorously defended by his disciples, and that he would not be taken prisoner without fighting. The chief priests and teachers of the law clung obstinately to the idea that our Lord's kingdom was a worldly kingdom, and therefore supposed that it would be upheld by worldly means. They had yet to learn the solemn lesson contained in our Lord's words to Pilate, "My kingdom is not of this world. . . . Now my kingdom is from another place" (John 18:36).

We would do well to remember this in all our attempts to extend the kingdom of true religion. It is not to be propagated by violence, or by bodily strength. "The weapons we fight with are not the weapons of the world" (2 Corinthians 10:4). "'Not by might nor by power, but by my Spirit,' says the LORD Almighty" (Zechariah 4:6). The cause of truth does not need force to maintain it. False religions, like Islam, have often been spread by the sword. False Christianity, like that of the Roman church, has often been enforced on people by bloody persecutions. But the real Gospel of Christ requires no such aids as these. It stands by the power of the Holy Spirit. It grows by the hidden influence of the Holy Spirit on people's hearts and consciences. There is no clearer sign of a bad cause in religion than a readiness to appeal to the sword.

2. Everything in our Lord's passion was according to God's Word

Second, let us notice in these verses how all things in our Lord's passion happened according to God's Word. His own speech to those who took him shows this in a striking manner: "the Scriptures must be fulfilled" (verse 49).

There was no accident or chance in any part of the close of our Lord's earthly ministry. The steps in which he walked from Gethsemane to Calvary were all marked out hundreds of years before. Psalm 22 and Isaiah 53 were literally fulfilled. The wrath of his enemies, his rejection by his own people, his being dealt with as a criminal, his being encircled by a band of evil men – all had been known before, all had been foretold. Everything that took place was only the working out of God's great design to provide an atonement for a world's sin. The armed men whom Judas brought to lay hands on Jesus were, like Nebuchadnezzar and Sennacherib, unconscious instruments in carrying out God's purposes.

Let us rest our souls on the thought that all around us is ordered and ruled over by God's almighty wisdom. The course of this world may often be contrary to our wishes. The position of the church may often be very unlike what we desire. The wickedness of worldly men and the inconsistencies of believers may often afflict our souls. But there is a hand above us, moving the vast machine of this universe, and making everything work together for his glory. The Scriptures are being fulfilled year by year. Not one detail in them will ever fail to be accomplished. The kings of the earth may take their stand, and the rulers may gather together against Christ (Psalm 2:2), but the resurrection morning will prove that, even at the darkest time, everything was being done according to the will of God.

3. The faith of true believers may give way

Third, let us notice in these verses how much the faith of true believers may give way. We are told that when Judas and his company laid hands on our Lord, eleven disciples "deserted him and fled" (verse 50). Perhaps up to that moment they were buoyed up by the hope that our Lord would work a miracle and set himself free. But when they saw no miracle worked, their courage failed them entirely. Their former protestations were all forgotten. Their promises to die with their Master rather than disown him were all cast to the winds. The fear of present danger got the better of faith. The sense of immediate peril drove every other feeling out of their minds. They all "deserted him and fled."

There is something deeply instructive in this incident. It deserves the attentive study of all professing Christians. Happy is the one who notes the conduct of our Lord's disciples, and gathers wisdom from it!

Let us learn from the flight of these eleven disciples not to be over-confident in our own strength. The fear of other people does indeed bring a snare. We never know what we may do if we are tempted, or to what extent our faith may give way. Let us be clothed with humility.

Let us learn to be charitable in our judgment of other Christians. Let us not expect too much from them, or set them down as having no grace at all, if we see them overtaken in a fault. Let us not forget that even our Lord's chosen apostles deserted him in his time of need. Yet they rose again by repentance, and became pillars of the church of Christ.

Finally, let us leave the passage with a deep sense of our Lord's ability to sympathize with his believing people. If there is one trial greater than another, it is the trial of being disappointed in those we love. It is a bitter cup, which all true Christians have frequently to drink. Ministers fail them. Relations fail them. Friends fail them. One cistern after another proves to be broken, and to hold no water. But let them take comfort in the thought that there is one unfailing Friend, namely Jesus, who is able to sympathize with our weaknesses, and has tasted all our sorrows. Jesus knows what it is to see friends and disciples failing him in the time of need. Yet he bore it patiently, and loved them despite everything. He is never tired of forgiving. Let us try to be the same. Jesus, at any rate, will never fail us. It is written, "his compassions never fail" (Lamentations 3:22).

[The question has often been asked, "Who was the 'young man' mentioned at the end of this passage, who was seized and who fled naked?" St. Mark is the only evangelist who relates this detail; and he has given us no clue to further knowledge as to who it was, or why the event is mentioned.

No satisfactory answer to these questions has yet been given. The most that can be said of any of the explanations attempted is that they are conjectures and speculations.

Petter, in his commentary on Mark, says:

Some have thought that it was one of the twelve disciples, viz. James the son of Alpheus, the Lord's brother, or kinsman of our Saviour (whose appearance was perhaps like our Lord's). This is the view of Epiphanius and Jerome. Others have thought that it was John, the beloved disciple. This is the view of Ambrose, Chrysostom and Gregory. But it could be neither of them, nor any other of the twelve, because it is said immediately before, that they "all fled" upon the taking of our Saviour, whereas this young man followed our Saviour at this time. It is more likely that it was some good young man, who dwelt near the garden of Gethsemane, who hearing the noise and stir that was made about the taking and binding of our Saviour, did arise suddenly out of his bed to see what was the matter, and perceiving that they had cruelly taken and bound our Saviour, and were leading him away, did follow after him to see what would be done with him, whereby it appears that he was a well-wisher to our Saviour.

Theophylact and Euthymius think it probable that it was some young man who followed our Lord from the house where he ate the Passover with his disciples. Some think that it was the Evangelist Mark himself.

Some have thought that St. Mark's purpose in relating the event is to show the cruelty, rage and ferocity of those who took our Lord. They were ready to lay hands on anyone who was anywhere near him, and to make prisoners indiscriminately of all who even appeared to be connected with him.

Some have thought that the whole business shows the utter desertion of our Lord. "This young man," says Claius, "would rather escape naked than be taken as one of the followers of Christ."

Some have thought that it is related to show the real peril in which the disciples were, and to make it plain that they saved their lives only by their flight.

One eminent divine regards the whole event as strongly figurative. He sees in it an antitype of what took place on the day of atonement, and at the cleansing of a leper. He considers the young man escaping to represent the goat let go free, and the bird let loose; while our Lord represents the goat offered up (Leviticus 16:22) and the bird slain (Leviticus 14:7).

I offer no opinion on any of the above explanations, excepting that I look on the last as eminently fanciful and unsatisfactory. Bullinger remarks sensibly, "It does not interest us much to know who this young man was, and it would not bring any very great fruit to us if we did know. If it had been useful and wholesome for us to know, the Spirit of God would not have been silent, seeing that he is often marvelously diligent in relating very minute things."]

Christ condemned before the high priest (14:53–65)

The book of Ecclesiastes tells us that one of the evils under the sun is when "fools are put in many high positions, while the rich occupy the low ones" (Ecclesiastes 10:6). We can imagine no more complete illustration of his words than the state of things we have recorded in this passage. We see the Son of God, "in whom are hidden all the treasures of wisdom and knowledge" (Colossians 2:3), arraigned as a criminal before "all the chief priests, elders and teachers of the law" (verse 53). We see the heads of the Jewish nation combining together to kill their own Messiah, and judging him who will one day come in glory to judge them and all mankind. These things sound amazing, but they are true.

1. Christians foolishly thrust themselves into temptation
First, let us observe in these verses how foolishly Christians sometimes thrust themselves into temptation. We are told that when our Lord was led away prisoner, "Peter followed him at a distance, right into the

courtyard of the high priest. There he sat with the guards and warmed himself at the fire" (verse 54).

[In the expression "warmed himself at the fire" it is worthy of note that the Greek word which we translate "fire" is not the same as that translated "fire" in John 18:18. It would rather bear the meaning of "light," or a fire so blazing as to give light.

The remark is not without interest, as it explains how easily Peter was recognized and discovered by those who sat around him, as one of Christ's disciples. The bright light of the fire shining on him made concealment impossible.]

There was no wisdom in this act. Having once deserted his Master and fled, he ought to have remembered his own weakness and not have ventured into danger again. It was an act of rashness and presumption. It brought on him fresh trials of faith, for which he was utterly unprepared. It threw him into bad company, where he was not likely to get good but harm. It paved the way for his last and greatest transgression – his threefold denial of his Master.

But it is a truth of experience that ought never to be overlooked, that when a believer has once begun to backslide and leave his first faith he seldom stops short at his first mistake. He seldom makes only one stumble. He seldom commits only one fault. A blindness seems to come over the eyes of his understanding. He appears to throw overboard his common sense and discretion. Like a stone rolling downhill, the further he goes on in sinning, the faster and more decided is his course. Like David, he may begin with idleness and end with committing every possible crime. Like Peter, he may begin with cowardice, go on to foolish trifling with temptation and then end with disowning Christ.

If we know anything of true saving religion, let us always beware of the beginnings of backsliding. It is like the letting out of water, first a drop and then a torrent. Once out of the way of holiness, there is no saying to what we may come. Once giving way to petty inconsistencies, we may find ourselves one day committing every sort of wickedness. Let us keep far from the brink of evil. Let us not play with fire. Let us never fear being too particular, too strict and too precise. No request in the Lord's prayer is more important than the last but one, "Lead us not into temptation."

2. What Christ endured from lying lips

Second, let us observe in these verses how much our Lord Jesus Christ had to endure from lying lips when he was on trial before the chief priests. We are told that "many testified falsely against him, but their statements did not agree" (verse 56).

We can easily conceive that this was not the least heavy part of our blessed Saviour's passion. To be seized unjustly as a criminal, and put on trial when innnocent, is a severe affliction. But to hear people inventing false charges against us and coining slanders – to listen to all the malignant virulence of unscrupulous tongues let loose against our character, and know that it is all untrue – this is a cross indeed! "The words of a gossip are as wounds" (Proverbs 18:8, KJV). "Save me, O LORD, from lying lips and from deceitful tongues" (Psalm 120:2). All this was a part of the cup which Jesus drank for our sakes. Great indeed was the price at which our souls were redeemed!

Let it never surprise true Christians if they are slandered and misrepresented in this world. They must not expect to fare better than their Lord. Let them rather look forward to it, as a matter of course, and see in it a part of the cross which everyone must bear after conversion. Lies and false reports are among Satan's choicest weapons. When he cannot deter people from serving Christ, he labors to harass them and make Christ's service uncomfortable. Let us bear it patiently, and not count it a strange thing. The words of the Lord Jesus should often come to our minds: "Woe to you when all men speak well of you" (Luke 6:26). "Blessed are you when people insult you, persecute you and falsely say all kind of evil against you because of me" (Matthew 5:11).

3. Christ's testimony to his own Messiahship and second coming

Third, let us observe in these verses what distinct testimony our Lord here bore to his own Messiahship and second coming in glory. The high priest asks him the solemn question, "Are you the Christ, the Son of the Blessed One?" (verse 61). He receives at once the emphatic reply, "I am. And you will see the Son of Man sitting at the right hand of the Mighty One and coming on the clouds of heaven" (verse 62).

These words of our Lord ought always to be remembered. The Jews could never say after these words that they were not clearly told that Jesus of Nazareth was the Christ of God. Before the great council of their priests and elders, he declared, "I am the Christ." The Jews could never say after these words that he was so lowly and poor a person that he was not worth believing. He warned them plainly that his glory and greatness was all yet to come. They were only deferred and postponed till his second coming. They would yet see him in royal power and majesty, "sitting at the right hand of the Mighty One," coming in the clouds of heaven, a judge, a conqueror and a King. If Israel was unbelieving, it was not because Israel was not told what to believe.

Let us leave the passage with a deep sense of the reality and certainty of our Lord Jesus Christ's second coming. Once more at the very end of his ministry, and in the face of his deadly enemies, we find him asserting the mighty truth that he will come again to judge the world. Let it be one of the leading truths in our own personal Christianity. Let us live in the daily recollection that our Saviour is one day coming back to this world. Let the Christ in whom we believe be not only the Christ who died for us and rose again – the Christ who lives for us and intercedes – but the Christ who will one day return in glory, to gather together and reward his people, and to punish fearfully all his enemies.

Peter disowns Christ three times (14:66–72)

A shipwreck is a sad sight, even when no lives are lost. It is sad to think of the destruction of property, and disappointment of hopes which generally attend it. It is painful to see the suffering and hardship which the ship's crew often have to undergo in their struggle to escape from drowning. Yet no shipwreck is half so sad a sight as the backsliding and fall of a true Christian. Though raised again by God's mercy and finally saved from hell, he loses much by his fall. Such a sight we have brought before our minds in these verses. We are there told that most painful and instructive story, how Peter disowned his Lord.

1. How far and how shamefully a great saint may fall

First, let us learn from these verses how far and how shamefully a great saint may fall. We know that Simon Peter was an eminent apostle of Jesus Christ. He was one who had received special commendation from our Lord's lips, after a noble confession of his Messiahship: "Blessed are you, Simon son of Jonah. . . . I will give you the keys of the kingdom of heaven" (Matthew 16:17, 19). He was one who had enjoyed special privileges, and had special mercies shown to him. Yet here we see this same Simon Peter so entirely overcome by fear that he actually disowns his Lord. He declares that he does not know the one he had accompanied and lived with for three years! He declares that he does not know the one who had healed his own mother-in-law, taken him up onto the mountain of transfiguration, and saved him from drowning in the Sea of Galilee! And he not only disowns his Master once, but does it three times! And he not only disowns him simply, but does it cursing and swearing (verse 71)! And above all, he does all this in the face of the plainest warnings, and in spite of his own loud protestation that he would do nothing of the kind, but rather die!

These things are written to show the church of Christ what human nature is, even in the best of men. They are intended to teach us that, even after conversion and renewal of the Holy Spirit, believers are subject to weakness and liable to fall. They are meant to impress upon us the immense importance of daily watchfulness, prayerfulness and humility, so long as we are in the body. "So if you think you are standing firm, be careful that you don't fall!" (1 Corinthians 10:12).

Let us carefully remember that Simon Peter's case does not stand alone. The word of God contains many other examples of the infirmity of true believers, which we shall do well to observe. The stories of Noah, Abraham, David and Hezekiah will supply us with sad proof that "the infection of sin remains even in the regenerate," and that no one is so strong as to be beyond the danger of falling. Let us not forget this. Let us walk humbly with our God. "Blessed is the man who always fears the LORD" (Proverbs 28:14).

2. How small a temptation may cause a great fall

Second, let us learn from these verses how small a temptation may cause a saint to have a great fall. The beginning of Peter's trial was nothing more than the simple remark of "one of the servant girls of the high priest" (verse 66). "You also were with that Nazarene, Jesus" (verse 67). There is nothing to show that these words were spoken with any hostile purpose. For anything we can see, they might fairly mean that this girl remembered that Peter used to be a companion of our Lord. But this simple remark was enough to overthrow the faith of an eminent apostle, and to make him begin to disown his Master. The chief and foremost of our Lord's chosen disciples is thrown down, not by the threats of armed men, but by the saying of one powerless girl!

There is something deeply instructive in this fact. It ought to teach us that no temptation is too small and trifling to overcome us, if we do not watch and pray to be upheld. If God is for us we may remove mountains and get the victory over a host of foes. "I can do everything through him who gives me strength" (Philippians 4:13). If God withdraws his grace, and leaves us to ourselves, we are like a city without gates and walls, a prey to the first enemy, however weak and contemptible.

Let us beware of making light of temptations because they seem little and insignificant. There is nothing little that concerns our souls. A little yeast works through the whole batch of dough. A little spark may kindle a great fire. A little leak may sink a great ship. A little provocation may bring out from our hearts great corruption, and end in bringing our souls into great trouble.

3. Backsliding brings saints into great sorrow

Third, let us learn from these verses that backsliding brings saints into great sorrow. The conclusion of the passage is very affecting. "Peter remembered the words Jesus had spoken to him: 'Before the cock crows twice you will disown me three times'" (verse 72). Who can pretend to describe the feelings that must have flashed across the apostle's mind? Who cna conceive the shame, confusion, self-reproach and bitter remorse which must have overwhelmed his soul? To have fallen so foully! To have fallen so repeatedly! To have fallen in the face of such plain warnings! All these must have been cutting thoughts. The iron must indeed have entered into his soul. There is deep and solemn meaning in the one single expression used about him – "he broke down and wept" (verse 72).

The experience of Peter is only the experience of all God's servants who have yielded to temptation. Lot, Samson, David and Jehoshaphat in Bible history, Cranmer and Jewell in the records of the English church – they have all left evidence, like Peter, that "the faithless will be fully repaid for their ways" (Proverbs 14:14). Like Peter, they went terribly wrong. Like Peter, they repented truly. But, like Peter, they found that they reaped a bitter harvest in this world. Like Peter, they were freely pardoned and forgiven. But, like Peter, they shed many tears.

Let us leave the passage with the settled conviction that sin is sure to lead to sorrow, and that the way of most holiness is always the way of most happiness. The Lord Jesus has mercifully provided that it shall never profit his servants to walk carelessly and to give way to temptation. If we will turn our backs on him we shall be sure to smart for it. Though he forgives us, he will make us feel the folly of our own ways. Those that follow the Lord most fully will always follow him most comfortably. "The sorrows of those will increase who run after other gods" (Psalm 16:4).

Mark
Chapter 15

Christ condemned before Pilate *(15:1–15)*

These verses begin the chapter in which St. Mark describes the killing of "the Lamb of God, who takes away the sin of the world." It is a part of the Gospel story which should always be read with particular reverence. We should recall that Christ was cut off, not for himself, but for us (Daniel 9:26). We should remember that his death is the life of our souls, and that unless his blood had been shed, we would have perished miserably in our sins.

1. Proof that the times of the Messiah had come
First, let us note in these verses what a striking proof the Jewish rulers gave to their own nation that the times of the Messiah had come.

The chapter opens with the fact that the chief priests bound Jesus and "turned him over to Pilate," the Roman governor (verse 1). Why did they do so? Because they no longer had the power to put anyone to death, and were under the dominion of the Romans. By this one act they declared that the prophecy of Jacob was fulfilled. The scepter had departed from Judah, and the ruler's staff from between his feet; he to whom it belongs must have come (Genesis 49:10). Yet there is nothing whatever to show that they remembered this prophecy. Their eyes were blinded. They either could not or would not see what they were doing.

Let us never forget that wicked people are often fulfilling God's predictions to their own ruin, and yet do not know it. In the very height of their madness, folly and unbelief, they are often unconsciously supplying fresh evidence that the Bible is true. The unhappy scoffers who make a joke of all serious religion, and can scarcely talk of Christianity without ridicule and scorn, would do well to remember that their conduct was long ago foreseen and foretold. "In the last days scoffers will come, scoffing and following their own evil desires" (2 Peter 3:3).

2. Christ's meekness and lowliness

Second, let us note in these verses the meekness and lowliness of our Lord Jesus Christ. When he stood before Pilate's bar and was "accused of many things," he did not answer. He was content to endure the sinners speaking against him, not answering them (Hebrews 12:3). Though he was innocent of any transgression, he submitted to hear groundless accusations made against him without a murmur. Great is the contrast between the second Adam and the first! Our first ancestor Adam was guilty, and yet tried to excuse himself. The second Adam was guiltless, and yet made no defense at all. "As a sheep before her shearers is silent, so he did not open his mouth" (Isaiah 53:7).

Let us learn a practical lesson from our Saviour's example. Let us learn to suffer patiently, and not to complain, whatever God may think fit to lay upon us. Let us take care that we do not offend in our speech when we are tempted (Psalm 39:1). Let us beware of giving way to irritation and ill-temper, however provoking and undeserved our trials may seem to be. Nothing in the Christian character glorifies God so much as patient suffering. "How is it to your credit if you receive a beating for doing wrong and endure it? But if you suffer for doing good and endure it, this is commendable before God. To this you were called, because Christ suffered for you, that you should follow in his steps" (1 Peter 2:20–21).

3. Pilate's wavering

Third, let us note in these verses the wavering and undecided conduct of Pilate.

It is clear from the passage that Pilate was convinced of our Lord's innocence. He knew that "it was out of envy that the chief priests had handed Jesus over to him" (verse 10). We see him feebly struggling for a time to obtain our Lord's acquittal, and so to satisfy his own conscience. At last he yields to the importunity of the Jews, and "wanting to satisfy the crowd" hands Jesus over to be crucified – to the eternal disgrace and ruin of his own soul.

A man in high places without religious principles is one of the most pitiable sights in the world. He is like a large ship tossed to and fro on the sea without compass or rudder. His very greatness surrounds him with temptations and snares. It gives him power for good or evil, which if he know not how to use it aright, is sure to bring him into difficulties, and make him unhappy. Let us pray much for great men. They need great grace to keep them from the devil. High places are slippery places. No wonder St. Paul recommends intercession "for kings and all those in authority" (1 Timothy 2:1). Let us not envy great men. They have many special temptations. How hard it will be for a rich man to enter the kingdom of God. "Should you then seek great things for yourself? Seek them not" (Jeremiah 45:5).

4. The guilt of the Jews

Fourth, let us note in these verses the great guilt of the Jews in the matter of the death of Christ. At the eleventh hour the chief priests had an opportunity of repenting, if they took it. They had the choice given them whether Jesus or Barabbas should be let go free. Coolly and deliberately they persevered in their bloody work. They chose to have the Prince of Life put to deah. The *power* of putting our Lord to death was no longer theirs. The *responsibility* of his death they publicly took upon themselves. "What shall I do with him?" was Pilate's question. "Crucify him!" was the awful answer. The agents in our Lord's death were undoubtedly Gentiles. But the guilt of our Lord's death must always rest chiefly on the Jews.

We are amazed at the wickedness of the Jews at this part of our Lord's story – and no wonder. To reject Christ and choose Barabbas was indeed an astounding act! It seems as if blindness, madness and folly could go no further. But let us take care that we do not unwittingly follow their example. Let us beware that we are not found at last to have chosen Barabbas and rejected Christ. The service of sin and the service of God are continually before us. The friendship of the world and the friendship of Christ are continually pressed upon our notice. Are we making the right choice? Are we clinging to the right

Friend? These are solemn questions. Happy are those who can give them a satisfactory answer.

5. The release of Barabbas a symbol of the Gospel

Fifth, let us note in these verses what a striking symbol the release of Barabbas gives of the Gospel plan of salvation. The guilty is set free and the innocent is put to death. The great sinner is delivered, and the sinless one remains bound. Barabbas is spared, and Christ is crucified.

We have in this striking fact a vivid picture of the manner in which God pardons and justifies the ungodly. He does it because Christ suffered in their place, the just for the unjust. They deserve punishment, but a more powerful substitute has suffered for them. They deserve eternal death, but a glorious surety has died for them. We are all by nature in the position of Barabbas. We are guilty, wicked and worthy of condemnation, but "when we were without hope," Christ the innocent died for the ungodly. And now God for Christ's sake can be just, and yet "the one who justifies those who have faith in Jesus" (Romans 3:26).

Let us bless God that we have such a glorious salvation set before us. Our plea must always be, not that we deserve to be acquitted, but that Christ has died for us. Let us be careful that, having such a great salvation set before us, we really make use of it for our own souls. May we never rest till we can say by faith, "Christ is mine. I deserve hell. But Christ has died for me, and believing in him I have a hope of heaven."

Christ mocked and crucified (15:16–32)

This passage is one of those which show us the infinite love of Christ towards sinners. The sufferings described in it would fill our minds with mingled horror and compassion if they had been inflicted on one who was only a man like ourselves. But when we reflect that the sufferer was the eternal Son of God, we are lost in wonder and amazement. And when we reflect further that these sufferings were voluntarily endured to deliver sinful men and women like ourselves from hell, we may see something of St. Paul's meaning when he says, "the love of Christ ... surpasses knowledge" (Ephesians 3:18–19), and "God demonstrates his own love for us in this: While we were still sinners, Christ died for us" (Romans 5:8).

We shall find it useful to examine separately the several parts of our Lord's passion. Let us follow him step by step from the moment of his condemnation by Pilate to his last hour on the cross. There is a deep meaning in every detail of his sorrows. All were striking pictures of spiritual truths. And let us not forget, as we dwell on the wonderful story, that we and our sins were the cause of all these sufferings. "Christ died for sins once for all, the righteous for the unrighteous, to bring you to God" (1 Peter 3:18). It is the death of our own surety and substitute that we are reading about.

First, we see Jesus delivered into the hands of the Roman soldiers as a criminal condemned to death. He, before whom the whole world will one day stand and be judged, allowed himself to be sentenced unjustly, and given over into the hands of wicked men.

And why was this? It was so that we, poor sinful humans, believing in him might be delivered from the pit of destruction and the torment of the prison of hell. It was so that we might be set free from every charge on the day of judgment, and be presented before God the Father without fault and with great joy.

Second, we see Jesus insulted and made a laughing-stock by the Roman soldiers. They "put a purple robe on him" in derision, and put "a crown of thorns" on his head in mockery of his kingdom (verse 17). "They struck him on the head with a staff and spat on him" (verse 19), as one utterly contemptible, and no better than "the refuse of the world" (1 Corinthians 4:13).

And why was this? It was so that we, vile as we are, might have glory, honor and eternal life through faith in Christ's atonement. It was done so that we might be received into God's kingdom with triumph at the last day, and receive the crown of glory that does not fade.

Third, we see Jesus stripped of his garments and crucified naked before his enemies. The soldiers who led him away divided up his clothes and "cast lots to see what each would get" (verse 24).

And why was this? It was so that we, who have no righteousness of our own, might be clothed in the perfect righteousness that Christ has worked for us, and not stand naked before God on the last day. It was done so that we, who are all defiled with sin, might have a wedding-garment to wear as we sit down by the side of angels, and not be ashamed.

Fourth, we see Jesus suffering the most ignominious and humiliating of all deaths, namely the death of the cross. It was the punishment reserved for the worst of criminals. The man on whom it was inflicted was regarded as cursed. It is written, "Cursed is everyone who is hung on a tree" (Galatians 3:13).

And why was this? It was so that we, who are born in sin and are objects of wrath, might be treated as blessed for Christ's sake. It was done to remove the curse which we all deserve because of sin, by laying it on Christ. "Christ redeemed us from the curse of the law by becoming a curse for us" (Galatians 3:13).

Fifth, we see Jesus reckoned a transgressor and a sinner. "They crucified two robbers with him" (verse 27). He had committed no sin, and no deceit was found in his mouth (1 Peter 2:22), yet he was "counted with the lawless ones" (Mark 15:28, NIV footnote, ed. note).

And why was this? It was so that we, who are miserable transgressors, both by nature and practice, may be reckoned innocent for Christ's sake. It was done so that we, who are worthy of nothing but condemnation, may be counted worthy to escape God's judgment and be pronounced not guilty before the assembled world.

Sixth, we see Jesus mocked when dying, as one who was an impostor and unable to save himself.

And why was this? It was so that we, in our last hours, through faith in Christ may have strong consolation. It all happened so that we may enjoy strong assurance – may know whom we have believed, and may go down the valley of the shadow of death fearing no evil.

Let us leave the passage with a deep sense of the enormous debt which all believers owe to Christ. All that they have, and are, and hope for, may be traced up to the doing and dying of the Son of God. Through his condemnation they have acquittal – through his sufferings, peace – through his shame, glory – through his death, life. Their sins were imputed to him. His righteousness is imputed to them. No wonder St. Paul says, "Thanks be to God for his indescribable gift!" (2 Corinthians 9:15).

Finally, let us leave the passage with the deepest sense of Christ's unutterable love to our souls. Let us remember what we are, corrupt, evil and miserable sinners. Let us remember who the Lord Jesus is, the eternal Son of God, the maker of all things. And then let us remember that for our sakes Jesus voluntarily endured the most painful, horrible and disgraceful death. Surely the thought of this love should constrain us daily to live not unto ourselves but unto Christ. It should make us ready and willing to offer our bodies as living sacrifices to him who lived and died for us (Romans 12:1). Let the cross of Christ be often before our minds. Rightly understood, no object in all Christianity is so likely to have a sanctifying as well as a comforting effect on our souls.

Christ's death, and the signs accompanying it *(15:33–38)*

We have in these verses the death of our Lord Jesus Christ. All deaths are solemn events. Nothing in a person's whole history is so important as the end. But never was there a death of such solemn moment as that which is now before us. In the instant that our Lord drew his last breath, the work of atonement for a world's sin was accomplished. The ransom for sinners was at length paid. The kingdom of heaven was thrown fully open to all believers. All the solid hope that mortals enjoy about their souls may be traced to Jesus' death on the cross.

1. Visible signs and wonders

First, let us observe in these verses the visible signs and wonders which accompanied our Lord's death. St. Mark mentions two in particular, which demand our attention. One is the darkening of the sun for three hours. The other is the tearing of the curtain which divided the holy of holies from the holy place in the temple. Both were miraculous events. Both had, no doubt, a deep meaning about them. Both were calculated to arrest the attention of the whole multitude assembled at Jerusalem. The darkness would strike even thoughtless Gentiles, like Pilate and the Roman soldiers. The tearing of the curtain would strike even Annas and Caiaphas and their unbelieving companions. There were probably few houses in Jerusalem that evening in which people would not say, "We have heard and seen strange things today."

What did the miraculous darkness teach? It taught the great wickedness of the Jewish nation. They were actually crucifying their own Messiah, and killing their own King. The sun himself hid his face at the sight. It taught the great sinfulness of sin in the eyes of God. The Son of God himself had to be left without the cheering light of day, when he became sin for us and carried our transgressions.

[It is almost necessary to remark that the darkness which covered the heaven on the day of the crucifixion could not possibly have been occasioned by an eclipse of the sun, because the Passover was always held at full moon. It is evident that the darkness was miraculous, and caused by some special interference with the course of nature.]

What did the miraculous tearing of the curtain mean? It taught the abolition and termination of the whole Jewish law of ceremonies. It taught that the way into the holiest of all was now thrown open to all mankind by Christ's death (Hebrews 9:8). It taught that Gentiles as well as Jews might now draw near to God with boldness, through Jesus the one High Priest, and that all barriers between man and God were forever thrown down.

May we never forget the practical lesson of the torn curtain! To attempt to revive the Jewish ceremonial in the church of Christ, by returning to altars, sacrifices and a priesthood is nothing better than closing up again the torn curtain and lighting a candle at noon.

May we never forget the practical lesson of the miraculous darkness! It should lead our minds on to that blackest darkness which is reserved for all obstinate unbelievers (Jude 13). The darkness endured by our blessed surety on the cross was only for three hours. The chains of darkness which will bind all who reject his atonement and die in sin, will be forevermore.

2. Christ made a curse for us

Second, let us observe in these verses how truly and really our Lord Jesus Christ was made a curse for us, and bore our sins. We see it strikingly brought out in those marvelous words which he used at the ninth hour, "My God, my God, why have you forsaken me?" (verse 34).

It would be useless to pretend to fathom all the depth of meaning which these words contain. They imply an amount of mental suffering, such as we are unable to conceive. The agony of some of God's holiest servants has been occasionally very great, under an impression of God's favor being withdrawn from them. What then may we suppose was the agony of the holy Son of God – when all the sin of all the world was laid on his head – when he felt himself reckoned guilty, though without sin – when he felt his Father's countenance turned away from him? The agony of that time must have been something past understanding. It is a high thing. We cannot perfectly explain and find it out.

One thing, however, is very plain, and that is the impossibility of explaining these words at all unless we accept the doctrine of Christ's atonement and substitution for sinners. To suppose, as some dare to do, that Jesus was nothing more than a man, or that his death was only a great example of self-sacrifice, makes this dying cry of his utterly unintelligible. It makes him appear less patient and calm in a dying hour than many a martyr, or even than some heathen philosophers. One explanation alone is satisfactory. That explanation is the mighty scriptural doctrine of Christ's vicarious sacrifice and substitution for us on the cross. He uttered his dying cry, under the heavy pressure of a world's sin laid upon him, and imputed to him.

3. Being temporarily forsaken by God

Third, let us observe in these verses that it is possible to be forsaken by God for a time and yet to be loved by him. We need not doubt this when we read our Lord's dying words on the cross. We hear him saying to his Father, "Why have you forsaken me?" and yet addressing him as "my God." We know too that our Lord was only forsaken for a time, and that even when forsaken he was the beloved Son in whom, both in his suffering and doing, the Father was "well pleased."

There is deep practical instruction in this, which deserves the notice of all true Christians. No doubt there is a sense in which our Lord's feeling of being "forsaken" was special to himself, since he was suffering for our sins and not for his own. But still after making allowance for this, there remains the great fact that Jesus was for a time "forsaken

by the Father" and yet for all that was the Father's "beloved Son."
As it was with the great head of the church, so it may be in a modi-
fied sense with his members. They too, though chosen and beloved
of the Father, may sometimes feel God's face turned away from
them. They too, sometimes from illness of body, sometimes from
special affliction, sometimes from indifference in discipleship, sometimes from God's sovereign will to draw them nearer to himself,
may be constrained to cry, "My God, my God, why have you forsaken
me?"

Believers who feel "forsaken" should learn from our Lord's experience not to give way to despair. No doubt they ought not to be content
with their position. They ought to search their own hearts, and see
whether there is not some secret thing there which causes their consolations to be small (Job 15:11). But they should not write bitter things
about themselves, and hastily conclude that they are cast off forever, or
are self-deceivers and have no grace at all. Let them still wait on the
Lord and say with Job, "Though he slay me, yet will I hope in him"
(Job 13:15). Let them remember the words of Isaiah: "Who among you
fears the LORD . . . ? Let him who walks in the dark, who has no light,
trust in the name of the LORD and rely on his God" (Isaiah 50:10). And
of David: "Why are you downcast, O my soul? Why so disturbed
within me? Put your hope in God, for I will yet praise him, my Saviour
and my God" (Psalm 42:11).

Christ's burial (15:39–47)

The death of our Lord Jesus Christ is the most important fact in
Christianity. On it depend the hopes of all saved sinners both for time
and eternity. We need not therefore be surprised to find the reality of
his death carefully placed beyond dispute. Three kinds of witnesses to
the fact are brought before us in these verses: the Roman centurion,
who stood near the cross; the women who followed our Lord from
Galilee to Jerusalem; and the disciples, who buried him. They were all
witnesses that Jesus really died. Their united evidence is above suspi-
cion. They could not be deceived. What they saw was no swoon, or
trance, or temporary unconsciousness. They saw that same Jesus, who

was crucified, lay down his life, and become obedient to death, even death on a cross. Let this be established in our minds. Our Saviour really and truly died.

1. Honorable mention of women

First, let us notice in this passage what honorable mention is here made of women. We are specially told that, when our Lord died, "some women were watching from a distance" (verse 40). The names of some of them are recorded. We are also told that they were the same who had followed our Lord in Galilee and cared for his needs, and that there were "many other women who had come up with him to Jerusalem" (verse 41).

We should hardly have expected to have read such things. We might well have supposed that when all the disciples but one had deserted our Lord and fled, the weaker and more timid sex would not have dared to show themselves his friends. It only shows us what grace can do. God sometimes chooses the weak things of the world to shame the strong. The last are sometimes first, and the first last. The faith of women sometimes stands upright when the faith of men fails and gives way.

But it is interesting to note throughout the New Testament how often we find the grace of God glorified in women, and how much benefit God has been pleased to confer through them on the church, and on the world. In the Old Testament we see sin and death brought in by the woman's transgression. In the New, we see Jesus born of a woman, and life and immortality brought to light by that miraculous birth. In the Old Testament we often see woman proving a hindrance and a snare to men. The women before the flood, the stories of Sarah, Rebecca, Rachel, Delilah, Bathsheba, Jezebel, are all painful examples. In the New Testament we generally see women mentioned as a help and assistance to the cause of true religion. Elizabeth, Mary, Martha, Dorcas, Lydia and the women named by St. Paul to the Romans are all cases in point. The contrast is striking, and we need not doubt intentional. It is one of the many proofs that grace is more abundant under the Gospel than under the law. It seems meant to teach us that women have an important place in the church of Christ, one that ought to be assigned to them, and one that they ought to fill. There is a great work that women can do for God's glory, without being public teachers.

Happy is that congregation in which women know this, and act on it!

2. Jesus has friends of whom we know little

Second, let us notice in this passage that Jesus has friends of whom little is known. We cannot conceive a more remarkable proof of this than the person who is here mentioned for the first time, Joseph of Arimathea. We know nothing of this man's former history. We do not know how he had learned to love Christ, and to desire to do him honor. We know nothing of his subsequent history after our Lord left the world. All we know is the touching collection of facts in this chapter. We are told that he "was himself waiting for the kingdom of God," and that at a time when our Lord's disciples had all deserted him he "went boldly to Pilate and asked for Jesus' body" (verse 43), and buried it honorably in his own tomb. Others had honored and confessed our Lord when they saw him working miracles, but Jospeh honored him and confessed himself a disciple, when he saw him a cold, blood-sprinkled corpse. Others had shown love to Jesus while he was speaking and living, but Joseph showed love when he was silent and dead.

Let us take comfort in the thought that there are true Christians on earth of whom we know nothing, and in places where we should not expect to find them. No doubt the faithful are always few. But we must not hastily conclude that there is no grace in a family or in a parish because our eyes do not see it. We know in part and see only in part, outside the circle in which our own lot is cast. The Lord has many "hidden ones" in the church who, unless brought forward by special circumstances, will never be known till the last day. The words of God to Elijah should not be forgotten, "Yet I reserve seven thousand in Israel" (1 Kings 19:18).

3. The grave honored

Third, let us notice in this passage what honor our Lord Jesus Christ has placed on the grave by allowing himself to be laid in it. We read that he was "placed in a tomb cut out of rock," and a stone was rolled against the entrance (verse 46).

This is a fact that in a dying world we should always remember. Man is destined to die once. We are all going to one place, and we naturally shrink from it. The coffin and the funeral, the worm and corruption, are all painful subjects. They chill us, sadden us and fill our minds with heaviness. It is not in flesh and blood to regard them without solemn feelings. One thing, however, ought to comfort believers, and that is the thought that the grave is "the place where the Lord once lay." As surely as he rose again victorious from the tomb, so surely will all who believe in him rise gloriously on the day he appears. Remembering this, they may look down with calmness into the "place appointed for all the living." They may recollect that Jesus himself was once there on their behalf, and has robbed death of its sting. They may say to themselves, "the sting of death is sin, and the power of sin is the law. But thanks be to God! He gives us the victory through our Lord Jesus Christ" (1 Corinthians 15:56–57).

The great matter that concerns us all is to make sure that we are spiritually buried with Christ, while we are still alive. We must be joined to him by faith, and conformed to his image. With him we must die to sin, and be buried with him through baptism into death (Romans 6:4). With him we must rise again, and be given life by his Spirit. Unless we know these things, Christ's death and burial will profit us nothing at all.

Mark
Chapter 16

The power of love for Christ; the stone rolled away; mercy to backsliders *(16:1–8)*

1. The power of strong love for Christ

First, let us observe in this passage the power of strong love for Christ. We have a forcible illustration of this in the conduct of Mary Magdalene and the other Mary, which St. Mark here records. He tells us that they had "bought spices" to anoint our Lord, and that "very early on the first day of the week, just after sunrise, they were on their way to the tomb" (verses 1–2).

We may well believe that it required no small courage to do this. To visit a grave in the dim twilight of an eastern day-break would try most women under any circumstances. But to visit the grave of one who had been put to death as a common criminal, and to get up early to show honor to one whom their nation had despised, this was a mighty boldness indeed. Yet these are the kind of acts which show the difference between weak faith and strong faith – between weak feeling and strong feeling for Christ. These holy women had experienced our Lord's pardoning mercies. Their hearts were full of gratitude to him for light, hope, comfort and peace. They were willing to risk all consequences in testifying their affection to their Saviour. So true are the words of the Song of Songs: "Love is as strong as death. . . . Many waters cannot quench love; rivers cannot wash it away" (Song of Songs 8:6, 7).

Why is it that we see so little of this strong love for Jesus among Christians today? How is it that we so seldom meet with saints who will face any danger and go through fire and water for Christ's sake? There is only one answer. It is the weak faith, and the low sense of obligation to Christ, which so widely prevail. A low and feeble sense of sin will always produce a low and feeble sense of the value of salvation. A slight sense of our debt to God will always be attended by a slight sense of what we owe for our redemption. It is the person who feels much forgiven who loves much. "He who has been forgiven little loves little" (Luke 7:47).

2. Difficulties sometimes disappear as we approach them

Second, let us observe in this passage how the difficulties which Christians fear will sometimes disappear as they approach them. These holy women, as they walked to our Lord's grave, were full of fears about the stone at the door. "They asked each other, 'Who will roll the stone away from the entrance of the tomb?'" (verse 3). But their fears were needless. Their expected trouble was found not to exist. "When they looked up, they saw that the stone . . . had been rolled away" (verse 4).

What a striking picture we have in this simple narrative of the experience of many Christians! How often believers are oppressed and cast down by anticipation of evils, and yet, in the time of need, find the thing they feared removed and the "stone rolled away." A large proportion of a saint's anxieties arise from things which never actually happen. We look forward to all the possibilities of the journey towards heaven. We conjure up in our imagination all kinds of crosses and obstacles. We carry mentally tomorrow's troubles, as well as today's. And often, very often, we find at the end that our doubts and alarms were groundless and that the thing we dreaded most has never happened at all. Let us pray for more practical faith. Let us believe that in the path of duty, we shall never be entirely deserted. Let us go forward boldly, and we shall often find that the lion in the way is chained, and what seems a hedge of thorns is only a shadow.

3. Christ's friends need not be afraid of angels

Third, let us observe in this passage that the friends of Christ have no need to be afraid of angels. We are told that when Mary Magdalene saw an angel sitting in the tomb "they were alarmed" (verse 5). But they were at once reassured by his words: "Don't be alarmed. You are looking for Jesus the Nazarene, who was crucified" (verse 6).

The lesson, at first sight, may seem of little importance. We see no visions of angels today. We do not expect to see them. But the lesson is one which we may find useful at some future time. The day is drawing near when the Lord Jesus will come again to judge the world, with all the angels round him. The angels on that day will gather together his elect from the four winds. The angels will gather the weeds into bundles to burn them. The angels will gather the wheat of God into his barn. Those whom the angels take they will carry to glory, honor and immortality. Those whom they leave behind will be left to shame and everlasting contempt.

Let us try to live in such a way that when we die we may be carried by angels to Abraham's side. Let us try to be known by angels as those who seek Jesus, and love him in this world, and so are heirs of salvation. Let us give diligence to make our repentance sure, and so to cause joy in the presence of the angels of God. Then, whether we wake or sleep, when the archangel's voice is heard we shall have no need to be afraid. We shall rise from our grave and see in the angels our friends and fellow-servants, in whose company we shall spend a blessed eternity.

4. God's kindness to backsliders

Fourth, let us observe in this passage the great kindness of God towards his backsliding servants. The message which the angel conveys is a striking illustration of this truth. Mary Magdalene and the other Mary were to tell the disciples that Jesus "is going ahead of you into Galilee," and that "there you will see him" (verse 7). But the message is not directed generally to the eleven apostles. This alone, after their recent desertion of their Master, would have been a most gracious action. Yet Simon Peter, who had denied his Lord three times, is specially mentioned by name. Peter, who had sinned particularly, is singled out and noticed particularly. There were to be no exceptions in the deed of grace. All were to be pardoned. All were to be restored to favor – Simon Peter as well as the rest.

We may well say when we read words like these, "This is not how men behave." On no point perhaps are our views of religion so narrow, low and contracted as on the point of God's great willingness to pardon penitent sinners. We think of him as like ourselves. We forget that he delights to show mercy (Micah 7:18).

Let us leave the passage with a determination to open the door of mercy very wide to sinners, in all our speaking and teaching about religion. Not least, let us leave it with a resolution never to be unforgiving towards other people. If Christ is so ready to forgive us, we ought to be very ready to forgive others.

Proofs of the resurrection; kindness to great sinners; the weakness of believers *(16:9–14)*

1. Proof of Christ's resurrection

First, let us note in these verses what abundant proof we have that our Lord Jesus Christ really rose again from the dead. In this one passage St. Mark records no less than three distinct occasions on which he was seen after his resurrection. First, he tells us, our Lord appeared to one witness, Mary Magdalene – then to two witnesses, two disciples walking into the country – and lastly to eleven witnesses, the eleven apostles all assembled together. Let us remember, in addition to this, that other appearances of our Lord are described by other writers in the New Testament, beside those mentioned by St. Mark. And then let us not hesitate to believe that of all the facts of our Lord's history there is none more thoroughly established than the fact that he rose from the dead.

There is great mercy in this. The resurrection of Christ is one of the foundation-stones of Christianity. It was the seal of the great work that he came on earth to do. It was the crowning proof that the ransom he paid for sinners was accepted, the atonement for sin accomplished, the head of him who had the power of death crushed, and the victory won. It is as well to remark how often the resurrection of Christ is referred to by the apostles. "He was delivered over to death for our sins," says Paul, "and was raised to life for our justification" (Romans 4:25). "He has given us new birth into a living hope," says Peter, "through the resurrection of Jesus Christ from the dead" (1 Peter 1:3).

We ought to thank God that the fact of the resurrection is so clearly established. The Jew, the Gentile, the priests, the Roman guard, the women who went to the tomb, the disciples who were so backward to believe, are all witnesses whose testimony cannot be contradicted. Christ has not only died for us, but has also risen again. To deny it shows far greater credulity than to believe it. To deny it you must put credit in monstrous and ridiculous improbabilities. To believe it you have only to appeal to simple undeniable facts.

2. Christ's singular kindness to Mary Magdalene

Second, let us mark in these verses our Lord Jesus Christ's singular kindness to Mary Magdalene. We are told that "When Jesus rose early on the first day of the week, he appeared first to Mary Magdalene, out of whom he had driven seven demons" (verse 9). To her before all other descendants of Adam was granted the privilege of being first to behold a risen Saviour. Mary, the mother of our Lord, was still alive. John, the beloved disciple, was still on earth. Yet both were passed over on this occasion in favor of Mary Magdalene. A woman who at one time had probably been chief of sinners, a woman who at one time had been possessed by seven demons, was the first to whom Jesus showed himself alive when he rose victorious from the tomb. The fact is remarkable, and full of instruction.

[There is nothing in the New Testament to justify the common notion that Mary Magdalene had been a sinner against the seventh commandment more than other commandments. There is no scriptural warrant for calling hospitals and asylums intended for fallen women "Magdalene Hospitals." No better authority can be discovered for the common idea on the subject than tradition.

At the same time it is only fair to say that there seems strong probability for supposing that the sins of Mary Magdalene had been very great. There was probably some grave cause for her being possessed by seven demons, though the nature of it has not been revealed to us.]

We need not doubt, for one thing, that by appearing "first to Mary Magdalene" our Lord meant to show us how much he values love and faithfulness. Last at the cross and first at the grave, last to confess her Master while living, and first to honor him when dead, this warm-hearted disciple was allowed to be the first to see him when the victory was won. It was intended to be a perpetual memorial to the church that those who do honor Christ, he will honor, and that those who do much for him on earth will find him even on earth doing much for them. May we never forget this. May we always remember that for those who leave all for Christ's sake there is "a hundred times as much in this present age" (Mark 10:30).

We need not doubt, for another thing, that our Lord's appearing "first to Mary Magdalene" was intended to comfort all who have become penitent believers after having run into great excesses of sin. It was meant to show us that, however far we may have fallen, we are raised to complete peace with God if we repent and believe the Gospel. Though before far off, we are brought near. Though before enemies, we are made dear children. The old has gone, the new has come (2 Corinthians 5:17). The blood of Christ makes us completely clean in God's sight. We may have begun like Augustine, and John Newton, and been ringleaders in every kind of iniquity. But once brought to Christ, we need not doubt that all is forgiven. We may come near boldly, and have access with confidence. Our sins and iniquities, like those of Mary Magdalene, are remembered no more.

3. Weakness in the faith of the best Christians

Third, let us note in these verses how much weakness there is sometimes in the faith of the best Christians. Three times in this very passage we find St. Mark describing the unbelief of the eleven apostles. Once, when Mary Magdalene told them that our Lord had risen, "they did not believe it" (verse 11). Again, when our Lord had appeared to two of them as they walked, we read of the rest of them, "they did not believe them either" (verse 13). Finally, when our Lord himself appeared to them as they were eating, we are told that "he rebuked them for their lack of faith and their stubborn refusal to believe" (verse 14). Never perhaps was there so striking an example of people's unwillingness to believe what runs counter to their early prejudices. Never was there so remarkable a proof of people's forgetfulness of plain teaching. These eleven men had been told repeatedly by our Lord that he would rise again. And yet, when the time came, all was forgotten, and they were found unbelieving.

Let us however see in the doubts of these good men the overruling hand of an all-wise God. If people who were so unbelieving at first, were convinced at last, how strong is the proof supplied us that Christ indeed rose. The very doubts of the eleven apostles are the confirmation of our faith today.

Let us learn from the unbelief of the apostles a useful practical lesson for ourselves. Let us stop feeling surprise when we find doubts arising in our own hearts. Let us stop expecting perfect faith in other believers. We are still in the body. We are people of similar feelings to the apostles. We must not think it strange if our experience is sometimes like theirs, and if our faith, like theirs, sometimes gives way. Let us resist unbelief strongly. Let us watch, and pray, and strive to be delivered from its power. But let us not conclude that we have no grace because we are sometimes harassed with doubts, nor suppose that we have no part or lot with the apostles because at times we feel unbelieving.

Let us not fail to ask ourselves, as we leave this passage, whether we have risen with Christ, and been made to share spiritually in his resurrection. This, after all, is the one thing needed. To know the facts of Christianity with the head, and to be able to argue for them with the tongue, will not save our souls. We must yield ourselves to God as those alive from the dead (Romans 6:13). We must be raised from the death of sin, and walk in newness of life. This and this only is saving Christianity.

The apostles' commission; the terms of the Gospel; the promise to faithful laborers *(16:15–18)*

1. Christ's parting commission

First, we ought to notice in these verses the parting commission which our Lord gives to his apostles. He is addressing them for the last time. He marks out their work till he comes again, in words of wide and deep significance: "Go into all the world and preach the good news to all creation" (verse 15).

The Lord Jesus wants us to know that all the world needs the Gospel. In every quarter of the globe people are the same, sinful, corrupt and alienated from God. Civilized or uncivilized, in China or in Africa, they are by nature everywhere the same, without knowledge, without holiness, without faith and without love. Wherever we see a child of Adam, of whatever color, we see one whose heart is wicked, and who needs the blood of Christ, the renewing work of the Holy Spirit and reconciliation with God.

The Lord Jesus wants us to know that the salvation of the Gospel is to be offered freely to all mankind. The good news that "God so loved the world that he gave his one and only Son" (John 3:16) and that "Christ died for the ungodly" (Romans 5:6) is to be proclaimed freely "to all creation." We are not justified in making any exception in the proclamation. We have no warrant for limiting the offer to the elect. We come short of the fullness of Christ's words, and take away from the breadth of his sayings, if we shrink from telling anyone, "God is full of love to you, Christ is willing to save you." "Whoever wishes, let him take the free gift of the water of life" (Revelation 22:17).

Let us see in these words of Christ the strongest argument in favor of missionary work both at home and abroad. Remembering these words, let us be untiring in trying to do good to the souls of all mankind. If we cannot go to the heathen in China and India, let us seek to enlighten the darkness which we shall easily find within reach of our own door. Let us labor on, unmoved by the sneers and taunts of those who disapprove of missionary operations, and hold them up to scorn. We may well pity such people. They only show their ignorance, both of Scripture and of Christ's will. They understand neither what they say nor what it is they are talking about.

2. The terms on which the Gospel should be offered
Second, we ought to notice in these verses the terms which our Lord tells us should be offered to all who hear the Gospel. "Whoever believes and is baptized will be saved, but whoever does not believe will be condemned" (verse 16). Every word in that sentence is of deep importance. Every expression in it deserves to be carefully weighed.

We are taught here the importance of baptism. It is an ordinance generally necessary to salvation, where it can be had. Not "whoever believes" simply, but "whoever believes and is baptized will be saved." Thousands no doubt receive not the slightest benefit from their baptism. Thousands are washed in sacramental water who are never washed in the blood of Christ. But it does not follow therefore that baptism is to be despised and neglected. It is an ordinance appointed by Christ himself, and when used reverently, intelligently and prayerfully is doubtless accompanied by a special blessing. The baptismal water itself conveys no grace. We must look far beyond the mere outward element to him who commanded it to be used. But the public confession of Christ, which is implied in the use of that water, is a sacramental act which our Master himself has commanded; and when the ordinance is rightly used, we may confidently believe that he seals it by his blessing.

We are taught here, furthermore, the absolute necessity of faith in Christ to salvation. This is the one thing needed. "Whoever does not believe" will be lost forevermore. They may have been baptized and made members of the visible church. They may be regular communicants at the Lord's table. They may even believe intellectually all the leading articles of the creed. But all this will be useless if they lack saving faith in Christ. Have we this faith? This is the great question that concerns us all. Unless we feel our sins, and feeling them flee to Christ by faith and lay hold on him, we shall find at length we had better never have been born.

We are taught here, furthermore, the certainty of God's judgments on those who die unbelieving. "Whoever does not believe will be condemned." How awful the words sound! How fearful the thought that they came from the lips of him who said, "My words will not pass away." Let no one deceive us with vain words. There is an eternal hell for all who will persist in their wickedness, and leave this world without faith in Christ. The greater the mercy offered to us in the Gospel, the greater will be the guilt of those who obstinately refuse to believe. "If only they were wise and would understand this and discern what their end will be!" (Deuteronomy 32:29). He who died on the cross has given us plain warning that there is a hell, and that unbelievers will be damned. Let us take care that his warning is not given to us in vain!

3. Gracious promises of special help

Third, we ought to notice in these verses the gracious promises of special help which our Lord holds out in his parting words to his apostles. He knew well the enormous difficulties of the work which he had just commissioned them to do. He knew the mighty battle they would have to fight with heathenism, the world, and the devil. He therefore cheers them by telling them that miracles will help their work forward. "These signs will accompany those who believe: In my name they will drive out demons; they will speak in new tongues; they will pick up snakes with their hands; and when they drink deadly poison, it will not hurt them at all; they will place their hands on sick people, and they will get well" (verses 17–18). The fulfillment of most of these promises is to be found in the Acts of the Apostles.

The age of miracles no doubt is long passed. They were never meant to continue beyond the first establishment of the church. It is only when plants are first planted that they need daily watering and support. The whole analogy of God's dealings with his church forbids us to expect that miracles would always continue. In fact, miracles would cease to be miracles if they happened regularly without cessation or intermission. It is well to remember this. The remembrance may save us much perplexity.

But though the age of physical miracles is past, we may take comfort in the thought that the church of Christ will never lack Christ's special aid in its times of special need. The great head in heaven will never forsake his believing members. His eye is continually on them. He will always time his help wisely, and come to their aid at the time that he is wanted. "When the enemy comes in like a flood, the Spirit of the LORD will put him to flight" (Isaiah 59:19, NIV footnote, ed. note).

Finally, let us never forget that Christ's believing church in the world is of itself a standing miracle. The conversion and perseverance in grace of every member of that church is a sign and wonder as great as the raising of Lazarus form the dead. The renewal of every saint is as great a marvel as the driving out of a demon, or the healing of a sick man, or the speaking with a new tongue. Let us thank God for this and take courage. The age of spiritual miracles is not yet past. Happy are those who have learned this by experience, and can say, "I was dead, but am alive again; I was blind, but I see."

Christ's ascension; the word of preachers confirmed by signs (16:19–20)

These words form the conclusion of St. Mark's Gospel. Short as the passage is, it is a singularly suitable conclusion to the story of our Lord Jesus Christ's earthly ministry. It tells us where our Lord went when he left his world and ascended on high. It tells us what his disciples experienced after their Master left them, and what all true Christians may expect until he appears again.

1. Where Christ went

First, let us note in these verses the place to which our Lord went when he had finished his work on earth and the place where he is at this present time. We are told that "he was taken up into heaven and he sat at the right hand of God" (verse 19). He returned to that glory which he had with the Father before he came into the world. He received, as our victorious mediator and Redeemer, the highest position of dignity and power in heaven which our minds can conceive. There he sits, not idle but carrying on the same blessed work for which he died on the cross. There he lives, always interceding for all who come to God by him, and so able to save them completely (Hebrews 7:25).

There is strong consolation here for all true Christians. They live in an evil world. They are often worried and upset about many things, and are very depressed by their own weakness. They live in a dying world. They feel their bodies gradually failing and giving way. They have before them the awful prospect of soon launching forth into a world unknown. What then will comfort them? They must lean back on the thought of their Saviour in heaven, never slumbering and never sleeping, and always ready to help. They must remember that though they sleep, Jesus wakes – though they faint, Jesus is never weary – though they are weak, Jesus is almighty – and though they die, Jesus lives forevermore. Blessed indeed is this thought! We travel on towards a dwelling where our best Friend has already gone, to prepare a place for us (John 14:2). The Forerunner has entered in and made everything ready. No wonder St. Paul exclaims, "Who is he that condemns? Christ Jesus, who died – more than that, who was raised to life – is at the right hand of God and is also interceding for us" (Romans 8:34).

2. Christ's blessing on all who work faithfully for him

Second, let us note in these verses the blessing which our Lord Jesus Christ bestows on all who work faithfully for him. We are told that when the disciples went out and preached, the Lord "worked with them and confirmed his word by the signs that accompanied it" (verse 20).

We know well from the Acts of the Apostles, and from the pages of church history, the manner in which these words have been proved true. We know that bonds and afflictions, persecution and opposition, were the first fruits that were reaped by the laborers in Christ's harvest. But we know also that, in spite of every effort of Satan, the word of truth was not preached in vain. Believers from time to time were gathered out of the world. Churches of saints were founded in city after city, and country after country. The little seed of Christianity grew gradually into a great tree. Christ himself worked with his own workers, and in spite of every obstacle his work went on. The good seed was never entirely thrown away. Sooner or later there were "signs."

Let us not doubt that these things were written for our encouragement, on whom the end of the world has come. Let us believe that no one will ever work faithfully for Christ and find at last that his work has been altogether without profit. Let us labor on patiently, each in our own position. Let us preach, and teach, and speak, and write, and warn, and testify, and rest assured that our labor is not in vain. We may die ourselves, and see no result from our work. But the last day will assuredly prove that the Lord Jesus always works with those who work for him, and that there were "signs" though it was not given to the workers to see them. Let us then "stand firm," letting nothing move us, always giving ourselves fully to the work of the Lord (1 Corinthians 15:58). We may go on our way heavily, and sow with many tears; but if we sow Christ's precious seed, we shall "return with songs of joy, carrying sheaves" with us (Psalm 126:6).

And now let us close the pages of St. Mark's Gospel with self-inquiry and self-examination. Let it not content us to have seen with our eyes, and heard with our ears the things here written for our learning about Jesus Christ. Let us ask ourselves whether we know anything of Christ "dwelling in our hearts by faith." Does the Spirit "witness with our spirit" that Christ is ours and we are his? Can we really say that we are "living the life of faith in the Son of God" and that we have found by experience that Christ is "precious" to our own souls? These are solemn questions. They demand serious consideration. May we never rest till we can give them satisfactory answers! "He who has the Son has life; he who does not have the Son of God does not have life" (1 John 5:12).